IN THE Wake OF THE Dhow

In the Wake of the Dhow

The Arabian Gulf and Oman

Dionisius A. Agius

ITHACA
PRESS

IN THE WAKE OF THE DHOW
The Arabian Gulf and Oman

Published by
Garnet Publishing Limited
8 Southern Court
South Street
Reading
RG1 4QS
UK

First Edition 2002

ISBN 0 86372 259 8

British Library Cataloguing-in-Publication Data
A catalogue record for this book is available from the British Library

Jacket design by Garnet Publishing
Typeset by Samantha Barden

Printed in Lebanon

Contents

ABBREVIATIONS

ARCHIVAL

Aan	Aanwinsten le Afdeling (Dutch General State Archives, The Hague)
AGSFC	The Arab Gulf States Folklore Centre (Doha, Qatar)
AHG	Arquivo Historico de Goa
AHU	Arquivo Historico de Ultramarino
ANTT	Arquivos Nacionais da Torre do Tombo, Lisbon
ARA	Algemeen Rijksarchief den Haag (Dutch General State Archives, The Hague)
BL	British Library
BM	British Museum
BM Or	British Museum Oriental
BMp	British Maps
BN	Bibliothèque Nationale, Paris
CDRAD	Centre for Documentation and Research in Abu Dhabi
DLH	Directeuren van de Levantse Handel (Archives of the Board of Directors of the Dutch Levant-Trade – Dutch General State Archives, The Hague)
DM	Dutch Maps
DMM	Dār al-Makhṭūṭāt li-Masqaṭ (Ministry of National Heritage and Culture, Muscat)
EBD	English Basra Diary (Bombay State Archives)
FRPPG	Factory Records, Persia and the Persian Gulf (English East India Company)
GD	The Gombroon Diaries (English East India Company)
IOL	India Office Library
IOR	India Office Records
KLI	Khudābukhsh Library, India (Archives of the University of Alexandria, Faculty of Arts)
LAS	Library of the Academy of Sciences, St Petersburg
SPDD	Secret and Political Department Diaries (Bombay Archives)
SRBG	Selections from the Records of the Bombay Government
UAFAL	Archives of the University of Alexandria, Faculty of Arts Library
VOC	Verenigde Oost-Indische Compagnie

LINGUISTIC

Ad	Adeni
Ak	Akkadian
Ar	Modern Standard Arabic
Aram	Aramaic
CA	Classical Arabic
Dh	Dhofari
Egy	Egyptian
Eng	English
GA	Gulf Arabic
Gr	Greek
Had	Hadrami
Hin	Hindi
Ir	Iraqi
Kt	Kuwaiti
Lat	Latin
Leb	Lebanese
Mal	Malay
Meh	Mehri
NP	Neo-Persian
Per	Persian (Fārsī)
Port	Portuguese
SA	South Arabian
Skt	Sanskrit
Som	Somali
Sw	Swahili
Syr	Syriac
Tig	Tigré
Tun	Tunisian
Ur	Urdu
Yem	Yemeni

LITERARY

AD	Anno Domini
AH	Anno Hegirae
b/bin/Ibn	son of
c	circa
cc	corpo cronológico
cf	confer (compare)
coll	collective

d	died in/dates
ed	edited
EI2	Encyclopaedia of Islam (second edition)
fl	floruit (flourished)
fn	footnote
fol(s)	folio(s)
Ibn	son of
lit	literally
MS	manuscript
nd	no date
NE	north-east
np	no publisher's name
OED	Oxford English Dictionary
pl	plural
r	recto
s	singular
sv	sub voce (under the word or heading)
SW	south-west
trans	translated
v	verso
vol(s)	volume(s)
vs	verse

Symbolic

*	hypothetical origin
>	becoming
<	resulting from
=	equivalent to
/ /	phonetic transcription
[?]	doubtful origin

Transliteration System

CONSONANTS

'	ء	r	ر	f	ف
b	ب	z	ز	q	ق
t	ت	s	س	g	گ
th	ث	sh	ش	k	ك
ch	چ	ṣ	ص	l	ل
j	ج	ḍ	ض	m	م
ḥ	ح	ṭ	ط	n	ن
kh	خ	ẓ	ظ	h	ه
d	د	c	ع	w	و
dh	ذ	gh	غ	y	ي

VOWELS

Long		Short	
ā	ا	a	َـ
ū	و	u	ُـ
ī	ي	i	ِـ
ō		o	
ē		e	

Doubled	
iyy (final form = /i/)	ِيّ
uww (final form = /u/)	ُوّ

Diphthongs	
ay	َيْ
aw	َوْ

ACKNOWLEDGEMENTS

I should like to express my particular gratitude to the Leverhulme Trust for funding this research. Generous thanks are also due to the British Council of Kuwait, Bahrain, Qatar and the United Arab Emirates as well as the Ministry of Information and Culture of Bahrain and Qatar for offering me grants to carry out my fieldwork and archival research.

Tom Vosmer of the Western Australian Maritime Museum, Fremantle and William Donaldson of the Department of Islamic and Middle Eastern Studies, University of Edinburgh were of invaluable assistance in reading the entire text, providing me with copious comments. The book has benefited enormously from their constructive and knowledgeable criticism.

I would like to offer my particular thanks to H. E. Tariq Almoayed, Minister of Information and Culture in Bahrain; H. E. Hamad bin Suhaim Al Thani, Minister of Information and Culture in Qatar; Sheikha Houssa Al Sabah, curator of the Kuwait Museum of Islamic Heritage; Sheikha Naila Al Khalifa, curator of the National Museum in Bahrain; Khaled Al Mulla, curator of the Qatar National Museum; Jumaa Abdullah Al Qubaisi, director of the National Library, Abu Dhabi; Mohamed Morsy Abdulla, director of the Centre for Documentation and Research in Abu Dhabi; Mohamed Said Nasser Al-Wahaibi, director general of culture and heritage and Ali Al-Shanfari, director of antiquities, Ministry of Culture and Heritage, Muscat; Sheikh Abdullah bin Khalifa Al Majally, member of the consultative council, Masirah; Saeed Masaud Muhammed Al-Mashini, director of the Cultural Centre, Salalah; British Council directors M. A. Frankel (Kuwait), John Wright (Bahrain), John Shorter (Qatar), Andy Mackay, David Latta and Robert Sykes (United Arab Emirates) and Clive Bruton (Oman).

In the gathering of information for this book many people helped me, and my deepest debt is to all the master-builders, captains, navigators, seamen, pearl divers, fishermen and guides whom I acknowledge in the text. I owe thanks to those who gave me the opportunity to search for and discuss archival material for my research, in particular Sheikh Seif Marzuq Al-Shamlan, maritime historian in Kuwait; Yacoub Y. Al-Hijji, maritime historian and boat researcher, Center for Research and Studies on Kuwait; Khalid al-Sindi, archaeologist and historian of antiquities and Abd Allah Khalifa Al Shamlan, maritime historian in Bahrain; Jassem Zaini, curator and Jassem Al Rais, assistant head, Department of Museum and Antiquities, Doha;

Mustafa Aqeel, Department of History, University of Qatar; Abdalrahman Al Mannai, folklorist, Muhamed Saeed al-Balushi and Hasan al-Muhannadi, both researchers at the Centre for Gulf Folklore Studies, Doha; Susanna Dos Santos (Portuguese Archives), Liesbeth van Til-Schaefer (Dutch Archives), Grace Kuruvilla and Barbara De Keijzer (Anglo–Indian Archives), Chantal Uguen (French Archives), Frauke Heard-Bey (German Archives) and Daad Barakat (Ottoman Archives) of the Centre for Documentation and Research at Abu Dhabi; Hussain Sulaiman Qandil, archaeologist, Department of Archaeology and Museums, Dubai; Ayesha Mubarak A. Obaied, head of the Department of Archaeology and Museums, Dubai; Abdul Aziz Al Musallam, folklorist and director of heritage, Department of Culture and Information, Sharjah; Rashid Obeid Al Shouq, folklorist and storyteller, Sharjah; Abdullah Abulhoul, former head of Police and Customs, Dubai and his son Mansour Abulhoul, a graduate in Arabic and Politics at the University of Leeds; Obeid Al Murar, translator at the Presidential Court, Abu Dhabi; Khair bin Antara, director of handicrafts, Ministry of Culture and Heritage, Muscat; Musallam al Maʾni and Seif Ali Suleiman al-Mamari, translators at the Royal Air Force of Oman, Muscat; Najeeb Ahmed Al-Mani and Abdallah Hamed al-Nabli, Royal Navy of Oman; Ali Ahmed Al-Shahri, researcher in antiquities, Salalah; Eric Kentley, National Maritime Museum, Greenwich, London; Delia Cortese, Bernard Quaritch Antiquarian Booksellers, London; Brian MacDermot, Mathaf Gallery; Isabel Sinden, Victoria and Albert Museum (Picture Library); Roger Fenby, BBC World Service; members of the sixth campaign of the Oman Maritime Heritage Project with whom I collaborated as an oral historian in South East Oman and the Royal Air Force of Oman who assisted me with flights to Musandam Peninsula and Masirah Island.

The original drawings were the work of my daughter Safja Marija Agius (Toronto) to whom I am immensely grateful. I would also like to thank John Whale who provided me with photographs of his superb oil paintings and finally, my wife Anne who with great patience read several drafts of my manuscript. Thank you all.

NOTE

With the exception of names of interviewees, consultants and officials I have adopted the Library of Congress transliteration system for names of Arab/Muslim rulers, dynasties, religious and political movements and technical terms. All bibliographical Arabic entries (ie names of authors, titles of works) follow the Library of Congress system. Christian dates are normally preceded by Islamic dates if the subject concerns the Islamic period; in other instances only the date of the Christian era is inserted. I have maintained the Arabic script where technical terms quoted from Arabic sources relating to parts of a dhow had no vocalisation. In the text and bibliographical references the word Ibn, 'son', occurs at the initial position with classical Muslim writers, eg Ibn Ḥawqal, but an abbreviated 'b' is employed in the middle of a name, eg Abū Bakr Muḥammad b Ḥusayn. When, however, referring to names of sheikhs or other personalities in documents or historical texts of the modern period I used the conventional 'bin' in the middle of the name, eg Ḥamad bin ʿIsā Āl-Khalīfa. The article 'al-' was used with all authors and 'Āl' (family) for tribal names of sheikhs. Otherwise, I followed the country's official transliteration system of recording names: in this case no diacritic points were used and names may appear with 'al'/'Al' (without a hyphen) or 'al-'/'Al-' (with a hyphen).

Preface

I have long been fascinated by the works of writers on medieval travel and geography and it was here that I found interesting and valuable information on Arab seafaring, ship types and nautical terms. The fourth/tenth-century geographer al-Muqaddasī (d 378/988) in particular triggered my interest in the nomenclature of ship types and this became the focus of my present research on the dhow in the Arabian Gulf and Oman.

This book represents the first part of my ongoing research: Seafaring in the Arabian Gulf and Oman (SFAGO), which entails both a study of the nomenclature of dhow types and of parts of the dhow. The sail, sailing techniques and navigational instruments are dealt with in a subsequent publication. The aim of this work, the first part of the project, has been to establish an historical and linguistic link between the present traditional seagoing vessels and coastal boats of the Gulf and Oman, and those of the medieval Islamic period. I had conducted several field trips to the Arabian Gulf, visiting Kuwait in 1990, then Bahrain in 1991 and Qatar in 1992; for these trips I was sponsored by the British Council and the Ministry of Information and then visited the Emirates in 1994 for which I was awarded a travel grant by the British Council. My next plan was to visit Oman, a vast country with a long tradition of dhow-building and seafaring. The work in Oman was made possible by a two year Leverhulme Research Fellowship from 1996 to 1998. The grant came in time to see the project coming to its fruition. In addition to the fieldwork, I consulted manuscripts at the National Heritage Museum in Muscat, the Bodleian Library in Oxford and several documents at the Centre for Documentation and Research at Abu Dhabi, the Centre for Gulf Folklore Studies in Doha (Qatar), the Bahrain Centre for Studies and Research, and the Centre for Research and Studies on Kuwait.

This volume spans the period from the seventeenth to the twentieth century. Historically, the taking of India and the Persian Gulf by the Portuguese is very significant because of the political and cultural influence they had in the area; most important from the point of view of my research is their contribution to shipbuilding techniques. The Dutch and the English, on the other hand, both played an important role in the commercial activity between the East and the West, but particularly important was the British involvement in controlling piratical and slave-trading activities. They also helped the Gulf Arabs in the making of the present states. My main focus however, was to find historical and linguistic links between the nomenclature of ships in the Gulf and Oman. The Portuguese, Dutch and English documents pertaining to the area provided a wealth of information on the history of the Arabian/Persian Gulf and India but were also a rich source on the nomenclature of ships. All the sources which I consulted were copies deposited in the Centre for Documentation and Research in Abu Dhabi: i) Portuguese – Arquivo Historico de Goa, Arquivo Historico de Ultramarino, and Arquivos Nacionais da Torre do Tombo (Portuguese National Archives), ii) Dutch – the Directeuren van de Levantse Handel (Archives of the Board of Directors of the Dutch-Levant Trade in the Dutch General State Archives) and the Verenigde Oost-Indische Compagnie (Archives of the Dutch East India Company), and iii) British documents – extensive use has been made of the factory records containing the Gombroon Diaries (India Office Library), English Basra Diary (Bombay State Archives) and Selections from the Records of the Bombay Government.

One of the difficulties I experienced in my field trips was in finding good reliable guides who could act as interpreters when needed. When I succeeded it was worth every minute of the interview, though only a crazy researcher is determined to drive a Toyota truck around in temperatures as high as 122ºF in the shade, particularly when I once had to jump from my truck as it plunged into quicksand. I waited for hours in the middle of nowhere under a scorching sun until two Bedouins picked me up to get help from a nearby village. Another unfortunate occurrence entailed the loss of some of my field-notes when my tent blew away. Fortunately some of the notes were retrieved with the help of the team members, but it still entailed some reconstruction from memory. The Omanis attributed this misfortune to the local *jinn*s (or genies), which were supposed to haunt the area, and insisted on performing ceremonies (with frankincense and myrrh) to drive out the demons. I am pleased to report that the *jinn*s did not come back!

In the course of my fieldwork, the guides had to be prepared to translate from the regional dialects into standard Arabic. They also had to make the necessary contacts with the people I needed to interview and get all the official papers organized for me. Only twice was I refused entry to a place because of sensitive military installations or political instability. Much time was wasted before the real work could start. After obtaining the appropriate permission from the *wālī*s (governors) or sheikhs (heads) of towns or villages I set off, taking with me all that was needed: camera, tape recorder and field notes.

The fieldwork consisted of interviews, of which I conducted 204. The results obtained from each were checked against those from other sources, technical or non-technical, thus producing a reasonably accurate study. At the outset I made a decision that my work would be a linguistic inquiry drawing on different historical, literary and technical sources. There was no doubt in my mind that this would be a difficult task to accomplish. My subjects were shipwrights, captains, merchantmen, seamen, pearl-divers and fishermen, not to mention boat researchers, archaeologists, maritime historians and *rāwī*s (storytellers). Handling interviews with some seamen was at times delicate, for the moment they became microphone conscious they tended to withhold information. Occasionally, it was hard to convince interviewees that I was not a government agent and that they could talk freely of what they knew about dhows and their experiences on board the dhows, sailing, for example, to south-west India and East Africa. I conducted open interviews giving interviewees the freedom to participate in an informal talk rather than rigid structured interviews with specific questions. With the open-interview method I could gather detailed information, with each question leading to another. An advantage of this was that when answers were ambiguous I could clarify things there and then without worrying whether or not I would complete a set of questions. It was not easy to establish dates. For example in Oman, the modern age starts when Sultan Qaboos came to power in 1970, before which, the towns and villages had hardly any roads, electricity or running water. When I asked old seamen when was the last time they saw a certain dhow I got as vague an answer as when I asked them about their age. Most of my subjects were over fifty years old as the aim of my research was to record the end of the days of the sail which came about in the early 1970s. The oldest man I interviewed was 114 years old, a former pearl-diver from Bahrain. He was born during the times of Isa bin Khalifa Al Khalifa (1869–1932), the great-great-grandfather of the present ruler, Hamed bin Isa Al Khalifa (1999–). I also included some of the younger generation in my survey, as I wanted to know how much they were informed about dhows, and dhow-building in general. There I found much of the seafaring heritage gradually disappearing, dying with the previous generation.

Difficulties did occur with some of the elderly informants (in their late eighties) who could not remember facts clearly, and allowances have been made for this. Other problems were to do with establishing a consensus of fact from at least three or more interviewees. The process of weeding out statements that were contradictory and exaggerated was essential and crucial to my study. At Fins, south-east of Oman, I was talking to a gathering of about 18 fishermen when, after posing a question about some parts of a dhow, all of them started to talk at the same time and argue about who would answer my question. The answer was simple but it only became clear after one of them pushed himself forward and drew the boat with his finger in the sand. But generally speaking most of the interviewing went smoothly. Some just talked, gesticulating with their hands, pointing at parts of the vessel as if they were talking to an expert. With this latter category of interviewees it was difficult to coordinate interviewing and simultaneously taking notes, let alone photographing. There was no solution to this and sometimes I had to rely on my memory when I sat down in the evenings at the hotel (or in the tent when no hotel was available), going over the recorded tapes and field notes. This exercise was essential on a daily basis. The Gulf people are wonderful people and helpful in all imaginable ways and they never minded me going back to ask them over and over again the same questions, in order to verify what I had tape-recorded or written in my field notes. Back home I checked their results against those from other sources in order to ensure a reasonable accuracy.

The time spent in the largest Gulf state of Oman was very worthwhile as I managed to gain a great deal of the technical information not previously found. Admittedly some of the data on the nomenclature of ship types did conflict with the notes made on my earlier field trips to other Gulf states. The fishermen I interviewed though, were absolutely clear on what seemed to me a complex matter. Most of my day trips relied on the guides who drove me around and acted as interpreters. Their help was quite often indispensable, particularly on one or two occasions as we could only reach some fishing villages by boat and by no other means. But also being on my own visiting ports where Iranian, Indian, Pakistani and African cargo dhows lay at anchor, was extremely fruitful and rewarding. Talking to captains and merchant sailors was an added experience and their information on sea-trade links between the Gulf and the Indian Ocean and East Africa, did not seem to change much from what has been described by western travellers during the past hundred years, nor did it in some ways alter from what Muslim travellers reported in the medieval period.

I often set off walking on the shores of the Emirates and Oman searching for fishing or pearling boats left abandoned on the beach. It was a remarkable experience to find relics of a not too distant past lying there before your eyes. I spent hours sketching and photographing these boats. The fact that some of the boats have their stem and sternposts stitched to the hull is evidence of a technique that served its purposes well. I found out later that because these parts tended to break with the frequent pulling of the boat ashore and pushing it to the sea, they were easier for fishermen to repair by stitching rather than nailing them to the hull. Up until the 1940s, the planks of a vessel were stitched together. No nails were ever used. This information is corroborated by that found in the travellers' accounts written in the medieval period and diaries and reports in the Portuguese, Dutch and English documents up to the nineteenth century. It was a pitiful sight to see the abandoned boats on the beach but even more sad to find out that Arab dhows are increasingly becoming relics of the past. My study came at the right time, before these traditional boats finally disappear. They are gradually being replaced by the fibreglass fishing dhows which, from the locals' perspective, are economical to maintain, lighter, and swifter on the sea. But there is now an increasing demand to build wooden racing boats styled after the traditional dhows. Shipbuilders all over the Gulf have once more adapted to creating a craft type that will perhaps save the proud heritage of an Arab seafaring community.

As the research progressed I came across some information which was worth pursuing: it was about the lack of sunken ships found in the Gulf and Oman and there was word of an underwater expedition which was about to search for sea artefacts in waters adjacent to the ruins of Qalhat in south-east Oman, eight miles north of Sur. The expedition would be sponsored by the Oman Maritime Heritage Project, Earthwatch and the Western Australian Maritime Museum in Fremantle. The expedition's director, Tom Vosmer, told me that his team was hopeful of finding a wreck, after an earlier survey in the area discovered a number of stone anchors lying on the seabed near Qalhat harbour. I was very excited about the idea of finding a sunken ship, an Arab or Indian dhow (or for that matter a Portuguese ship), because there are so few of them about. The information that can be extracted from a shipwreck is immense; this could be the link between the fragmented data found in medieval documents, and data collected from locals and the present traditional dhows. The underwater archaeology team chose Qalhat for diving because it was for many centuries the gateway to the Gulf and the Indian Ocean; it was the entrepôt of the monsoon trade and was much frequented by merchant ships as pointed out in the diaries of Pliny the Elder (d 79 AD), Marco Polo (d 1323), Ibn Baṭṭūṭa (d 770/1368) and Alfonso d'Alboquerque (d 1515). Also, the many fine examples of broken pottery and glass shards littered amongst the ruins suggest that Qalhat was once a thriving port town. I therefore joined the team not in the capacity of a diver (much as I would love to have done so) but as an oral historian, travelling a distance of 373 miles, and gathering information from local seamen, fishermen and storytellers on their present and past activities. I wanted to establish how much of the information given to me on names of ship types and hull shapes could be corroborated by the findings of written technical and non-technical sources and, in the case of anchors, how much of the information corresponded with the discoveries of the underwater archaeology team. The experience added a wider dimension to my research and it was evident at the end of the expedition that the archeologist, the historian and the linguist get better results if they work as a team.

My fieldwork took me as far as the borders of Dhofar with Hadhramaut. I decided that this would be the cut-off point, firstly because Dhofar is politically part of Oman and secondly the dhows beyond the west of Dhofar are a study on their own. This second reason is important because the dhows of East Africa, the Yemen and Hadhramaut form a typology together, different in many ways to the Arabian Gulf and Oman, though an attempt has been made to discuss their features comparatively. The present research does not include the Iranian littoral of the Gulf even though many dhows there share similar features with the Arabian Gulf. Nonetheless, I have classified some types as Perso-Arab dhows when there has been evidence of this being so.

One of the most innovative aspects of this book is the oral history, which has enabled me to comment on all the sources I consulted, with much more accuracy than would have been possible without the fieldwork data. Nautical jargon remains relatively untapped. Names of ship types, and technical terms for parts of a dhow, have been discussed by non-Arabists but certainly not historical linguisticians. The traditions of seafaring and shipbuilding form part of a network of cultural and trade exchange that exists among the diverse linguistic and ethnic communities of the Arabian/Persian Gulf, Southern Arabia, East Africa and Western India. A linguistic inquiry into this subject area would shed new light on material that has already been examined from a more conventional historical perspective.

Essentially, this is a study of what the mariners had to say about their knowledge of dhows and nautical terms, rather than a study relying on written sources. You will find in this book the geographical conditions of each dhow type, the historical background to the life pattern of the dhows in their roles as cargo, pearl-diving, fishing, pirate and slaving vessels. It has been the aim to document the dhow as part of a seafaring community, and its contribution to the prosperity of the area before the discovery of oil.

Dionisius Albertus Agius
Leeds 2002

Map 1
The Northern Arabian Gulf States and East Oman

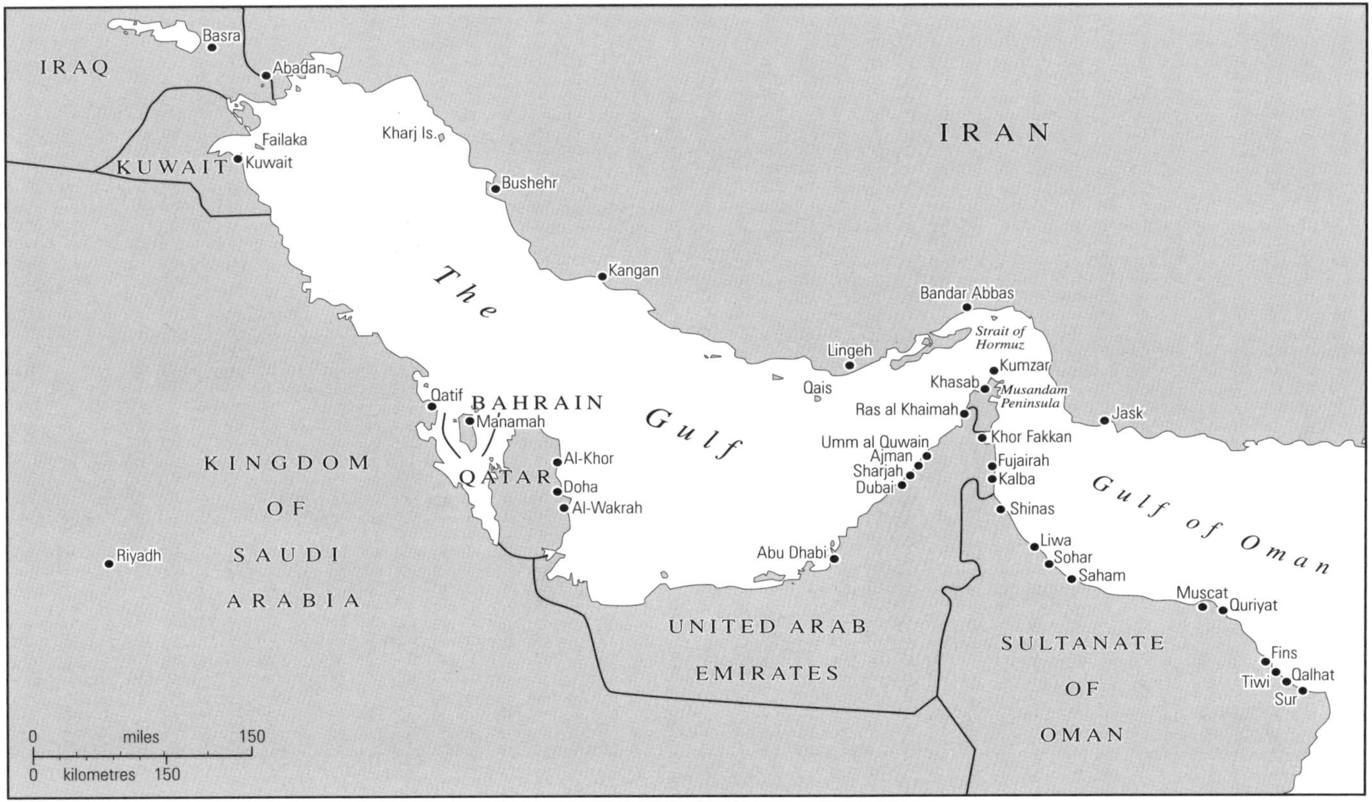
IRAQ
Basra
Abadan
KUWAIT
Kuwait
Failaka
Kharj Is.
Bushehr
IRAN
Kangan
The Gulf
Bandar Abbas
Strait of Hormuz
Lingeh
Qais
Kumzar
Khasab
Musandam Peninsula
Ras al Khaimah
Jask
Qatif
BAHRAIN
Manamah
QATAR
Al-Khor
Doha
Al-Wakrah
Umm al Quwain
Ajman
Sharjah
Dubai
Khor Fakkan
Fujairah
Kalba
Shinas
Gulf of Oman
KINGDOM OF SAUDI ARABIA
Riyadh
Abu Dhabi
Liwa
Sohar
Saham
Muscat
Quriyat
UNITED ARAB EMIRATES
SULTANATE OF OMAN
Fins
Tiwi
Qalhat
Sur
0 miles 150
0 kilometres 150

Map 2
The Arabian Gulf States and the Southern Arabian Coast

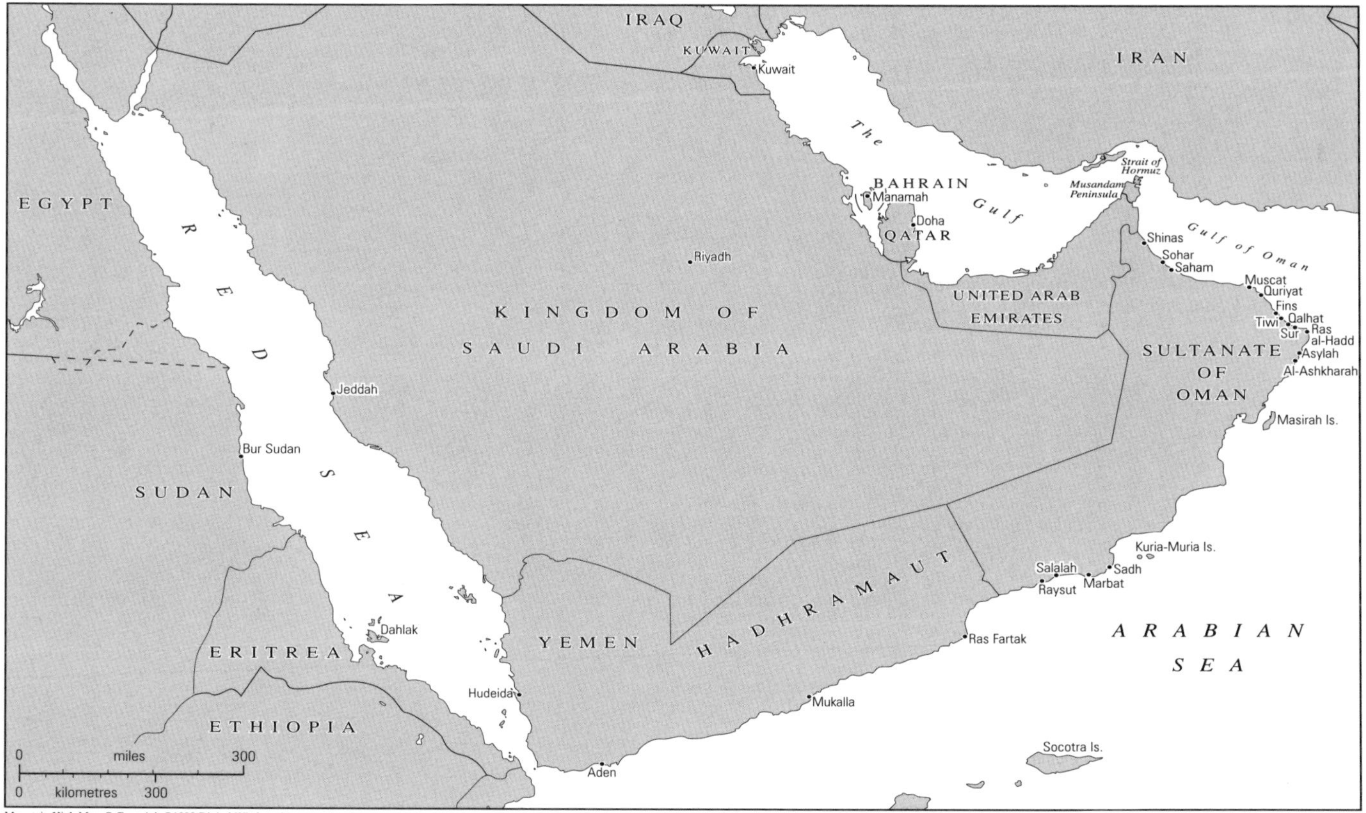

1
THE FIELDWORK

يالله يالله يالله
قلنا يالله
هو لو يا سيدي
هو لو يا فزعة الله

Let us sail !
Let us go forth !
O Lord, we proceed
in thy fear, O Allāh.

(Songs of the Sea – the raising of the sails)[1]

Dhows are very much a part of the material culture of the Arab world and Indian Ocean. In this book the reader will find many references to the term material culture which is normally taken to refer to objects such as articles of clothing, cooking utensils, building materials etc. Here, however, the term material culture represents both the inanimate object – the dhow – and the animate – the people associated with the dhow and their interaction with it. The names given and the way in which objects are used, peculiar to one society, may be adopted by other societies through cultural contact. Thus, material culture can be defined in terms of the transmission of the ideas and attitudes shared by one community, which make up its culture, from one generation to the next. Language is the chief agent of cultural transmission and although my primary interest is in the nomenclature, many of the objects which make up the material culture are fascinating in themselves and often of great aesthetic value as examples of visual art.

The present research is a study of the nomenclature of dhow types and parts of a dhow in the Arabian Gulf and Oman with the aim of establishing an historical and linguistic link from the medieval Islamic period to the present time. The book focuses on: a) technical and non-technical information from Arabic and western sources (though it is not my intention to present an in-depth study of boat architecture because this falls beyond my expertise), b) written and pictorial references to ship types in medieval and post-medieval sources and, c) fieldwork based on interviews with various people among the

1 'Yāllāh, yāllāh, yāllāh/gulnā yāllāh/huwa law yā sīd-ī/huwa law fazʿat Allāh' (al-Rifāʿī 1985: 140).

seafaring communities and with researchers in the field. The archival work included references to names of ship types, maritime ethnography and maps, the results of which have been of great value to my research. Thus by integrating the data available I applied a holistic approach, bringing together a variety of sources on boat typology, shipbuilding and sea activity.

At the outset I made a decision that in order to present a unified picture of traditional dhows in the Gulf and Oman and their origins and connections with the Indian Ocean and the Arabian Sea, I would need a fair amount of oral history, not only to corroborate the findings of earlier maritime historians and boat researchers as well as references to Muslim ships in medieval and post-medieval sources, but also to fill gaps not covered by the spoken word and documentary evidence. Of course there are always doubts about the legitimacy of oral history, the reliability of memory, and whether a person's account is representative of a period or community. However, what people do not say can be just as telling in certain circumstances as what they do say.

The late nineteenth and early twentieth-century studies of Wüstenfeld (1880), al-Dujaylī (1912, 1913), Ritter (1919), Kindermann's monograph (1934) and Zayyāt (1949) are indispensable sources on ship types. Kindermann based his research into Muslim ship types on classical and medieval Arabic sources and contemporary oral and written histories, and his studies are fundamental for the boat researcher albeit sometimes information is lacking or inaccurate. Māhir (1967) and al-Nakhīlī (1974) discuss the different types of Muslim craft in Classical Islam but with little or no information on the modern period. Shihāb (1987) studies ship types from the Indian Ocean, namely East Africa, the Southern Arabian Coast and the Red Sea; his work is based on earlier studies of Arab craft and includes some useful line drawings. Also of interest is the social and cultural data on communities, settlements and sea trade provided by western travellers to the Arabian/Persian Gulf and Oman: Niebuhr (1774), Burckhardt (1829), Chesney (1850), Hunter (1877), Burton (1893), Miles (1919), Dickson (1949), Thesiger (1967) and others are of great importance. Mention is required of Lorimer's *Gazetteer* (1986), in which Lorimer, together with his assistants, collected a mass of detailed information during their numerous field trips. The bulk of the work was conducted between 1908 and 1915 and it was checked by locals appointed by various offices of the British administration in India and the Gulf. Some of the descriptive and statistical information on tribal and coastal communities is remarkable for the time, though one wonders about the accuracy of some reports in spite of them having been checked and revised by local officials.

Technical information is hard to find in early Arabic sources of the medieval period, while the western literature (Portuguese, Dutch and English in particular), is significantly representative of ship types, functions and hull design. There has been much discussion on the classification of dhows and the European influence on the design of these ships after the arrival of the Portuguese in the Arabian/Persian Gulf and Indian Ocean, which led to a change from stitched to nail construction. Records of experiments in nautical archaeology were very useful in the present research. Heyerdahl's (1971, 1982) construction and fitting-out of replicas of reed boats similar to those of the Egyptians and Sumerian and Akkadian periods, and in the case of Severin (1982) the stitched boat, built on the lines of a medieval Arab trading vessel, may both give clues to some of the gaps in the history of shipbuilding. They may not prove that such ships actually sailed the voyages that both boat architects have tried to emulate, but they certainly prove that the boats could have travelled these distances on the basis of the strength and durability of their construction. These experiments, together with attempts at pictorial reconstructions of the dhow of the Middle Ages (Nicolle 1989: 168–97) in the Arabian/Persian Gulf and the Indian Ocean, confirm that an unchanging tradition of shipbuilding persisted for a long time even as far as the coastal stitched boat of modern times. European designs in the sixteenth century however, played a decisive role in several practical considerations such as seaworthiness, weight, speed, war strategies, or mere decoration. Such information is hard to find in Muslim historical, geographical and travel accounts of the medieval period and, accordingly, any scattered data was fundamental for reconstructing a picture of ship types of the above areas.

I am not currently aware of any comparative study of seacraft in the Arabian Gulf and Oman. Regional descriptive studies by al-Qināʿī and al-Khuṣūṣī (1982), ʿAbdallāh (1987), Shihāb (1987), al-Ḥijjī (1988), and al-Shamlān (1990), cover classificatory types of Arab dhows, shipbuilding, and navigational techniques; moreover, a lexicographical study by al-Rūmī (1996) includes names of parts of ships and other nautical information. Other works of equal substance are those by western nautical researchers and maritime historians, such as Pâris (1841), Moore (1925), Hornell (1942), LeBaron Bowen (1949, 1952), Villiers (1952), Hourani (1963), Johnstone and Muir (1964), Prins (1972–4), Yajima (1976), Hawkins (1977), Howarth (1977), Facey (1979), and Grosset-Grange's (1993) glossary of classical and modern Arabic nautical terms in the Indian Ocean. I have consulted all these works, referring to them whenever I wanted to corroborate either my findings from fieldwork, or information collected from interviewees.

The linguistic survey will not only look at names of dhow types but at how categories are defined, and how distinctions are perceived and expressed. An examination of the origins of these terms will give us more insight into how the different vessels were classified. These are categorized primarily by hull shape, some cases of which, to the casual observer, show no apparent difference, whereas European ships and boats are generally classified according to the rig. As a result of regional dialectal differences, similar ship types go by different names. Ambiguity soon arises when synonymous terms and regional variations and modifications over time are added to the picture. Alan Villiers and Clifford Hawkins and other writers have commented on this fact and cite various examples of it. I noticed however, that in spite of their technical knowledge, informative and reliable as it is, they sometimes fail to get a solid grip on the Arabic terminology, leaving a gap in the overall historical and linguistic picture. This is partly due to lack of knowledge of Arabic historical and literary sources and a linguistic knowledge of Arabic, and also, not being able to communicate effectively with local seamen or shipwrights other than through an interpreter.

The study of the origins of the names of dhow types, as well as the terminology of the parts of a vessel, is an area that has been little explored. Some scattered lists are found in the works already referred to (Hawkins, Hourani, Johnstone and Muir etc.) and in some Arabic works (al-Qināʿī and al-Khuṣūṣī, ʿAbdallāh, Shihāb, etc.). It was not my aim merely to collect and catalogue names of ship types in a lexicographical manner. Firstly it was important to discover the exact significance of the terms still in use off the Arabian Gulf and Omani coasts today, then to look them up in dictionaries. My aim in consulting lexica was to clarify, synchronically and diachronically, the term in question in the light of its context as portrayed in historical, geographical and travel accounts. This approach is of significant value to all researchers working in this field. It must be said however, that Arabic lexica (classical and modern) are not the best tools for the boat researcher. Often the term in question has not been included in dictionaries because lexicographers were not bothered with dialectal usages, a general problem which is found with many technical terms of the material culture. The dictionary of colloquial Anglo-Indian words, *Hobson-Jobson*, compiled by Yule and Burnell (1994; first published 1866), is generally good for the meaning and derivation of some names of ship types, but limited and sometimes unreliable. The best sources for tracing technical terms are historical and maritime works, the latter being rare in Arabic. These works may not describe the terms, but may contain information that could help the researcher in understanding their function. The Portuguese, Dutch and English documents were vital for the reconstruction of names of types in their historical context and looking for linguistic clues as to their origins.

An examination of the Arabic technical language brought to light a great many borrowings because Arabic was always flexible enough to borrow from other languages and cultures. The number of terms coming from Fārsī (Persian), Hindi and a few presumably from Portuguese, point to a mixing of diverse linguistic seafaring communities who introduced shipbuilding techniques together with traditions of seafaring. I found that with some names of dhow types, Arabic absorbed a wealth of foreign linguistic culture to such an extent that it is difficult to get to the roots of words and as Kindermann (1934: viii) rightly observed, it is difficult to establish which language a particular word belongs to in the first place. Arabic has a highly-developed morphology based in principle on a tri-consonantal root varying with a vowel-pattern system. This, unfortunately, is not a sign of strength in the area of technical and scientific terminology, and can in fact be problematic.

Gathering information about dhows has traditionally been a frustrating experience because of the difficulty of language, although this was not primarily a problem I came across in my own interviews and I rarely needed an interpreter. My educated spoken Arabic was sufficient to communicate with the coastal communities. Taking notes on the different parts of the dhow however, turned out to be more complicated than I originally thought as their nomenclature varied from Kuwait down to the Dhofari coast on the Arabian Sea. Some of the information I unearthed through my reading did not correspond with that given by my informants. This does not suggest that what I read was wrong; after all, some authors had, like me, recorded their findings from interviews. Lt Commander Vaughan and many others who gained first-hand information were often disappointed with their findings on dhow types and their sources of information often conflicted with one another. It was only after travelling to different shipyards and maritime centres that I discovered that one type of dhow might have different regional names and in other instances the same name might apply to other types of dhow. The same was true with names of the parts of a dhow. Technical terms varied regionally and this detail was not well recorded by previous researchers. I spent a lot of time sorting out discrepancies with my informants and had many headaches listening to the tapes, trying to figure out which was which. I was wrong to think that shipbuilders and ship owners necessarily provide accurate information on the nomenclature of ship types. Travelling to south-west India, East Africa and other maritime centres in the Gulf and the Arabian Sea, brought these builders and owners in contact with different types of ships, and new ideas led to alterations even though the hull design remained traditionally the same. Local fishermen, unlike the builders, are sedentary. Their knowledge on types of local boats, though not technical, relies on what their ancestors handed down to them. It is this dichotomy of adaptation versus tradition which I found intriguing and interesting.

Studying the names of ship types and hull designs entailed understanding the background of the builders, captains, sailors and fishermen. When I started my present project I believed that boat-building was not essentially ethnic in character and that there were no barriers to seafaring activity. Now, at the end of my project, the question of ethnicity has become crucial to my theory that the Fārsī content (some Indian) found in a ship's part names and to a lesser extent the nomenclature of ship types, indicates a strong Iranian element among settlers on the Arabian littoral. The way to test this was to establish from my interviewees their ancestral background and, even though some of their tribal names were easily detectable as being Iranian, I wanted to hear the story through their own words. This was not an easy task, basically because of the long historical and political rupture between Sunnī and Shīʿite Muslims, Iran of course being mainly Shīʿite and the rest of the Arabian Gulf mainly Sunnī. From medieval documents I learnt that historically among seafaring communities living on the Arabian coast, there had been an association with the Shīʿite belief, so I specifically asked locals about their religious and cultural background. Only a few were prepared to talk and then they were not happy that I was recording their conversations. From these recordings, and the silence of others, it does tend to confirm my hypothesis of a strong traditional Persian maritime heritage in the Gulf and Oman over the centuries. In Kuwait, Bahrain and Oman on the coast, there is evidence of a number of Shīʿite mosques which at one time served settlers who were engaged in seafaring. Many of the older generation still live in the neighbourhood of these mosques. The reference to Fārsī-Arabic speaking groups known as the Baḥārna in Bahrain (a minority in Kuwait), does suggest an active ethnic presence linked to Iran. The tradition of carving floral and geometric designs on the dhow's stem or sternposts could have its origins in Iran. This tradition extended to many towns and villages in the Gulf. They are also found on small and larger doors and in Sur I noticed that some doors had palm tree patterns. The tradition of carving doors is now becoming limited to wealthy families.

Indian Ocean seafaring has at times been dominated by Arabs and Persians, many of whom were shipbuilders and traders who had settled on the west Indian coast. Historically, maritime Muslim accounts, for example *Akhbār al-Ṣīn wa l-Hind*, compiled some time in 235/850, illustrate the importance of Indian navigation and its influence on Muslim navigation. Mention of Muslim captains and seamen mainly from Oman and Siraf, are found in sea adventures compiled by Buzurg b Shahriyār (d 399/1009) in the *Kitāb ʿajāʾib al-Hind*. The stories are of voyages made in India and China, similar to another collection of stories found in the *Silsalat al-tawārīkh* by al-Sīrāfī (fl third/ninth century) and 'The Voyages of Sindbād the Sailor' in the *One Thousand and One Nights*. The Muslim seafaring communities, linguistically diverse as they were, belonged to an Indian Ocean civilization of which the Arabian/Persian Gulf formed part. It is not surprising that

Muslim geographers in the early medieval period spoke of the Gulf as 'the arm of the Indian Ocean'. Fernand Braudel's imagery of the Mediterranean sea as a physical and human unit fits very well into the framework of the present research, not restricting the concept solely to history but extending it to the way in which a community shares a language and culture in common, and that material cultural terms reflect not only the language of a community but a whole set of systems such as economic and social changes, movements of people, climatic and cultural conditions, religion and politics, creating not only elements of cohesion but also contrasts.

Medieval works show how extended the Arabic language was, not only among Arabs but also non-Arabs and the Indian Ocean communities in particular. A too Arabocentric view of the Gulf and Oman can be corrected. Indian shipping, shipbuilding techniques and traders, play an important role in the dhow world and one may argue a strong case for considering the Arabian/Persian Gulf as part of the Indian Ocean civilization which in the days of sail, trading under the seasonal Monsoon winds, formed a natural unity.

Studying the nomenclature of material culture, one becomes aware that not only does the language exist as an abstract system, codified in grammar books and dictionaries, but that it is integral with everyday life and belongs ultimately to its community users. The everyday interaction of the speaker with material culture is reflected in how a technical term operates in a cultural relationship. In this respect the language of the dhow in the Arabian Gulf and Oman as portrayed in the names of dhow types, their parts, the boat-builders, the language of the sailors, and the relationship between the seafaring communities and the dhow world, presents a dynamic study in the understanding of Arab seafaring within the Indian Ocean civilization. The findings in this book show that the study of the nomenclature of types of dhow and technical terms for parts of a dhow, is a discipline that underpins the identity and language of a people, demonstrating their specialized skills and artistic imagination to produce objects for use both within their community and for the outside world.

2
The Maritime Setting

ثم سافرت من بلاد عمان إلى بلاد هرمز... ووصلنا إلى هرمز الجديدة... وهي مدينة حسنة كبيرة..
لها أسواق حافلة وهي مرسى الهند والسند ومنها تحمل سلع الهند إلى العراقين وفارس وخراسان

I travelled next from the land of ʿOmān to the land of Hurmuz . . . We came to New Hurmuz . . . It is a fine large city, with magnificent bazaars, as it is the port of India and Sind, from which the wares of India are exported to the two ʿIrāqs, Fārs and Khurāsān.

(Ibn Baṭṭūṭa, 1995, II: 400 [230–1][1]

The history of the Arabian/Persian Gulf and Oman from the sixteenth to the nineteenth century is complex, partly because of the volatility of the Arab tribes in the area but mainly due to the lack of Arabic and Persian records, and to a lesser extent, Ottoman sources.[2] On the other hand, the history of European policy in the Indian Ocean and Arabian/Persian Gulf is well documented but inevitably we are left with a picture which is incomplete and unbalanced. This is difficult to correct. What I have attempted here is an historical overview by setting up the maritime scene in the area from the seventeenth century to the present day,[3] based on European (namely Anglo-Indian) records, as a background for the study of dhow type-names and dhow activity, in the Arabian/Persian Gulf and the Indian Ocean.

The foundations of the English and Dutch companies

The Portuguese naval success in the Indian Ocean and the Arabian/Persian Gulf was impressive throughout the sixteenth century. Their superiority was marked by well-armed ships, compared with the small Muslim merchant and war vessels which were inferior in technology and equipment. Soon

1 Ibn Baṭṭūṭa visited Oman and the Persian Gulf in 729/1329.

2 B. J. Slot's *The Arabs of the Gulf 1602–1784* (Abu Dhaḅi – The Hague: CDRAD, 1991) is one of the best works on the early history of the Gulf states. It revolves around three themes: tribes, traders and tollhouses, focusing on the people of the coasts and sea.

3 Lorimer's (1986) reports are among the best of the sources. For a very readable and general good discussion on the rise of the Gulf states, see R. Said Zahlan's work, *The Making of the Modern Gulf States* (Reading: Ithaca Press, 1998; a revised and updated edition of 1989).

after the Portuguese had integrated into the local political and commercial environment of the Indian Ocean, they faced a new challenge: the arrival of English and Dutch ships at the end of the sixteenth century. It was an encounter which proved disastrous to the Portuguese both in terms of manpower and naval skills; moreover, it was fatal to their economic prosperity. The founding of both the English East India Company, incorporated by royal charter in 1600, and the Dutch Verenigde Oost-Indische Compagnie in 1602, created powerful and prestigious organizations, combining, as they did, trade and political objectives. They had begun to acquire a commercial footing in India between 1600 and 1612 and in Oman in the following years. The creation of these companies coincided with the reign of Ṣafavid political power (under Shāh ʿAbbās I; 996–1038/1588–1629) and its rival, the Ottoman Empire, which was at the start of an economic decline. The Ottomans were to suffer several setbacks from the competition of western manufactured goods and superior commercial techniques (Inalcik 1973: 445). It had been Portuguese policy to maintain an equal balance of rivalry between the Persians and the Ottomans, without committing themselves to either. But Shāh ʿAbbās was far ahead of the Portuguese. He sought contact with the west to create a European alliance against the Ottomans. It was the alliance between Persia and England which marked the end of Portuguese power. The Portuguese had lost their grip on all the coastal towns of Malabar in India, and in the Arabian/Persian Gulf and Oman; they were practically destroyed after the fall of Hormuz in 1622 (illus. 1). Thereafter, both the British and Persians occupied Hormuz and the English East India Company settled at Bandar Abbas.

1

Ruins of the Portuguese fort on the east coast of Fujairah, United Arab Emirates

The fall of the Portuguese was due perhaps to violence and bad conduct in dealing with the Muslims; certainly, the fact that no trade company was founded, as their English and Dutch rivals were to do, could be explained by their chaotic administration, general lack of discipline and in later years their succumbing to various plagues and diseases (Lorimer 1986, I, ia: 39). The loss of the island of Hormuz was a symbolic defeat for the Portuguese. It was not just a political incident; it marked the entry of the English and the Dutch into the world market, who further consolidated their power throughout the seventeenth century. The Persians had settled on the Arabian coast at Muscat, Khor Fakkan, Julfar and Khasab in 1634, sometimes with the help of the English East India Company, and built themselves fortresses there.[4] Bandar Abbas (Gombroon), on the Persian coast, was a remarkably good place for the English company's trade with the Persian markets inland. Oman played an important role in bringing Portuguese control to an end. The Imām Nāṣir Āl Yaʿrubī (1034–59/1624–49) in 1646 concluded a trade treaty with the British, the result of which started a relationship which was to grow from strength to strength in future centuries. Sulṭān bin Sayf Āl Yaʿrubī (1059–1131/1649–1718), his successor, built up an impressive navy (presumably with the help of the British) and established a good network of overseas trade, the only source of prosperity for Oman.

By the mid eighteenth century, the Dutch and the English companies and later, the French Compagnie des Indes Orientales established in 1664, traded eastern goods to points in Europe passing through many lands in the Middle East and the Mediterranean. The route was long and broken into short stages and losses were often incurred by the companies, but economically and politically the arrangement proved much more secure. From the statistics published by Amin (1967: 155), it is difficult to interpret the meaning of the figures for Dutch and English representatives attached to foreign residences: there were 114 Dutch in Bandar Abbas in 1740 and about 130 in Kharg after 1756,[5] while the number of British in Bandar Abbas in 1751 was only 11. The large Dutch presence could possibly suggest a number of merchants involved in trade (probably many were not even Dutch), and not residing members, as government agents would have been. It seems, therefore, that the English establishment gives a true representation of the number of chief officials (with a small clerical staff) residing in Bandar Abbas at the time. Contemporary documents on economic matters of this period are many though they are one-sided and our knowledge of the economic system, apart from external trade, remains vague.

4 CDRAD/Dutch Archives, VOC Bahrain, ARA 132, 1756 fol 30; Slot 1993: 97.

5 See section on Dutch figures in ARA – VOC, vol 5168–214.

The following commodities mentioned in the Dutch economic documents reveal to what extent the luxury and bulk goods transported by the Dutch were marketed at the inter-regional level and then carried to Europe: camphor, copper, lacquer and porcelain, from Japan and China; zinc from Taiwan; pepper from Sumatra and Wingurla; indigo from Souratta; sugar from Jakarta (Batavia); cinnamon, woollen fabrics, benjuin (used in medicines and perfumes), iron, steel, candied ginger, anise, silk-type material and arrack, from Sri Lanka (Ceylon); pewter from Malacca; various linens from the Bengal and the Surat coast; coffee (cauwa) from Mocha; cardamom, sandalwood, radix, gum lac, gold, borrie, dried ginger, nutmeg, cloves and mace from various places.[6]

London and Amsterdam became leading centres in the West for re-exporting eastern goods to Europe and America. The great trading regions of the Arabian/Persian Gulf, the Indian Ocean, China and south-east Asia had established a system of interdependent economic relations, a profitable chain which still exists today. Relations between the English and Dutch companies seem to have been cordial up to the second half of the eighteenth century, a time when England established good relations with the Arab tribes on the Arabian littoral of the Gulf. The English built factories in Bandar Abbas, Isfahan, Basra and other places in Persia and Iraq in order to distribute English products in the Gulf and to use the Basra factory for the company's dispatches, the safest route being through Basra and Aleppo and from there to the Mediterranean. The company bestowed regular gifts of money and goods on the Arab tribes.[7] From this time the trading power of the French Company started to gradually fade away. The overland route proved of great value for the English and Dutch companies which prospered, and with difficulty, strengthened their political ties with the Bedouin Arabs, and made the number of factories built on the Persian coast financially viable.

Tribal settlements on the coast

Little is known about the general state of the economy of the Arab and Persian settlements on the coasts of the Gulf during the sixteenth and seventeenth centuries. Nomadic cattle-breeding and occasional sea trade, as in the past, had brought some sources of 'income' which supplemented the poor food of their own production and provided textiles for clothing. Agriculture on the coast was next to none. The port towns of Bandar Abbas, Bushehr, Bandar Kong, Basra and Muscat had, as of old, well-established

6 CDRAD/Dutch Archives, VOC Bahrain, ARA 132, 1756 fol 34.

7 IOR – FRPPG, vol 18 dispatch no 1229, Basra 6 November 1784; vol 14 dispatch no 2330, Bandar Abbas 2 March 1724; vol 15 dispatch no 670, Basra 19 May 1741.

principal caravans that went inland.[8] The income from transit trade was taxed by the rulers of states like Muscat, Basra and Hormuz.[9] Some tribes from semi-independent territories would ask for contributions from ships sailing through their waters; piratical raids were organized to rightfully attack foreign (European, Indian etc) ships if payments were not made. The Portuguese and their allies seem to have been the main target; the English and Dutch in India or Persia who sailed in dhows were spared, though errors occurred.[10] In general, annual income from importing and exporting brought large portions of wealth to locals in a number of coastal settlements; the foreigners had a smaller share of the profit. Arab and Persian seamen joined the foreign merchant navies; others worked for local traders who owned ships, and who sold food, water and firewood.[11]

Two other sources of income connected with the sea were fishing and pearling; at one time both yielded great profits, but not during the presence of the European companies in the area. It was much later in the late nineteenth century that the pearl industry made considerable profits in Kuwait, Bahrain, Qatar and Trucial Oman (partly the Emirates). Fishing, on the other hand, brought a steady, though relatively small, income. Apart from feeding the inhabitants on the coast, some dried fish was sold to passing ships, caravans and of course, most importantly, was used for feeding cattle and fertilizing the date palm trees. Fishing, pearling, and particularly transit trade, served as a power base for the Arab tribes who settled on the northern Arabian littoral of the Gulf. By the eighteenth century we see their importance growing as economic and political powers at a time when the Europeans started, with their fast sailing ships, to open a new route around the Cape of Good Hope.

Trade between Bombay and Basra initiated the rise of the ʿUtbī maritime power in the mid eighteenth century. The rise of the ʿUtūb, the ancestors of the ruling families of Kuwait and Bahrain, marks the beginning of their political supremacy in the Arabian/Persian Gulf. The Arab tribes living along the Arabian littoral were influential and their political and economic relationship with the Persians in the north-east, the Ottomans in Iraq, the Arabs in the south, namely Oman, and the English Company, became increasingly difficult. In fact the Banī Khālid tribe was the strongest power in

8 ARA – VOC, vol 1304, fols 479, 488–9.

9 ARA – VOC, vol 1304, fols 490–1.

10 CDRAD/British Archives, GD, G/14/9, 1756; /15/10, 1756; /4/12, 1756.

11 ARA – VOC, vol 2448, fols 1994–9; one letter (dated 1717) mentions a local ship loaded with firewood being stopped by Arab ships; see CDRAD/Dutch Archives, VOC, vol 1913 Bandar Abbas 1717, fol 50.

the Gulf in the first half of the eighteenth century, their influence growing from Kuwait to Oman. As one letter from the Dutch Verenigde Oost-Indische Compagnie reports in 1741: 'The Arabs dominate all lands from the entrance on the Gulf till the Euphrates'.[12] The ʿUtūb family who came from al-Aflaj in Najd (central Arabia), first settled in Kuwait and lived under the protection of the sheikh of the Banī Khālid until 1752. Upon his death the ʿUtūb built independent states: in Kuwait, in about 1716; Zubara in Qatar in 1766, and then Bahrain in 1782. The Gulf and the desert routes operated so well that ʿUtbī vessels to and from India ceased calling at Muscat to avoid paying taxes to the sultan. Instead they called at Zubara and Bahrain.

The factories of the English and Dutch companies were fortified and warships accompanied cargo vessels to protect them against piracy which was provoked by the Qawāsim,[13] a powerful seafaring community,[14] most feared by the Gulf states and the European powers in India. The Companies arranged to have vessels for the Persian fleet procured from India during Nādir Shāh's reign (1148–60/1736–47).[15] Not Persian, but Indian and Portuguese captains navigated these warships; French sailors were also seen sailing on Arab dhows (Niebuhr 1774: 269–70). It was not uncommon to find Europeans engaged in seafaring; renegades who had deserted from the armies in the East professed Islam and took refuge under Muslim rulers. The Arabs, though not mentioned in connection with Gulf warships and cargo vessels, were good seamen: they were employed by Nādir Shāh for his naval fleet on the Caspian Sea. However, many Arabs were making a living from pearl-diving which was becoming increasingly important in Bahrain at the end of the eighteenth century.[16]

From the mid to the end of the eighteenth century the state of affairs in the Arabian/Persian Gulf was one of turmoil. After the death of Nādir Shāh in 1747, anarchy broke out among several major Arab forces namely those of Bushehr, Bandar-e Rig and Banī Kaʿb of Dawraq, including other Arab Huwala tribes who lived on the southern coast of Persia viz. Qishm, Qais and Hormuz (Abu Hakima 1965: 79). The Shāh, Karīm Khān (1163–93/1750–79) failed to subdue the Arab incursions but succeeded in

12 CDRAD/Dutch Archives, VOC, vol 2546, 1741, fol 33.

13 See report from Bandar Abbas to the Court of Directors, London: IOR – FRPPG, vol 14 dispatch no 2384, Bandar Abbas 15 March 1727; see also Lorimer 1986, I, ia: 147.

14 The Qawāsim were part of the Huwala clan, their name originating from Shaykh Qāsim, whose grandfather Shaykh Rashīd bin Maṭar resided at Julfar (Ras al Khaimah) (Miles 1994: 269).

15 See report from Basra to Court of Directors, London: IOR – FRPPG, vol 15 dispatch no 671, Basra 16 December 1741.

16 CDRAD/Dutch Archives, ARA/Aanw no 1889– 23b.

taking Basra from the Ottomans in 1775; Basra was then the richest port of the Gulf and much envied by other ports in the region. The English left Basra just before the town was sacked by the Persians and reopened their factory in Bushehr.[17] The loss of their establishment in Basra was felt badly; their choice to leave was incumbent because of their having assisted the Ottomans in trade matters. Some time later, however, the English negotiated with the Persians through the intermediary of the sheikh of Bushehr to return to Basra, and though they were finally granted permission to reopen the factory in 1776, political tension remained between them and the Persians. Following Karīm Khān's death in 1779, Basra fell again into the hands of the Ottomans. The English were then able to administer Basra for some time, under Ottoman occupation, on more peaceful terms.[18]

Perhaps the most devastating blow to the economy of the Gulf in general was the spread of the plague in 1773 which struck Basra, and was then carried to Kuwait, Qatif and Bahrain, the estimated number of deaths rising to two million.[19] It was at this point that much of the trade destined for Basra began to go to Kuwait, and Zubara in Qatar. Meanwhile, Muscat became the emporium for trade in the second half of the eighteenth century: it owned a large number of trading dhows which sailed to Surat, Bombay, Goa and the Malabar coast, and also to Mocha and Jeddah on the Red Sea. Many vessels from Basra and the town ports of the Gulf called at Muscat to load and unload their goods (Parsons 1808: 207). The Oman–India–Gulf trade triangle was practically run by ʿUtbī and Muscat fleets (Saldanha 1908: 409).

It is in this context that we find mention of ship types in the area: none of the sources give descriptions of Arab vessels, nor for that matter anything about Persian or Ottoman vessels. Dutch and Indian (Bombay) records mention some local types of ships but give no information as to how large they were and it is only in context that we can guess what function they had. A *ghurāb* is often mentioned in reference to fighting, aggression and battles in general: a Muscat Arab ship attacked a *ghurāb* sailing from Bandar Abbas to Surat in India in 1717;[20] the Persian navy in Bandar Abbas chased a fleeing *ghurāb* in 1741.[21] There were *ghurāb*s, according to the British Gombroon Diaries, that carried from 14 to 20 guns on deck.[22] Also mentioned in the

17 EBD, vol 203, fols 45, 61, 93, 133; *Chronicle* 1927, II: 1209–10; ARA – DLH, no 165, letter from Aleppo, 16 June 1775.

18 Saldanha 1908, I: 308–9; ARA – DLH, no 165, letter from Aleppo 16 June 1779.

19 Letter from Mr Moore and company of the Basra Factory to the Court of Directors, London: IOR – FRPPG, vol 17 dispatch no 1061, Basra 16 January 1774.

20 CDRAD/Dutch Archives, VOC, vol 1913, Bandar Abbas 2 April 1717, fol 29.

21 CDRAD/Dutch Archives, VOC, vol 2680, 1741, fol 44.

22 CDRAD/British Archives, GD, G/29/5, 19 March 1769.

records is the *gallivat* or *gallouet*, belonging to the Persians, which operated as a warship or pirate ship: a number of these were reported in 1759 to have been cruising near Basra. The most powerful Arabs on the Persian littoral, the Banī Kaʿb, their stronghold being at Dawraq, used Persian *gallouet*s in 1774 to plunder Qatif, renowned for its pearl commerce.[23] However, Turkish *gallivat*s are mentioned in 1775.[24] They were, in Edward Ives' description, 'superior to any force the Turks or their neighbours have in these seas' (1758: 204). The most common type that appears in the Dutch documents was the *trankey*,[25] owned by Persians or Arabs[26] and mentioned with reference to transportation of soldiers and trading cargo, some being equipped with war ammunition.[27] The British Gombroon Diaries of this period often record *trankey*s belonging to Julfar Arabs: one document reports in 1760 how they 'continue to trouble the Gulph in *trankey*s and we fear that they molest small craft trading this way'.[28] They are described as 'very large' craft and armed for fighting.[29]

The sea-borne trade

European trading vessels reached the ports of Qatar and Kuwait and transferred their goods to caravans for the Baghdad–Aleppo desert route. The diaries of European travellers who used those caravans have left abundant information on the state and condition of such routes.[30] In particular, the Dane, Carsten Niebuhr (d 1815), surveyed whole territories of Arabia; his work is full of factual information, some things observed personally and some learned from others. His notes about caravan routes of the Bedouins through Iraq and Syria are incredibly detailed and accurate. There is no doubt that the desert route was very significant in building up the Gulf as a route for transporting Indian goods to the markets of the Ottoman provinces, the

23 IOR – FRPPG, vol 17 despatch no 1074, dated 1774.

24 Report from Mr Moore, Latouche Abraham to the Court of Directors, London: IOR – FRPPG, vol 17 dispatch no 1089, 15 August 1775.

25 There are other spellings, see Chapter 4.

26 On a few occasions the Dutch made reference in their letters to Persians and Arabs having a fleet of *tranquin*s (ie *trankey*s) as large as 100 or 110, see CDRAD/Dutch Archives, VOC 2546, fols 403–5, fol 1434.

27 CDRAD/Dutch Archives, VOC 2546, fols 33, 87, 403–5, 1434, 2133–6; VOC 2584, 1741 fols 2109–17; VOC 2680, OB 1747, 77 fol 825; Ibes 1758, 204, 214; ARA/Aanw no 1889–23b, fol 8; ARA/Aanw no 1889–23b, fol 11; IOR – FRPPG, vol 17 despatch no 1089.

28 CDRAD/British Archives, GD, G/29/17, 1760.

29 CDRAD/British Archives, GD, G/29/6, 29 November 1743; GD, G/29/7, 26 June 1751 and 19 September 1751; GD, G/29/13, 19 July 1761.

30 See Abu Hakima 1965: 168, fn 2.

Mediterranean and Europe. Of course, the Arabian/Persian Gulf had to compete, as it often did, with its rival the Red Sea, where European vessels carrying Indian goods called at Suez. Muscat was the best stopping place for a large number of vessels bound for the Gulf and the Red Sea. Bahrain was sought after, mainly for the quality of its pearls, a market which developed with Muscat and other ports.[31] In India, large dhows were built around the 1780s for the seafaring community in Bahrain, who imported Indian goods for their own use and for export to Baghdad and Aleppo. Zubara, east of Qatar, was also at this time a vital centre for pearl trading though perhaps on a smaller scale than Bahrain.[32] It was, indeed, the second centre of general commercial activities of the Āl Khalīfa and the other ʿUtbī families. It rivalled the other ports on the Persian littoral and was attacked by the Arabs living there (Lorimer 1986, I, ia: 146–7).

With the English company's establishment of a factory in Kuwait in 1793, we start to see the beginnings of commercial success largely depending upon transit trade, though the company was only using Kuwait as a centre for distributing mail. Several war threats, from Banī Kaʿb and other Arabs from the Persian coast, menaced the Āl Ṣabāḥ family who had by now established themselves in Kuwait. The family had to build its own war fleet against the enemy and also managed to persuade caravaneers and shipowners with imported goods bound for Muscat, Qatif, Bahrain and Zubara, to call at Kuwait to avoid the heavy duties levied at Basra. Imports were Surat blue goods, Bengal coarse white goods, Bengal soosies, coffee, sugar, pepper, spices, iron and lead, and other considerable quantities of Bengal and Surat goods such as cotton, yarn, camby, chanders, coffee and pepper, for the Baghdad and Aleppo merchants (Saldanha 1908: 107). The Āl Ṣabāḥ faced opposition from the British, who refrained from unloading at Kuwait the goods destined for Baghdad and Aleppo; politically, they considered Basra as the official sea port after Muscat, at least from 1763 to 1800.

The Qawāsim and piracy

The Trucial Coast of Oman (or the Pirate Coast as it was known by the

31 See Buckingham 1829: 454–7; Wellsted 1838, I: 264–5 and 1840: 115–23.

32 It is probably that the Āl Khalīfa family arrived at Zubara from Kuwait in 1766. Zubara became a stronghold of the ruling family, see Lorimer 1986, IIc: 1534, 1952; and also al-Riḥānī 1960, II: 207–35. The Persians were then in control of Bahrain and, fearing the Āl Khalīfa political and economic threat, launched an attack on Zubara but with a great loss. In retaliation, Aḥmad bin Muḥammad Āl Khalīfa (1782–96) attacked the Persians' main holds in Bahrain and successfully expelled them from Bahrain in 1783 (Belgrave 1975: 131). Following this victory, the ruling family moved from Zubara and settled on the island.

British in the nineteenth century), was the territory of several tribes most of whom rallied to the Qawāsim[33] of Ras al Khaimah who became adherents to Wahhābism.[34] The Wahhābīs[35] with their call for *jihād* (holy war) grew in importance in Arabia where they made their first appearance and then gradually infiltrated Trucial Oman. The new religious and political movement was, as Winder (1965: 14) rightly described it, 'a distant ancestor of later Arab nationalism'. Its appeal to the Qawāsim was the idea of the true identity of an Arab against the European infidel who was policing the coast against piratical activities and later the slave trade, activities which were imbued with different meanings for the Arabs. Certainly, military success was more appealing to the Qawāsim than embracing the iconoclastic and puritanical Islamic preaching of the Wahhābīs. The Trucial Coast ruler Shaykh Sulṭān bin Ṣaqr (d 1283/1866) of Sharjah played a double game with the British; he expressed fear of Wahhābī advance and requested British aid in case the threat persisted while at the same time he and Rashīd bin Ḥumayd of Ajman welcomed the Wahhābīs partly because they felt pressurized by a large proportion of the people who accepted Wahhābism without reservation. Omani expansionist policy as far as Bahrain, and Bandar Abbas, Hormuz and Qishm on the southern coasts of Persia under Sulṭān bin Aḥmad (1206–20/1792–1806), had now been threatened by the Wahhābīs. By 1833, practically all of the Arabian/Persian Gulf acknowledged Wahhābism. Britain's policy, however, made clear to the sheikhdoms and the Omani sultan, Saʿīd bin Sulṭān (1205–73/1791–1856), that it would not interfere in mainland affairs but would continue to exercise maritime security.[36]

The Qawāsim were at war with the sultan of Muscat (probably because of his good relations with the British) but continued to trade with neighbouring ports on both sides of the Gulf.[37] Following the decline of Persian ascendancy in the Gulf, the Qawāsim lived on the proceeds of raids and plunder, causing

33 The Qawāsim was a term used by the English and Dutch, substituting the name for 'pirates'. A study on the rise and fall of this tribal confederacy, using primary sources, was undertaken by the present sheikh of Sharjah, Sultan Muhammad al-Qasimi, in a work entitled *The Myth of Arab Piracy in the Gulf* (originally a PhD dissertation at the University of Exeter) and published in London 1986. An attempt is made in this book to correct the long myth that the Qawāsim were pirates; see other details in Miles 1994: 263 seq; particularly the Qawāsim pirates (312–6, 440), pursuing peace (306) and trade with English ports (307).

34 IOL – BM, Add 7358, fols 38–9.

35 The founder was Muḥammad bin ʿAbd al-Wahhāb (d 1207/1792), a native of the town ʿUyainah in the Najd. He and his disciples followed the legal school of Aḥmad b Ḥanbal (d 241/855), founder of the orthodox school of Islamic law.

36 See Wellsted 1838, I: 200; Miles 1994: 334 and Blunt 1985: 529–30.

37 IOR – SRBG, vol 24, fol 301.

havoc both on sea and land. They were able seamen and owned some 63 large dhows and a huge fleet of smaller ones. From 1806 to 1809, it was estimated that 19,000 men were working for the Qawāsim at sea (Lorimer 1986, I, ia: 183), with around 900 vessels. Two British expeditions were sent to fight them. The first ended with a temporary cessation of piracy after 'offensive measures to chastise the hostility of the pirates in the Gulf of Persia';[38] the second expedition in 1809 was more successful in its mission, the chief aim being to destroy piratical craft and to conclude a treaty whereby the safety of navigation in the Gulf was secured. The British government employed war vessels from the company and the navy, and about 1,000 European troops to combat the Qawāsim: they captured Ras al Khaimah after house-to-house fighting and some thirty large warships were destroyed in the harbour (ibid, 184).

Information about the types of war vessel used by the Qawāsim, and the natives in the Gulf at the time, is scanty. From the British Gombroon Diaries of the eighteenth century there is continuous mention of *dingey*s which were Persian and possibly Indian, but we know nothing about their hull design except that they were large sailing ships.[39] One particular vessel that appears in these diaries is the *dow* (or *dough*), which is almost always associated with the Qawāsim pirates and slave trading (illus. 2). The ship was large and armed, 'the largest of which mounts 14 guns', reports one letter.[40] The *dow*s carried slaves from Africa and Baluchistan and sometimes contraband cargoes of drugs or liquor or gold; the prospect of large profits for smuggling outweighed the risk of capture by military patrol boats. The name *dow* (or as it is known today *dhow*) became the stereotype nomenclature given by the English for any type of native Arab, Persian or Indian vessel (see Chapter 3). One other vessel mentioned in connection with slave trading was the *sanbūq* (ibid, I, iib: 2496, 2498), recognizable by its low curved stem and high stern. Two other types that occur in the records are the *baqqāra* and *battīl*,[41] both of

38 Extract from a letter to Jonathan Duncan, President at Bombay from W. T. Money, Marine Superintendent: CDRAD/British Archives, GD – SPDD, no 232, fols 5669–70, M. 215–6 (dated 10 May 1808).

39 CDRAD/British Archives, GD, G/29/6, 20 November 1743; GD, G/29/7, 24 December 1746; GD, G/29/7, 30 October 1747.

40 Extract of a letter to Alexander Walker, resident of Basra from Lieutenant W. Maxfield, Commander of the Cruiser *Sylph*: CDRAD/British Archives, GD – SPDD, no 232, fols 5669–70, M. 215–6 (dated 14 April 1808); see also letter to the Court of Directors from William Digges Latouche: GD, G/29/21, 7 November 1782 and letter to Samuel Manesty, resident at Basra, from Nicholas Hankey Smith at Bushehr: GD, G/29/23, 1 July 1797.

41 IOR – SRBG, vol 24, fol 474 (year 1856 [?]).

2
A drawing of a possible *dāw* on the wall of Fort Liwa, Oman

3
Battīls and *baqqāras*: the troops are preparing to land on the morning of 13 November 1809 (Temple 1911, no. 6)

which had already appeared in the Dutch reports of the eighteenth century.[42] A drawing extracted from Temple (1811: no 6) shows several *battīl*s and *baqqāra*s engaged in battle, though curiously enough they are being used by the British and their aides (probably Arabs and Persians) (illus. 3); most probably these dhows were well known for their speed and often outsailed the European vessels. The *battīl*, for example, was renowned for being a swift war vessel while the *baqqāra* was smaller but with a lot of manoeuvrability, particularly when approaching the shore (see Chapter 5). The same report also records *baghla*, a double-ended piratical type of vessel with gun ports on deck for cannons; there is a model *baghla*, dated about 1830, in the Science Museum in London. The vessel was also a slave trader (Lorimer 1986, I, iib: 2494, 2502). One letter mentions a *baghla* carrying eighty bags of treasure on board '60 of which were safely carried away and brought up to Bushire [Bushehr]'.[43]

The treaty which implied, among other things, the safety of navigation in the Gulf, was not honoured by the Qawāsim. Piratical offences committed by them never stopped between 1811 and 1816. They attacked and robbed several large native vessels belonging to Basra and Kangun on the Persian coast, and right out in the Arabian Sea and the Gujarat coast: in 1813, a Persian vessel was captured, likewise in the waters between Muscat and Bandar Abbas in 1814, and several attacks on British vessels occurred in 1815 and 1816. The list of offences, according to Lorimer (ibid, I, ia: 183), was too long to mention, and a third expedition was organized against the Qawāsim settlement in Ras al Khaimah and other ports in 1819 and 1820. The British landed there after destroying several piratical craft and other large vessels; similar operations took place in Bahrain, Lengeh and Kangun. Continuous monitoring of Trucial Oman was set up by the British to counteract any revival of piratical activity. The severe punishment inflicted on the pirates during the ensuing period was a death-blow to piracy in the Gulf and by 1835 it was almost eradicated. But it was not until 1853 that Britain and the sheikhdoms of the Gulf finally agreed to the Perpetual Maritime Truce, agreeing to stop piracy. Elsewhere, the British company stationed at Muscat used its influence to control, and then end, the slave trade. Patrol boats had the power to stop and arrest 'all moorish ships and vessels sailing about without an English pass'.[44] Captain Sawyer reports to have encountered several piratical fleets around 1856: 'the surrendered pirate commanders

42 CDRAD/Dutch Archives, VOC 3184, 7, 11–12, 27, 33 [fols 8, 17–18, 51, 61] (year 1766).

43 Letter to Captain H. Lowe from S. Hennell (resident): CDRAD/British Archives, GD, R/15/1/115, 19 January 1848.

44 CDRAD/Dutch Archives, VOC 2088, 1726–8, fol 3420 (April 1727).

were sent to Bombay where the principal one was tried, found guilty, and condemned to death'.[45]

Slave trade

The suppression of piracy had almost come to an end when reports of large numbers of slaves from East Africa being shipped on dhows to various Gulf ports, started to reach the Political Agent in Bushehr in 1837. The traffic had assumed terrifying proportions and the fight to suppress slavery became a complex and long-drawn-out affair. The practice of slavery among the Arab and Persian seamen contributed to the commercial supply of African blacks for centuries.[46] Slavery had always been an institution sanctioned by religious law and custom; Arabs and Persians saw their age-old practices as good as perhaps the bonds of servitude practised in British India. Lt Colonel John Johnson (quoted by Hawley 1995: 96–7) on his visit to Muscat in 1817, observed that the Arab owners adopted the slaves with full rights of sharing their master's property at their death: 'They are perfectly trustworthy and instances are not wanting in which they have been left sole heirs of the property . . .'. The slave trade yielded great profits not only for the Arab and Persian *nākhōda* (sea captain) and the slave traders who accompanied them on the dhows on their voyages down the east African coast, but also for the sheikhs, the dealers in the markets, and the caravaneers.[47] Slave labour was for the most part employed in household duties but others were engaged in productive work. There were among these, sailors, pearl divers, fishermen, boatbuilders and other skilled manual labourers.

45 IOR – SRBG, vol 24, fol 477 (1856 [?]).

46 One good example is found during the third/ninth century when thousands of black slaves, known as the Zanj, were brought (presumably from the east African coast) to the marshes of southern Iraq clearing the nitrous top soil for arable ground. They toiled for years under appalling conditions, exposed to fatal sicknesses as a result of the dampness and dirt; see Th. Nöldeke, *Sketches from Eastern History*, trans J. Sutherland Black (London, 1892), one of the earliest to write a topographical study of southern Iraq during the Zanj movement, see also A. Popovic, *La révolte des esclaves en Iraq au III/IXe siècle* (Paris, 1967) remains one of the best studies we have on the economic social factors that led to the Zanj insurrection.

47 Unquestionably, slave trade was one of the most profitable branches of shipping. It was portrayed in a genre of sea adventure stories about Arab and Persian pirates sailing on vessels and looting European or local ships which firstly began to emerge in Portuguese and Dutch chronicles and then in English chronicles. Novelists wrote about the romantic image of the piratical dhow but in the eyes of the Arabs and Persians it was a political stigma that the westerners, in particular the British, assigned to them in their effort to eradicate slavery.

As much as Islamic teaching actually favoured emancipation of slaves there is overwhelming evidence to point to the fact that the British, in the case of the Arabian/Persian Gulf, Oman and East Africa, had put pressure on the sheikhs and imams to revise the law and custom towards the total suppression of slavery and its eventual abolition. The first treaty to suppress it came from the ruler of Muscat in 1822[48] but it was in 1845 that the imam of Muscat, Saʿīd bin Sulṭān signed an agreement to prohibit 'under the severest penalties', the export of slaves from the Omani east African colonies and, 'to use his utmost influence with all the chiefs of Arabia, the Red Sea and the Persian Gulf' (Lorimer 1986, I, iib: 2477). Muscat had been until then the chief port of Arabia for slave trade. Similar agreements with the British were signed in 1847 by the five Trucial sheikhs of Ajman, Umm al Quwain, Sharjah, Dubai and Abu Dhabi to prohibit the carrying of slaves on board vessels owned by themselves or others; the sheikh of Bahrain signed a perpetual treaty of peace and friendship with Britain concerning slavery and maritime aggression.[49] The Sultan of Zanzibar, Barghash bin Saʿīd (d 1306/1888), agreed to stop maritime traffic and the public slave markets (Coupland 1938 and 1939). The island was the most notorious of the slave ports and though the 1847 treaty for the suppression of the traffic was signed by the sultan, slavery was still permitted from the mainland to the island to satisfy the demand from Oman for manual labourers.[50] The Ottomans and the Persians were to go further: they signed a treaty with the British government in 1880 and 1882 against the slave trade, authorizing British cruisers to visit, search and if necessary detain, merchant vessels (Lorimer 1986, I, iib: 2482–3). Yet English preventive operations between 1857 and 1873 had little success. Merchant dhows continued to ship slaves. As trade and the pearling industry expanded, shipping increased and black slaves became a feature of the Indian Ocean economy. Ironically, just as the English were taking the moral issue of the slave market so seriously, the demand for pearls by the British in India became increasingly pressing, thus accelerating the need for, and use of, forced labour in the Gulf. The black slaves were an important part of the economy; with such cheap labour they brought to the Gulf system muscle power and diving techniques that no Arab or Persian diver could beat.

48 It needs to be mentioned here that the abolition of domestic slavery in Britain came only in 1833.

49 The British Government was aware that the slave traffic would continue to flourish irrespective of any attempt to stop it 'unless the limitations within which it [was] still lawful to prosecute it [were] removed', BL – IOR, L/P and S/5/507 Muscat and Zanzibar Commission of 1860, fol 113.

50 BL – IOR, L/P and S/5/507 Muscat and Zanzibar Commission of 1860, fols 113–14 (document signed by Brigadier W. M. Cogilan).

In a few instances penal sanctions were imposed: two reports in 1884 mention *nākhōda*s and dealers caught in a slave trade operation who were sent to Muscat and imprisoned by the sultan, in Fort Jalali (illus. 4) or Fort Mirani (ibid, I, iib: 2493, 2496). If we look at two figures quoted by Lorimer's informants, in general the slave trade would still appear to have been active: Mr Blane, the British Resident at Bushehr estimated that in 1844, 3,500 slaves were carried from the east African coast to the Arabian/Persian Gulf, and Colonel Rigby, the Political Agent at Zanzibar reported one year later an annual export of 10,000. What became complicated in the British fight against slave traffic was that dealers in the late 1890s concealed their operations by the use of French flags.[51] Sur was then the chief emporium of this traffic from Africa (ibid, I, iib: 2497); the dhows, mostly *sanbūq* and *baghla*, carried the slaves to the Al-Batinah district north of Muscat, and to the rest of the Gulf up to Basra. The embarrassment of the French government was cataclysmic; the British launched a campaign against the French and the sultan of Muscat, to abolish the slave trade for good. Towards the end of the nineteenth century the sultan of Muscat, Fayṣal bin Turkī (1306–32/1888–1913) issued a decree granting the freedom of slaves in 1897 and by 1909 the status of slave was abolished completely. But this did not stop Arab traders from making further attempts. Slavery continued to exist, and despite increasingly successful efforts to abolish it, Arab slave dhows were found plying the Arabian Sea and the Gulf way into the 1940s, as some of my informants in the Emirates reported.[52]

The maritime economy

During most of the latter part of the nineteenth century, British intervention was confined to keeping peace in tribal disputes, in Trucial Oman in particular. The British Political Resident in the Gulf was the final arbiter in all maritime litigations. The mutual agreement for the preservation of peace at sea became crucial in the ensuing years when the pearl fisheries were the chief means of livelihood for the Gulf and Omani people. Between 1905 and 1907, the number of dhows employed in the pearl fisheries industry was about 4,500 and the number of seamen engaged in pearling was over 74,000 (Lorimer 1986, I, iib: 2220). The Arabian littoral was by far the most

51 CDRAD/French Archives, Mascate–Golfe Persique et les Pusissances, Dossier Général, vol 3, 1896–8, fols 105–8, 109–14, 121–33; see also Mascate–Zanzibar, boutres francisés, November 1891–April 1898, vol 26, fols 20–3; May 1898–July 1900, vol 27, fols 56–7; April 1902–August 1903, fols 48–9, 134.

52 In a personal communication (27 April 2000) Tom Vosmer noted that he has in possession a slave trade document dated 1963.

4
Fort Jalali prison, Muscat: originally constructed by the Portuguese in 1588

productive of all the banks which yielded the best quality of pearls. There were talks about Europeans operating deep-sea dredging which, if not prevented by the British Agents in consultation with the British and Indian Governments, would have destroyed colonies from which oysters on shallow beds were fished by natives.[53] Foreign intervention had to be monitored closely and though some pearl-fishing concessions were obtained over the years, 'the maritime security to the great benefit of the pearl fisheries', we read in Lorimer's report, 'has been fully maintained' (ibid, I, iib: 2243). This could have been the case at the turn of the century. Locals were on the alert and some suspicions were aroused when in the 1930s a foreign oil company diving team in Bahrain was engaged in underwater inspection of pipelines and piers. At a time when the industry was in decline, some Bahraini and Saudi merchants and *nākhōda*s thought that the Europeans and Americans were involved in bringing up oysters.

An economic, social and political life existed through maritime activity. The maritime economy did not solely depend on the pearl industry. Frank

53 One good example is the Bombay steamer *Johnstone Castle*, which was caught with diving equipment by a British gunboat on the Bahrain waters in 1882 (O'Shea 1947: 140–1).

Broeze (1997: 152) saw it resting on four other main pillars – fishing, shipping, shipbuilding and trade. He was referring mainly to the case in Kuwait but in fact his statement is equally true of Bahrain, Qatar and the north of Trucial Oman. To a large extent the five pillars are 'mutually supportive'. Boat and shipbuilders produce the types of craft specifically needed for fishing, pearling, shipping and trade. The *jālbūt* of the Gulf, characterized by its upright stem and transom stern and the Omani *badan* with its slim long hull were the most common fishing boats. Other boats such as the *sanbūq* (identified by the low scimitar-shaped bow) and the *shūᶜī* (with its straight stem ending in a double curve and transom stern) were typical of the fishing and pearling group. However, these boats were also employed in coastal trade outside the fishing season. The larger vessels such as the *baghla* of Kuwait and Bahrain,[54] the square galleon-shaped-stern *ghanja* of Sur and the double-ended Kuwaiti *būm* with a pointed stem, were the long-distance sailers. Kuwait in the 1920s was the leading shipbuilding site in the Arabian/Persian Gulf and 'no other dhows could be compared with the *būm* in terms of build and design', wrote the Lebanese traveller Amīn al-Rīḥānī (d 1359/1940) (1960, II: 183). The ordinary seamen who were hired for fishing and pearling were equally at home on the ocean-going dhows. The work of other seamen was seasonal; there were the Bedouins who, when not at sea, went back to their pasture land; Suri sailors were for centuries renowned for their seafaring skills and the Kuwaitis were increasingly gaining the reputation of being able seamen in the mid nineteenth century, as the Jesuit traveller, William Gifford Palgrave (d 1888) (1865, II: 386) testified: 'the mariners of Koweyt hold the first rank in daring, in skill and in trustworthiness of character'. But the seamen in fact were not Kuwaitis. Apart from those who came from various bedouin tribes, there was a mixture of Arabs from the coastal fishing villages along the Gulf who were attracted to a flourishing maritime activity in Kuwait, and a large number of the seamen were also Persians and African blacks.

The seamen embarked on their long journeys towards India before the monsoons blew south-west and made their homebound journey in winter with the northeast winds. Hundreds of trading dhows ran from one port to another in the Gulf and Oman; Kuwait, Bahrain, Muscat and Sur being general trade centres. Muscat, which eventually became the capital of the Āl Bū Saᶜīd sultans during the mid eighteenth century, had long been a port of

54 See for example mention of *baghla* from Kuwait carrying wheat and barley, CDRAD/Ottoman Archives. Muscat Documents 1819–40, MS no 4, fol 63 (13 Ramaḍān 1236/1820); on trading *baghla*s from Bahrain and Kuwait to the south-west Indian coast, see Stocqueler 1832, I: 1–3.

international significance, with reputable seafarers and *nākhōdas*.[55] Pearls, dried fish and dates were the main exports to distant ports. The outbound voyages were to two destinations; the vessels sailed eastward to the Makran coast, Karachi and down the Malabar coast from Bombay, Mangalore and Calicut to Quilon, bringing imports on their homebound journey: rice, cotton, silk embroidery, spices, coffee, sugar, tea, coir-rope, timber, metals, hardware, haberdashery, barley, wheat, ghee, rosebuds, rose water, firewood, almonds, currants, gram, walnuts, live cattle, sheep and goats. This list comes from Lorimer's report in the early years of the twentieth century and practically nothing changed until the 1960s when newer products were being imported on board the trans-oceanic liners from European and South African countries, and from Japan in the east. Some products up to this very day are still being imported from India, Iran and Pakistan on dhows which call on Dubai and Doha in Qatar and are then distributed throughout the Gulf, Saudi Arabia and Oman. The second traditional destination was Dhofar via Oman, Hadhramaut, Yemen and the east African coast. From East Africa all kinds of timber were bought but specifically the mangrove poles used for roof construction throughout the Arabian/Persian Gulf.

The pearl industry continued to flourish up to the early 1930s when a severe trade depression was caused by a decrease in demand in Europe and North America but also by the large scale manufacture of cultured pearls in Japan. But a more serious reason that precipitated the decline in the industry in the case of Bahrain and Kuwait, was the shocking working conditions imposed on the divers and their sons. The industry survived for a while through the difficult years of the 1930s and 1940s; the pearl oyster banks were productive but the divers were not receiving their proper share, 'many of whom had involved themselves in a form of financial slavery to the *nakhōdas*' (Belgrave 1975: 54). A considerable sum of money in a form of a *tisqām* (loan) was often borrowed from a *musaqqam* (financier), who secured loans from wealthy merchants. The money was to equip pearling boats, and supply food and water for the season but, importantly, advances were made to divers by the *nākhōdas* hired by the dhow owner, to maintain the divers' families while they were at sea. Such advances were sometimes excessive and by the end of the pearling season divers had to work almost free for their *nākhōdas* for another season, to pay off the loan. The following year the *nākhōdas*, irrespective of whether they received their loans back from the divers, still gave advances to support their families, otherwise they would not have worked for them, the result of which was a much deeper debt

55 Several references to Sīrāfī (from Persia) and Omani skilled sailors are found in the *ʿAjāʾib al-Hind*; see al-Rāmhurmuzī 1981: 4, 13, 21, 37, 57, 61, 80, 82–4.

(al-Shamlān 1975–8, II: 93). Meanwhile, *nākhōda*s were indebted to the merchants in having to pay high interest and the *nākhōda*s in their turn imposed interest on the divers (although this practice I was told was not according to the Islamic *sharīʿa*). What happened over the years was that diving debts were passed on from father to son thus increasing the debts. Only the reforms introduced by the Bahraini Shaykh Ḥamad (1351–61/1932–42) could bring to an end the thousands of debts and a law was passed that no debts could be inherited by the diver's heirs (ibid, II: 113–17).

For years the sea was the economic mainstay of the Arabian Gulf with pearl fishing generating much of the income. When the summer pearling season was over, pearl fishers spent the months of winter in fishing or dhow-building but also carried merchandise across the desert or to remote coastal villages. Others reverted to the agricultural life or became shepherds tending their herds of animals. The fishing industry emerged as almost the only traditional occupation in the Gulf and Oman. Then, as now, there were 700 species of fish, some of which were eaten locally, the rest being used as fertilizer and animal fodder. Fish oil was used for smearing wooden dhows to strengthen their planks and and to make them seaworthy. It was also used as a rust preventative on nails, anchors, etc. The decline of the pearling industry had reduced the demand for the large old-fashioned sailing dhows; but in spite of that, boatbuilding continued to be the most important manufacturing industry for fishing and until the 1950s the *baghla*, *ghanja* and *būm* were still operating as trading vessels to India and the Omani east African colonies. The east African coast had suffered trade losses because of Yaʿrubī rulers and the Gulf sheikhs who were involved in the wars with Persia in the late eighteenth century. It only recovered later under the rule of Saʿīd bin Sulṭān, who extended his suzerainty over all the Arab and Swahili colonies, the richest being the island of Zanzibar. The challenge of the tribes from inland Oman and Saudi Arabia weakened Oman's economy; it sank into poverty and debt until the early 1970s when oil was discovered.

A decline in maritime activity began to be felt in the Gulf with the advent of oil exporting in the late 1950s and 1960s. Oil in the Gulf was discovered in 1908 though not before the 1930s were major finds exploited. Kuwait was the first to assert its independence from the Ottoman Empire but was asking protection from Britain in 1915. Iraq and Iran struck oil and Kuwait, as a trading post, prospered between the two. Drilling operations in Bahrain started in 1932 and oil was discovered in 1934 followed by Kuwait in 1938, and Trucial Oman and Qatar in 1939. World War II (1939–45) interrupted any further drilling; the wells were sealed off to protect the area from possible German raids. The big economic change in the Gulf came in the 1960s when oil was first exported. Oil was struck in commercial quantities offshore on the coast of Abu Dhabi in 1960, Oman in 1964, and offshore in Dubai waters in 1966. One country after the other got its independence. Scepticism about the new states' chances of survival was high at the beginning because of the early history of similar federations frequently disintegrating, but in spite of disputes and failures in the past, the five pillars of the maritime economy of the Gulf States and Oman had been well established over the last hundred years. In particular, the pearling industry had laid the foundations of an economy that helped to establish a network of labour forces which were strong enough to last until the 1950s in spite of decades of trade depression. The discovery of oil cemented those foundations. The economic activity grew stronger over the years in spite of gaps of depression caused by tribal warfare or world economic decline, and was determined essentially by the maritime trade, a network which provided, in the words of Frank Broeze (1997: 182), 'an excellent apprenticeship for financial management', a time when the Gulf sheikhdoms made way for modernization in the post-oil period.

Only a few local industries survived after the discovery of oil, which also had repercussions for the number of trading dhows. Most of the affected industries were associated with household objects and perhaps limited to the style of life the nomads and fishermen lived, though some related to the traders' or pearl merchants' high social status. Omanis in particular have a long tradition of skilled craftsmanship more than the other Gulf States. Metalworking is a very old tradition: copper was extracted in Oman for centuries; copper was invariably used to manufacture household utensils, for example coffee pots, beakers, cooking pans, dishes, incense burners and products such as nails; silver items included jewellery, decorations on knife and dagger handles, ornamental rings for attaching to belts, and silver boxes and buttons, while gold jewellery retained its popularity throughout the ages. Pottery-making is an old tradition in Bahrain: the brown and red clay is extracted from the hills to produce coarse ware while white clay is for finer work, ie household pottery such as bowls, pots, water jars and utensils. Various other items were manufactured: camel or goat hides were used for water-bags, donkey or camel side-bags, and sandals; palm tree branches to build fishing canoes; palm tree fibre to make ropes and palm-fibre braiding for floor mats, prayer mats, baskets and food covers, bags and fans; tallis-making for the decoration of traditional dress, and finally rugs with rich vibrant red and black colours. Traces of this craftsmanship still survive today in Oman and Bahrain while in the rest of the Gulf much of the tradition is now confined to handicraft centres. Dhow-building, on the other hand, albeit in a modified form, is still a living tradition, the craft of which contains remnants of the once thriving maritime economy of the Arabian/Persian Gulf and Oman.

3
FUNCTIONAL AND GENERAL NOMENCLATURE

يا حافظ الأرواح في الألواح
يا منجّي الألواح في لجج البحر
تحفظ لنا هذا السنبوق
يا الله يا رزّاق يا الله يا حافظ

O you who preserve life (sailing) on a ship,
O you who rescue ships from the depths of the sea,
Save and guard our *sanbūq*;
O Allāh, provider and saviour ![1]

The most difficult part of my study on ship types in the Gulf was to find a pattern by which I could classify dhows under certain categories based on hull design, function and size. In general this worked, but with some problems. For example, what appeared complex to me with various names for one type of vessel and conversely one name for different types, was simple and straightforward for many of the Arabs (and a few Iranians) I interviewed. In general, they were not bothered with classifying their craft; only shipwrights and *nākhōda*s (owners and captains)[2] cared about refinements

1 'Yā ḥāfiẓ al-arwāḥ fī l-alwāḥ/yā munajjī l-alwāḥ fī lujaj al-baḥr/taḥaffaẓ la-nā hādhā l-sanbūq/yā allāh, yā razzāq, yā allāh yā ḥāfiẓ' – invocatory prayer on the stern of a *sanbūq* in Marbat (Dhofar), recorded by the author on 20 November 1996 (see illus. 5).

2 Classical Arabic: *nākhūdha* or *nākhudhā* (pl *nawākhidha*) in the early Muslim geographical and travel works is etymologically traced back to Fārsī (connected with Hindi + Urdu), ie *nākhodā* or *nākhudā*: *nāw*, 'boat, ship' + *khudā*, 'master', denoting 'captain or master of a boat or vessel', a word common in the Indian Ocean terminology. I have heard several pronunciations of the term in question but the most common among the Gulf Arabs was (phonetically) *nākhōda*, a spelling variety which I use in the present work. It found its way into modern Arabic and often refers to 'captain', though the original sense is understood to be a 'shipowner' in medieval Arabic, see Ibn Baṭṭūṭa 1968, IV: 250, a term which to the present time is used by mariners in south-east Oman and the south Arabian coast to mean the same; for navigator (and sometimes skipper) they employ the term *rubbān*. I came across some sailors in the northern Gulf who used *nākhōda* to mean skipper and shipowner, both functions 'often combined' in the nineteenth century (Yule and Burnell 1994: 548). In many instances, however, during my interviews with seamen in Kuwait, Bahrain, Qatar and the Emirates, *nākhōda* arbitrarily meant either captain or pilot of the dhow. Modern authors like Villiers (1948b: 401, 408) also used both meanings as representing the same term. A detailed discussion on the nomenclature of the dhow's crew is dealt with in my forthcoming work, *People of the Dhow*.

of nomenclature. In discussing ships in general with seamen, they do not often speak of specific types but use generic names representing some particular kinds commonly shared by either a regional register,[3] or used as the language of the Gulf at large. When, on the other hand, a shipwright or *nākhōda* discussed a ship with a strict maritime usage it signified a particular type of vessel, but this narrow definition did not invalidate the generic use of the term to encompass all types of seagoing vessels. Most of the nomenclature of types that I collected came from the older seamen; the younger Arabs are more involved with boat racing and even though the traditional dhow is still the favoured design for such a sport, much of the terminology is fading away in the memories of those who recall the days of sail. It is essential before discussing individual names of types, to look firstly at functional names which categorize dhows according to what they are used for, and secondly at how generic terms are applicable to dhows of a certain class or order.

Functional terminology

The Gulf mariners do not recognize dhows by their rigging but by whether the sailing or motorized vessel is *mudabbab* (double-ended) or *bir-rigᶜa* (square-sterned). To a European, rigging is what determines the type of a sailing vessel such as *cutter*, *barque* or *brig*. For the Gulf dhows on the other hand, the sails had a fore and aft rather than square-rigged arrangement. The lateen sail remained unchanged. By my second field trip to Bahrain in 1991, I became aware in the course of my interviews that the dhow has two names, one associated with its function, the categories of which I will describe in the following section, and the other designated by the shape of the hull which I will discuss in Chapters 4, 5 and 6 on the nomenclature of dhow types.

The functional terminology falls into four main categories: a) the *saffār* (pl *safāfīr*) or *qaṭṭāᶜ* (pl *qaṭāṭīᶜ*), an ocean-going vessel, namely referring to a cargo ship such as the *baghla* and *ghanja* or the *būm*, all operating by sail only. The word *safar* in the seamen's register of the Gulf denotes a sea voyage to a far distant land and hence *saffār*, 'an ocean-goer', a term more commonly used than *qaṭṭāᶜ*. The latter, however, argued Saeed Haddad, a poet and historian from Kalba on the east Emirati coast, fits well with the semantics of the motion of the vessel, ie 'cutting through the waves on the open sea';[4] b) the *ghawwāṣ* (pl *ghawāwīṣ*), a common term among Kuwaitis, Bahrainis, Qataris and Emiratis for a pearling dhow with sails and oars. In the past, until the

3 Most unusual were generic terms used in Qalhat in my trip of March 1998, for medium-sized ships, *mēl* and small vessels *minwar*, words I could not place anywhere else in the Gulf.

4 Interviewed on 17 April 1996.

1960s, hundreds of these dhows were seen in the Gulf. Retired pearl divers in Bahrain and Qatar to whom I spoke, recalled that in the 1930s and 1940s there were hundreds of pearlers like the *sanbūq* and the *jālbūt* of varying sizes, carrying thousands of divers during the pearling season. On the shores of Kuwait, Lorimer's *Gazetteer* (1986, IIc: 1049) reports, dhows 'almost touch[ed] each other's sides, for hundreds of yards and when launched they must [have] form[ed] an imposing fleet'. Not all pearling dhows ventured on long distance trips, the smaller types kept to the coast. The main pearl-diving season, *al-ghawṣ al-kabīr* was from June to early October, but before and after this season there was *al-ghawṣ al-bārid* or, as it was sometimes called, *al-ghawṣ aṣ-ṣaghīr* (the cold or short-diving season), the duration of which was determined by weather conditions; c) the *sammāk* (pl *samāmīk*), a fishing vessel which went out to sea in different fishing seasons. The *shūʿī* and *badan* are typical examples in this category. Sails and oars were both used, the latter being essential when approaching the shore or in less favourable winds; d) the *ṭawwāsh* (pl *ṭawāwīsh*) refers to a small rowing boat which a pearl merchant or skipper employed to ply from the vessel to the shore and back, or occasionally hoisted a sail to make a trip to a neighbouring port. A *hūrī* or a *kīt* (dug-out canoe), both of Indian origin, were among the common types.

Finally, it is appropriate to note that these functional names follow a morphological pattern having the template *faʿʿāl* for singular (*saffār*, *qaṭṭāʿ*, *ghawwāṣ*, *sammāk* and *ṭawwāsh*), and *faʿāʿīl* for the plural (*safāfīr*, *qaṭāṭīʿ*, *ghawāwīṣ*, *samāmīk* and *ṭawāwīsh*), which I found unique in the language of the dhow.

The dhow

The first question to be asked is: what is a 'dhow'? The term now implies a collective usage by English speakers to represent any Perso-Arab or Indian or east African vessel. It is not a name recognized by Arabs of today but the word, or variations of it, can be found in eighteenth-century documents, which suggests that the term was applied by Gulf Arabs and others to refer specifically to a vessel of the time (see Chapter 4). One theory maintains that it is of east African origin. In the nineteenth and early twentieth centuries, Zanzibar was the meeting place where the ships came in December from the Somali coast, the Red Sea and the south Arabian coast and, with the north-east monsoon, from the Arabian/Persian Gulf and India. The northbound return passage started in April with the south-west monsoon. The cargoes were mainly slaves and it was at this time that the British, based in Zanzibar combatting the African slave traffic, seemingly began to call the Perso-Arab or Indian lateen-rigged craft 'dhow', because of its resemblance with the local Zanzibari vessel called in Swahili *dau* (pl *madau*). Hornell (1946: 35) and others believed in the Swahili origin. But there is historical and linguistic evidence to show that the word may be of Fārsī origin, something which will be pursued further in Chapter 4. Meanwhile, it may be of interest here to show how I came up with my conclusions as to the origins of the word dhow.

When H. R. P. Dickson (1949: 483) enquired of many of his acquaintances about the name, he reports being informed by a Kuwaiti sheikh who mentioned seeing it in some records, but could not recall the place where it appeared. At the turn of the twentieth century Miles (1994: 414) claims to have seen a ship in Bahrain having 'a high stern and poop projecting considerably over the rudder', which locals identified as *dāw*. He said that it was a type that at one time belonged to Gulf pirates. This information and that of the Kuwaiti sheikh gave me a clue. I had recently searched for the term in the Anglo-Indian documents at the Centre for Documentation and Research in Abu Dhabi. In the extracts of the English East India Company that were originally kept in Bandar Abbas and Basra, I came across three names, 'dought', 'dough' and 'dow', in connection with war vessels dated 1761 and 1782.[5] One diary entry dated 1808 mentions Qawāsim pirates having '5 large cruising dows, the largest of which mounts 14 guns'.[6] It became clear to me after having found other documents with these name variants that they graphemically represented what I was looking for, namely the piratical dhow or the war dhow. I could not trace the name in earlier documents, namely Portuguese and Dutch records, and the fact that it is only recorded in Anglo-Indian documents confirms the English adoption of the generic term.

What we can establish from the Anglo-Indian records is that the craft was a local war vessel used by Arabs and Persians alike and that the name with its conventional spellings does appear to have a close phonetic resemblance to the Fārsī *dawh* meaning 'a small ship', as the classical Arabic lexicographer, al-Azharī (d 370/981) pointed out centuries ago. However, there still remains the question of whether the Fārsī term is local or foreign (see Chapter 4).

What needs to be examined in the light of what has been said earlier is the question of how the Swahili *dau* came about. Is it a local or borrowed name? What is the connection between this and the Gulf name? The fact that we can trace back a Fārsī name, phonetically similar to the one used in the Anglo-Indian records, does suggest a historical link even though their function

5 CDRAD/British Archives, GD, G/29/13 (6, 12, 16 October 1761); G/29/21 (7 November 1782).

6 CDRAD/British Archives, GD – SPDD, no 232, fols 5669–70, M. 215–6 (7 November 1808). So far this is the only document I could come across with such description and, therefore, Miles' (1994: 414) claim that a dhow could carry 400 men and 40 to 50 guns does seem unlikely.

differed over time. In any case, the word 'dhow' has become firmly rooted in travel and maritime literature, identified as a pilgrim boat which carried Muslims on their holy journey to Mecca, or as the piratical boat which attacked the foreign intruder, or the slave boat that staggered, laden with slaves, from one harbour to another in the Arabian/Persian Gulf and the Indian Ocean. In English literature the 'dhow' became the romantic ship of the nineteenth and twentieth centuries and was the one on which adventurers, spies and pirates travelled.

General nomenclature

Terms for ships or boats: ʿūd, lawḥ, khashaba

The first Arabic generic term I heard during my field trip to the Gulf was *ʿūd* (pl *aʿwād*) referring to a ship or boat, a word with the basic meaning of 'a piece of wood or timber'. I could not locate this ship term in any maritime Arabic literature, nor for that matter in the classical and modern Arabic dictionary. Also missing from the literature and lexica is the name *lawḥ* (pl *alwāḥ*) for a vessel, meaning literally 'a board or plank of wood'. The exception, however, is a Qurʾānic reference in Sūrat Qamar (LIV: 13): 'But We bore him on a vessel caulked with palm-fibre' [wa-ḥamalnā-hu ʿalā dhāti alwāḥi wa-dusur], which clearly shows the occurrence of the term *alwāḥ* for sea-craft. The term generally refers to seagoing vessels, and is pronounced *lōḥ* in Raysut and other fishing villages on the Dhofari coast of the Arabian Sea. The invocatory prayer I saw engraved on the wood of the stern of a *sanbūq* in Marbat (quoted at the beginning of this Chapter) clearly shows the usage of the term *alwāḥ* for ships among the Dhofaris up to the present day (illus. 5).[7]

I also found the name *khashaba*, comparable to *lawḥ*, employed on the west coast of Oman, denoting all types of vessels, small and large. The implication of the word is 'a piece of wood, plank, board etc.' (Lane 1984, I: 741) but there is no reference to it as a ship in classical Arabic. However, I found a mention of it in a nineteenth century bilingual English–Arabic lexicon. The author, George Percy Badger (d 1888), was interested in compiling material cultural terms of dialectal usage, namely Levantine and Egyptian, and *khashab* or *akhshāb* was the collective term he noted for 'a plank of wood' (1967: 960). The term is common among sailors and fishermen in Khasab in the Musandam Peninsula and in the fish market of Sharjah (using the plural *khshāb*). Other places I noticed its usage was on the Dhofari coast where the locals say *khashbe* or *khashabe*, and on the Masirah Island where seamen speak of *khashabāt* (plural not collective).[8] Sabi

7 See footnote 1.

8 Kindermann (1934: 11), on the authority of George Percy Badger, gives *khashabāt*.

5
Invocatory prayer on the *sanbūq*'s stern in Sadh, Dhofar (Oman)

Khamis,[9] a fisherman from Raysut, and Basheer Saeed Rabee[10] from Marbat, told me during my stay in Dhofar in November 1996, that *khashbe* for Dhofaris specifically meant a large ship that sails to India or the type of trading vessel that carries frankincense and myrrh. The notion of *khashaba* being a large vessel is well attested by western writers. Around the beginning of the twentieth century, the German boat researcher Ritter (1919: 137) tells us that among the Iraqis, *khishbe* (pl *khishbāt* and *khashūb*) stood for a large vessel.[11] Maritime historian Alan Moore (1920: 76) also, writing about the same subject, said that the people of Sur called a large vessel (ie *baghla*), *khashaba*. But other sources dealing with ships of the Red Sea speak of a smaller type of dhow: al-Quṭāmī,[12] wrote that *khashaba* was a small fishing

9 Interviewed on 19 November 1996.

10 Interviewed on 16 November 1996.

11 He was referring to the *baghla* (characterized by its square, galleon-type stern with rear windows and quarter galleries) but he says that it was much shorter than the Iraqi *muhēle* or Arabic *muhayla*, a very distinctive river boat, 80 feet long, the bow and stern being 12 feet above the water, see Dickson 1949: 483.

12 ʿĪsā l-Quṭāmī, author of pilot guides for deep-sea dhows and pearling vessels, known particularly for his *Dalīl al-mukhtār fī ʿilm al-biḥār* (1915), re-edited by his son ʿAbd al-Wahhāb in Kuwait 1964.

or cargo boat that sailed between Yemen and East Africa (1964: 99, 105, 118). In the context of the Gulf of Aden and the Red Sea, Aḥmad b Mājid (fl ninth/fifteenth century)[13] described the Tihama *khashab* (coll) as small and light and able to travel to Hormuz and India (Tibbetts 1981: 110–11). It is clear in another passage of Ibn Mājid's *Fawāʾid* that these *khashab* were ideal sailing ships because they were small and could pass through many channels and sail over reefs (ibid, 251).

The occurrence of the word *khashaba* in some medieval south Arabian sources points to either a generic or specific term in its own right. A Yemenite source of Ibn al-Daybaʿ (d 944/1537) recounts how the Franks (Europeans), being unable to take Aden, burnt *khashaba*s anchored at the port (1983: 263). Here he could be implying a type of craft, or be making a general reference to merchant vessels or warships which were collectively called *khashaba*. From the Hadrami chronicles, however, there is evidence to show that *khashaba* was used generically to mean 'sailing ship' and that it referred to warships (Serjeant 1974: 48, 51, 74).

The Arabic terms *ʿūd*, *lawḥ* and *khashaba*, semantically refer to 'a piece of wood, timber, or log'. Whether any of these terms was ever used to indicate a log raft is not known. It is my understanding, however, that if this terminology historically points to a ship or vessel of all types then it is almost certain it would have been used to refer generically to a log raft. The concept of log raft is an ancient one, recorded in Mesopotamia[14] and the south Arabian coast.[15] Thor Heyerdahl and friends tested prehistoric types of raft ship, and sailed them across oceans.[16] Log-canoes of the catamaran construction were seen by Palgrave (1865, II: 314) on the Musandam Peninsula in 1862. Bent (1900: 47) in his travel to Oman, relates having seen fishermen in Muscat 'paddling themselves about on a plank or two tied together'. Log rafts existed in several separate locales and their distribution must surely be universal (see Chapter 6).

13 Author of some forty works, most of which are navigational and practically all of which are in verse. His best known work, the *Kitāb al-fawāʾid fī uṣūl ʿilm al-baḥr wa l-qawāʿid* is about navigational techniques and on the topography of the Indian Ocean, translated by G. R. Tibbetts (1981). Despite the nature of this work the boat researcher would be disappointed to learn that only eight types of vessels are briefly mentioned and those that Ibn Mājid himself sailed in were never recorded, see Tibbetts 1981: 47, 56.

14 The researcher refers the reader to a fine study on water transport on the two long rivers, the Euphrates and the Tigris, made possible by the artefacts which constitute the major source of information about ship, as no real ships or wrecks have been identified in Mesopotamia, see De Graeve (1981); see also Hornell 1946: 20–34.

15 Pliny 6.176; *Periplus* 1912: 127; 1989: 162–3 [27].

16 The classic example is the Kon-Tiki expedition (1950); other examples are his trip to and adventures in the Maldives (1986).

Classical general terms: *markab* and *safīna*

The name *markab* (pl *marākib*) denotes any sailing or motorized vessel of different hull design and size, and is widely used in the Gulf and Oman. Its name occurred in many conversations with my interviewees when we were talking about shipowners (s *ṣāḥib al-markab*) and ships in general. In order to describe the size, function, cargo load and speed, my informants would use the term in the plural, ie *marākib*, followed by a descriptive word (adjective), the most common being:[17] i) *marākib kabīra* or *marākib ṣaghīra*, 'large or small ships', used to describe the size, and when length and width were mentioned they would give rough figures in feet; ii) *marākib thaqīla* or *marākib khafīfa*, 'heavily or lightly laden ships', concerned with weight, the limits of which, depending on the size of the hull and length of the ship, are decided by the shipowner or *nākhōda*; iii) *marākib māshiya*, 'fast-going ships', to do with speed and the lightness of the craft (boat race is *sibāq al-marākib*); and iv) *marākib shirāʿiyya* or *marākib bish-shirāʿ*, 'sailing ships'. Different types of dhow are used for different occasions. The term *markab* also refers to any modern foreign ship that calls on a Gulf harbour.

Frequently used in medieval texts, *markab* generally is understood to mean a merchant or transport ship. The distinction is clear among long-distance *marākib baḥriyya* (or *marākib safariyya*), 'deep-sea vessels', *marākib al-tujjār*, 'merchant ships' and *marākib ḥarbiyya*, 'warships' (Agius 1998: 192). The geographer al-Yaʿqūbī (d 277/891) calls the stitched boats *marākib khayṭiyya* (1892, VII: 390), a nomenclature not adopted in modern times; instead *kambārī* (pl *kambāriyyāt*) is used on the south Arabian coast (see Chapter 5). Otherwise, in the Gulf, I heard *marākib mukhayyaṭa*.

Markab is found in the early Arabic repertoire; it was the most general term for 'ship'. The basic meaning of the verb *rakiba*, 'to mount, ride' and by extension 'to embark in the ship; go on board the ship' (Lane 1984, I: 1142), is a long-established root in the Semitic languages. The Arabic *markab*, apart from the application to a vessel, ship or boat, is often referred to in classical Arabic literature as 'any kind of vehicle borne by a camel or other beast' (ibid, I: 1145), but not specifically as a ship. It is appropriate to note here that *markab* or *markaba* in the sense of 'carriage, vehicle', is used today in media Arabic. Moreover, *al-markab*, the principal star of the constellation Pegasus, gets its name because of 'the place of the saddle' (ibid). The term *markab* can be traced to Ugaritic–Canaanite origin, *markabtu* (Von Soden 1959–81, II: 612).

Another classical term frequently applied to a dhow is *safīna* (pl *sufun*, *safāʾin* or *safīn*). I came across it on the south Arabian coast (plural was

17 The pronunciation of adjectives varied from one region to another in the northern Gulf and in some cases from one interviewee to another. For this reason I have given here the modern standard Arabic transliteration.

sfēyen) where it referred to any cargo or fishing vessel. On my visit to Masirah Island in April 1998, one of my informants, Hilal Saeed Mohammed Ashamakhi,[18] an experienced sea captain,[19] drew my attention to a detail in differentiating between *safīna* and *markab*. He said that *markab* meant a large vessel but is never intended to denote a *safīna*, a distinction which was accepted by some of the interviewees. I found the name *safīna* less common in the northern Gulf, and on a few occasions in Kuwait and Bahrain it was used in a compound, such as *alāt as-safīna*, 'the ship's instruments'.

The frequent occurrence of *safīna* in pre-Islamic poetry suggests that the nomenclature has long been known among the Arabs and Persians, particularly in Mesopotamia (Iraq and parts of Iran today).[20] Both the Tigris and Euphrates, from the time of the Akkadian and Sumerian periods, were the home of navigation and sea-trade links with the northern Gulf, the Indian Ocean and the Red Sea. But the familiarity of this name with mariners is because it is found in verses from the Qurʾān, where it appears three times.[21] In strict maritime usage the word *safīna* in early medieval sources meant a transport and cargo vessel which, according to the historian al-Ṭabarī (d 310/922), carried troops, weapons, war equipment and food on the rivers Euphrates and Tigris and, as the need arose, served as a pontoon.[22]

On the etymology of *safīna*, it is not of Arabic origin but Semitic. Fraenkel (1962: 216) was the first to indicate that the word was borrowed from Aramaic. Further research has shown that the Arabic *safīna* originated from *çʿphîynâh* (sefeenaw), a (seagoing) vessel (ie roofed with a deck) coming from Hebrew[23] and Chaldean *çâphan* (saw-fan), and ultimately traced back to Akkadian *sapīn(a)tu*.[24]

18 Interviewed on 5 April 1998.

19 From the northern part of the Arabian Gulf to south-east Oman (practically up to Ras al-Hadd), you hear locals saying *nākhōda* for sea captain, a term which on the southern Arabian coast changes to *rubbān* (see note 2).

20 For a comprehensive reading on the subjects of maritime terms in pre-Islamic poetry, see Montgomery 1998 and for a discussion on pre-Islamic verses in the context of ships see Agius, *Classic Ships of Islam* (forthcoming).

21 Sūrat al-Kahf (XVIII: 71, 79) refers to an ordinary boat, and Sūrat ʿAnkabūt (XXIX: 15) specifically alludes to Noah's Ark.

22 Al-Ṭabarī 1965, XII, iii: 1550, 1844; XIII, iv: 1965–8 – *sufun al-rijjāla*, 'ships for foot-soldiers'; XIII, iv: 1968 – *sufun bi-mā fī-hā min al-rijjāla wa-l-silāḥ wa-l-ālāt*, 'transport ships for foot-soldiers, weapons and (war) machines'; XII, iv: 1966–7 – *sufun al-jusur*, 'boat bridges'.

23 Jonah I: 5; see also A. Jeffery, *The Foreign Vocabulary of the Qurʾān* (Baroda, 1938), pp 171–2.

24 It was wrongly derived by Von Soden 1959–81, II: 1027 from 'sapannu', see Agius 1984: 118, 147. Note also Greek *sagena*, Byzantine galley could be related to the Semitic root; see Agius 1997: 315.

Sanbūq: a medieval name

Sanbūq, is a term used loosely in the past by mariners to denote any sailing boat or, more recently, a motorized vessel. It seems to have been more closely identified as a fishing or cargo vessel however. For a long time it was identified as the pearling dhow, although the pearl divers I met in Bahrain and Qatar still considered the name to represent all types and sizes of vessel. The *sanbūq* was an extremely versatile craft, also employed in deep-sea trading. The name is medieval and we do not know whether it always represented an all-inclusive ship type as in the last few hundred years, or if it ever represented a more specific type. The earliest reference in relation to the name (CA *ṣunbūq*) goes back to the fourth/tenth-century Buzurg b Shahriyār, a sea captain and a storyteller, who refers to it in conjunction with the Persian Gulf and the Arabian Sea (al-Rāmhurmuzī 1883–6: 190). Ibn Baṭṭūṭa often speaks of an all-purpose type. On his trip to Basra it was a ferry canal boat (1968, II: 17), at Maqadishu and Ẓafār (probably now Salalah) it was a harbour boat (ibid, II: 181, 198) and in Jeddah it was a larger type of passenger boat which could cope with the winds of the Red Sea (ibid, II: 251). The historian al-Nuwayrī l-Iskandarānī (d c 775/1372) confirms more or less what was mentioned by his contemporary Ibn Baṭṭūṭa and locates the craft as belonging to the Red Sea and Indian Ocean.[25] When Aḥmad b Mājid wrote about *sanbūq* as the ship's boat he did not include it with his main corpus of ships that sailed the Indian Ocean because its function, as we understand, was purely as a lifeboat rather than a ship equipped for navigation. However, the Portuguese accounts in the sixteenth century seem to mention *sanbūq* (recorded as *sambucho* or *zambuco*)[26] as having two functions: one as a small coastal boat which is close to Ibn Mājid's classification and the other as a larger type that could probably sail from East Africa to the west coast of India. The point I am making here is that the name was applied by the Portuguese to any Muslim (Moorish) or Indian Ocean craft that represented different types and functions.[27] Remarkably, the name has been around for a thousand years at least, from the Red Sea to the Arabian/Persian Gulf, and in many coastal settlements of the Indian Ocean. It has been designated to types of different hull design and size, through time up to the present day.

25 UAFAL (Berlin) MS 667, fol 127r.

26 CDRAD/Portuguese Archives, ANTT, Múcleo Antigo 592, fols 2-5v [1522]; see also *Three Voyages of Vasco da Gama*, 1869: 75-109, *Commentaries* (Dalboquerque) 1875-84, I: 29, 93, IV: 206, *Book of Duarte Barbosa* 1918-21, I: 9.

27 The other name was *terrada*, a warship, see Agius 1999: 183–6.

A general term for cargo ship: *hammāl* or *maḥmil*

Ḥammāl (lit. 'a carrier') (pl *ḥammālīn*) is a general term for a transport ship and at one time was a common word among Emiratis (Abu Dhabi, Umm al Quwain and Khor Fakkan) and particularly Omanis, for all cargo transport vessels in Khasab, as Abdallah bin Ali Mohammed Al-Kumzari,[28] a dhow-builder, informed me. In Kuwait, a type called *ḥammāl bāshī*[29] was employed to ferry merchandise to the shore from anchored ships lying at a distance off the coast (al-Ḥijjī 1988: 47). The medieval name *ḥammāla* may not have been a generic term because it was a transport vessel, part of a war fleet on the Mediterranean, carrying grain, soldiers, workmen and servants (or slaves) (Ibn Mammātī 1299 AH: 239–40). Some of these ships were huge if we are to believe Abū Shāma's (d 665/1266) description of one which could carry 1,250 passengers[30] on board (al-Nakhīlī 1974: 40).

From the same root, *ḥamala*, 'to carry; to load up and take along' (Wehr 1966: 206), I heard *maḥmil* (originally 'a camel-borne litter') and other phonetic variants[31] for seagoing vessels and coastal boats. From Ibrahim Khamis Bu Haroon,[32] a lifelong boat-builder in Umm al Quwain, I learnt that the specific term for a large vessel was *meḥmel ʿūd*. *Maḥmil* (pl *maḥāmil*) is a term of purpose, perhaps as common as *khashaba*, *markab* and *safīna*, which denotes a cargo vessel and is used all over the Gulf coast. In Al-Khor, a fishing town east of Doha (Qatar), the *maḥmil* was always known to be a fishing vessel and until some thirty years ago, Ahmed Muhammed Munhadi,[33] himself from Al-Khor, said that there used to be one or two local dhow-builders who built craft with this name. In Sohar, on the Al-Batinah coast of Oman, the fishermen I talked to,[34] almost without exception, spoke of the *maḥmil* as a type on its own. I asked them if they could be more specific about the hull design of the vessel and its general size but I got vague answers, nor could any boat-maker help me because there were none in the area. One piece of information was that wood from local trees[35] was used to build the craft, as Abdalla Ahmed

28 Interviewed on 24 November 1996.

29 The reference is meant to open-ended vessels such as the *būqāʿa* or *būgāʿa* (a small flat-bottomed vessel with a straight sternpost) and the *būm* (distinguished by its long and straight stemhead), see Chapter 4.

30 Chinese junks could carry such a large number of passengers; Arab vessels were much smaller in general and Abū Shāma's information comes to us as a surprise.

31 The common ones are *miḥmil* or *miḥmal* in Bahrain and Qatar and *meḥmel* elsewhere.

32 Interviewed on 16 April 1996.

33 Interviewed on 20 April 1992.

34 Interviewed Abdalla Ahmed Saeed Al-Naqbi, Abdalla bin Fadil bin Abdalla Al-Shizawi, Ibrahim Muhammed Ali Al-Nawfali and others on 28 November 1996.

35 This would be *qaraṭ*, *sidir* and *sumur*; *sāj* (teak) would have come from India; for a discussion on local timber and its use with boats, see my forthcoming book *People of the Dhow*.

Saeed Al-Naqbi from Sohar and in his sixties, confirmed.[36] The late Egyptian historian Jamāl al-Dīn al-Shayyāl,[37] listed the *maḥmil* as a type of its own, used in Bahrain, but gave no details about the vessel itself (al-Nakhīlī 1974: 138).

The *ḥammāl* and *maḥmil* are terms for ships localized in the northern Gulf. There is no trace of them in the classical Arabic lexica; the only reference to be found is Moroccan *ḥmmāla*, 'a harbour dredger' (Brunot 1920b: 250).

The names *bānūsh* and *dūmeh*

The most common generic word for dhow in Bahrain is the *bānūsh* (pl *bawānīsh*), which generally represents the square-sterned vessel (illus. 6). Its design has the features of a Gulf *sanbūq* and *shūʿī* as will be shown in Chapter 5. There were different sizes with different functions: the smallest type was essentially used for fishing but also transport, ferrying passengers from Firda (port in Manamah) to Saudi Arabia; the middle-sized boat was used for both fishing and pearling and the larger type was a ferry boat (also called *ʿabra*) which carried passengers from one port to another on the Arabian and Iranian coasts. I saw one or two of these ferry boats during my trip to Bahrain in April 1991. Hardly any of them exist today owing to the construction of the causeway between Saudi and Bahrain in the late eighties; the fishing *bānūsh*, however, remains as popular as it was in the past. But the name is not confined to Bahrain. I came across it in Abu Dhabi, although there the hull design is that of a double-ended canoe employed as a racing boat. Here is a good example of a boat with a hull design of a purpose-built *hūrī* (see Chapter 6) but which subsumes a generic name. The demand for *bānūsh* racing-type canoes is becoming increasingly popular, as Sultan Al Zaabi,[38] a shipwright at al-Butteen boatyard in Abu Dhabi, explained: 'Emiratis are becoming more and more keen on boat racing, which, as in the rest of the Gulf, has become a national sport'. The other place I heard the name *bānūsh* was in Salalah where it referred to a craft that had no sails and was rowed by up to ten men. Like other boats, the *bānūsh* was at one time sewn together with coconut fibre; nautical researcher Clifford Hawkins (1977: 135) notes having seen small sewn 'banouches' on the deck of south Arabian double-ended *sanbūq*s.

36 Interviewed on 28 November 1996.

37 Al-Shayyāl has meticulously collected data about names of ship types from medieval Arabic sources and was also interested in the Gulf dhows, particularly those of Bahrain, information which presumably he collected during his fieldwork there. His manuscript, which was consulted by al-Nakhīlī (1974), is located at the library of the Faculty of Arts of the University of Alexandria.

38 Interviewed on 12 April 1997.

6
The *bānūsh* under repair in Muharraq, Bahrain

One name which warrants further investigation came to light when an 87-year-old Bahraini model boat-maker[39] told me that in his youth the locals commonly referred to some boats with no sails as *dūmeh*. Only one shipwright could remember this term and I was not surprised to learn that none of the younger Bahrainis had ever heard it. However, when I was in Masirah some local fishermen recollected the generic name *dūmi shirāᶜ* for a sailing double-ended ocean-going craft. So far, I have been unable to find any historical-linguistic clue as to the origins of the names *bānūsh* and *dūmeh*.

The most common terms: *lanch* and *ṭarrāda*

By far the commonest generic term I heard was *lanch/lanj* (pl *lanchāt* or *lanjāt*), or in south-east Oman *ling/lang* (pl *lingāt/langāt*) for a fishing vessel. In Bahrain, *lansh* (given as such by my informants) is almost as common as *bānūsh* though the latter is a more inclusive term for *shūᶜī*. According to Ibrahim Rashid Shattaf of Ajman,[40] a boat-builder, *lanch* or *leng* (as pronounced in the east of the Emirates) is a term much preferred by the

39 Mohammed Abdallah Al Saqar, interviewed on 22 April 1991.

40 Interviewed on 16 April 1996.

younger generation.[41] Any large Arab or Indian vessel in Dubai is invariably referred to as *lanch* by the Indian seamen and dhow carpenters, irrespective of its shape or function, though admittedly some understood the term to mean all transom vessels with an engine installed. The fishing boats called *ling* or *lang*, which I saw in Masirah, had a straight bow. Originally, the boats were double-enders, but some twenty years ago the pointed sterns were cut square so as to mount an engine at the back. The only *lanch* that can be classified as a type on its own is the one in Kuwait and Dubai. The Kuwaiti type was still being built in the early 1980s, as the boat researcher al-Ḥijjī (1988: 44) claimed. It has a base of up to 40 feet and its prow stems out at a lower and sharper point. Of similar description was the *lanch* I saw under construction in Dubai in 1995. The word *lanch* (and its phonetic variants) is apparently of Malay origin,[42] 'a kind of small vessel often mentioned in the Portuguese histories of the 16th and 17th centuries' (Yule and Burnell 1994: 502).

Other untypical fibreglass dhows, resembling European craft, are generally called *ṭarrāda* or *ṭarrād* (CA *ṭarrada*, 'to pursue, follow') (pl *ṭarrādāt*), unrelated semantically to the naval *ṭarrāda*, 'cruiser or warship' (Hārūn *et al.* 1960-1, II: 560), and the medieval *ṭarīda* (pl *ṭarāʾid*) which functioned in the Mediterranean as a transport ship carrying food for the troops but primarily designed to carry horses.[43] The root *ṭarada*, 'to chase, hunt etc.' is quite appropriate to the medieval meaning while the semantics of the modern *ṭarrāda* are most likely connected with the southern Iraqi *tarada* (as conventionally spelt in travel works) or, more likely, *ṭarrād*, a small and swift boat or canoe.[44]

Generic terms for smaller boats: *zawraq* and *qārib*

Terms for the smaller types of boats like the *zawraq* (pl *zawāriq* or *zawārīq*) and *qārib* (pl *qawārib*), are common among all seamen I have spoken to; both being equivalent to a skiff or barque. The *zawraq* is in fact a lifeboat though no person I spoke to attached any importance to its name because it never really belonged to the Gulf. In the classic days of Islam a *zawraq* appears to

41 One type mentioned by the older men was *bākhire* (pl *bawākhir*), 'a steamship'. Of course the term is now out-of-date, but historically attempts to change from sailing to steam-dhows were made in the early twentieth century, though it seems Gulf seamen preferred the sail until the sixties when dhows gradually became motorized.

42 OED 1982, I: 1579, *lantcha* and *lanchara* or *lanchare*; *lanchar-an* from Malay *lanchār*, 'swift' (Yule and Burnell 1994: 502).

43 See Kindermann 1934: 57-8; al-Maqrīzī 1957-64, III, i: 113, 129; IV, ii: 686; Ibn Mammātī 1943: 339; Ibn Baṭṭūṭa 1968, IV: 107; see also other details of *ṭarīda*-types in Agius 1998: 193-4.

44 See Thesiger 1967: 34; Heyerdahl 1982: 26; Young 1989: 26.

have been popular and functioned as a canal boat near Basra, as we find in the accounts of the historian al-Ṭabarī, and the geographers al-Iṣṭakhrī (fl c 340/951) and Ibn Ḥawqal (fl c 367/977).[45] The Mediterranean *zawraq* was a larger type with a different function.[46] There is no evidence that the name is of Arabic origin; the lexicographer al-Jawālīqī (d 539/1144) traced it back to Fārsī (1969: 173).

In contrast to this term, *qārib* is a pan-Arab word but one which does not represent any particular type of boat in the Gulf, Indian Ocean, or on the south Arabian coast. Its general purpose is to transport cargo from ship to shore and for ferrying people. It is pronounced *gārib* (pl *gawārib*) in Qatar and *kārib* (pl *qawārib*)[47] in south-east Oman. However, *qārib* is sometimes used in Sharjah in the sense of a small double-ended boat, but meaning a dug-out canoe in Raysut, Marbat, and Sadh and pronounced *ghārib*.[48]

In medieval Islam we find references to a *qārib*: in the Indian Ocean at Barahnakār,[49] when Ibn Baṭṭūṭa (1994, IV: 875) was on a ship approaching the shore, some natives came to meet the crew and passengers in little boats, *qārib*s 'each of which was a single log hollowed out', a description which fits the meaning of the nomenclature used on the Dhofari coast. In the medieval Mediterranean its usage as a multi-purpose boat is well documented: (a) war canoe, (b) transport vessel for soldiers and pilgrims, (c) cargo boat carrying cereals, food and water, (d) fishing and pearl-diving vessel[50] and, of course, as an auxiliary boat in time of danger (al-Zabīdī 1968, IV: 18). Etymologically the word may be connected with the Byzantine Greek κάραβως (Liddell and Scott 1953: 877), borrowed, one assumes, by Greek-speaking Arabs and other

45 Al-Ṭabarī 1965, XI, iii: 1168; XIII, iv: 2074; al-Iṣṭakhrī 1870, I: 80; Ibn Ḥawqal 1873, II: 159.

46 It had two to three sails, fitted with up to 30 oars. Particularly mentioned by al-Nuwayrī l-Iskandarānī were the *zawraq*s, war vessels, employed by archers. They were swift and targeted larger ships which they set on fire. Moreover, compared to other medieval war vessels *zawraq*s had excellent manoeuvrability, to turn around in danger and flee from the enemy. Details on the war-*zawraq* in the Mediterranean are given by al-Nuwayrī l-Iskandarānī, KLI (no 667) MS II 359/60, fols 123v – 124r, 261r; (no 738) MS 2335, fol 260r.

47 As in Qatar, in Qalhat, Tiwi, Fins and sometimes Sur it is common to hear an initial velar plosive /k/, perhaps a Fārsī influence, and an initial uvular plosive /q/, when switching the word into the plural.

48 The affrication of voiced uvular plosive /q/ realizing as voiced uvular fricative /gh/ is quite common in the Dhofar region.

49 Beckingham (Ibn Baṭṭūṭa 1994, IV: 874, fn 1) sees Barahnakār as the name of a people who have not yet been identified while Gibb and Tibbetts perfectly understand it as being a place-name.

50 Al-Nuwayrī l-Iskandarānī, KLI (no 738) MS 2335, fols 260r, 262r – 262v; Ibn Miskawayh 1914-5, II: 176-8; Ibn Baṭṭūṭa 1968, II: 161, 231, 244.

Greek speakers in Syria and Egypt during the early centuries of Islam, and giving rise probably to the Portuguese *caravo* from which came the Spanish (and Portuguese) *caravela* (Pellegrini 1978: 817-8), the word having infiltrated the Gulf via Iraq, and the Red Sea via the south Arabian coast, or perhaps both routes simultaneously.

General terms for 'crossing': *ʿabra*, *ʿabbāra*, *ʿabrī* and *ʿabriyya*

There is no other generic term of purpose more fitting than *ʿabra* (pl *ʿabrāt*), from classical Arabic *ʿabara*, 'to cross, ferry', hence ferry boat. In Bahrain the *ʿabra* was until the sixties operated with sails and oars, and more recently, is propelled by an inboard diesel engine. The term was used for any ferry which carried passengers from the island to the Iranian coast, and to Ras Tannourah on the Saudi Arabian coast. This craft also served in general, to transport merchandise as well as rocks, stones and sand. At one time, the large Dubai *ʿabra* ferried passengers from the harbour to Bandar Abbas (Prins 1972-4: 161). Still popular today is the small *ʿabra* on the Dubai creek, a double-ended boat between 18 and 25 feet long, and which ferries from 15 to 20 passengers, from one side of the harbour to the other (illus. 7). Most of these *ʿabra*s I saw in April 1996 were motorized, with just a few being oared by old Iranian seamen. In Masirah, the locals call the ferry boat that crosses from the capital Hilf, to Hannah (mainland Oman), a *ʿabbāra* (pl *ʿabbārāt*). But in Iraq a *ʿabra* was constructed like a raft[51] (Kindermann 1934: 90). Talking to 80-year-old Ali Mohammed Matar,[52] a fisherman from Khasab in the Musandam Peninsula, he said that until fairly recently *ʿabra*s were used to transport people from Mina in Khasab, to the other side of the port or sometimes to Qadah, west of Khasab; these square-sterned *ʿabra*s were small, some 8 feet long, and carried 2 to 4 passengers.

The term *ʿabra*, therefore, can cover, wrote Hawkins (1977: 81), 'all manner of small craft which can be anything from a decrepit all-purpose boat in Aden to the sleek ferries of Dubai Creek'. There is some truth in that. Some specific features about the craft are recorded by Hunter (1877: 83) who

51 Similar to a *kelek*, an old type of raft transport mentioned by Strabo (1917 Book XVI [4m 2]) still in use apparently in modern times on the Euphrates. Chesney (1850, II: 635) describes it as being '16' to 18' long by 14' or 16' broad, and is supported by about 32/34 skins; but the longer ones are 30 or even 40 feet in length and have at least 50 skins and some are so large as to require 300 skins'. The *kelek*s were cargo rafts from Mosul to Baghdad and generally operated by 2 oars midstream. When the *kelek* reached its destination the materials were sold for firewood, and the skins were reused for another journey.

52 Interviewed on 26 November 1996.

7
The ʿ*abra* by the Sheikh's office in Khor, United Arab Emirates. The Bur Dubai Mosque is in the background

described it as a small boat of 5 to 15 tons built at Mukalla; Moore (1925: 123 says it was a vessel with a lowered bow and elevated stern and Serjeant (1974: 134) mentions a ʿ*abriyya sambūk* (his spelling) typical of the district of Mahra and the people of Sur. The name distinguishes itself from any ordinary *sanbūq* (see Chapter 5) for it is longer and wider with a long prow (*rās ṭawīl*) and employed particularly for hunting sharks. On the south Arabian coast ʿ*abrī* (or ʿ*ibrī*) and ʿ*abriyya* are terms used to refer to a specific type of boat. I was told in Salalah and Masirah that the terms were often used in the past to mean a small sailing boat which was stitched with coir and could carry up to five passengers. In Sur the general term applied to deep-sea cargo ships was ʿ*abrī* or ʿ*abriyya*.

Grouping dhow types

The purpose of hull designs depends on several practical considerations such as seaworthiness, weight, speed and sometimes for merely decorative purposes. Technological differences may vary from one vessel to another. However, to the local builder and user, this has no particular relevance. In the case of fishing dhows, the hull design is region-specific but sometimes, as we shall see, more than one name may be used to define a ship. In the ensuing Chapters (4, 5 and 6), we will look not only at names of ship types but also at how the categories are defined and the distinctions perceived and expressed. It is perhaps not an ideal way in which to focus on categories; some types do not fit exactly into the group I have chosen. But in grouping them this way, I believe the reader will be able to form a picture of the dhows in relation to each other, their function at sea and perhaps, most important of all, to see them through the eyes of the seamen and boat-builders themselves.

4
THE LARGE OCEAN-GOING DHOWS

ولا تَتَصَوَّرونَ الْبوم طَيْراً

فَما هُوَ غَيْرُ فُلْكٍ ذي شِراعِ

Do not think that the *būm* is a bird;
but (did you know) it is a ship with sails![1]

(Khālid al-Faraj, a Kuwaiti poet)

Large vessels

The deep-sea vessels, the *baghla*, *ghanja* and *kūtiyya* of Indian design, have striking features characterized by their carved ornamentation at the stem with rear windows and quarter galleries which Gulf builders, Omanis and Kuwaitis in particular, have adapted into local types. These dhows looked similar to each other and it would not have been possible for the layman to identify one from the other.

The aristocratic *baghla*

The *baghla*, 'the aristocrat of all the dhows', as Hawkins (1977: 85) called it, was the largest type and the most ornate of all Arab dhows: it was rigged with two or three masts, fully decked with a low bow and a high unswept quarterdeck. The parrot-shaped sternhead facing inward was frequently surmounted by a brass peg, a form of ornament (illus. 8). The light superstructure attached to the stern served as the living quarters for the captain, his wives, family and personal attendants and some elite passengers. The rudder was hung from the sternpost by gudgeons and pintles, controlled by chains which were attached to the steering wheel. The *baghla* must have been a beautiful craft to look at with its chestnut-brown sides, the richly ornamented carved transom stern pierced by five windows elaborated with foliar scrolls and close-set arabesques (Hornell 1942: 13).

It is generally believed that the *baghla* was in use around the beginning of the seventeenth century after Omani sailors visited shipbuilding yards that belonged to the English East India Company in Bombay (Qināʿī and Khuṣūṣī 1982: 122). At the beginning of the nineteenth century, trading *baghla*s were employed by Arab and Indian merchants on trips between the Gulf and the west Indian coast (Stocqueler 1832, I: 1–3). Some *baghla*s were sailing in the

1 'Wa lā tataṣawwarūna l-būma ṭayran/fa-mā huwa ghayru fulkin dhī shirāʿin'.

8
The parrot-shaped pollard of the *baghla Al Hashemi II*, Kuwait

lower parts of the rivers Euphrates and Tigris, carrying cargoes of dates to the upper parts of the Gulf[2] (Chesney 1850, II: 645). These craft were much smaller and weighed no more than 70 tons.[3]

The *baghla* is recorded as having been built in the nineteenth century at Cochin and other places on the Malabar coast, and in Kuwait until the early twentieth century. The cost of building such a vessel was enormous and carpenters were hard to find in the Gulf. Consequently, the Kuwaitis stopped building this craft in favour of the *būm*-type (see below) which was more cost-effective. Not only were the *baghla*s cargo vessels but some, according to Edye (1835: 12–13) and Low (1877, I: 169), were armed with guns on the stern for defence against pirates. Some had a long life; one built in 1750, was apparently still sailing in 1837 (Low 1877, I: 169). One peculiar type of *baghla* was a double-ender which had the characteristic pollard-like stemhead

2 A line drawing of a ship with a projecting stern frame was identified by Kapel as a *baghla* at the Jabal al-Jussasiyah in Qatar, see Kapel 1983, 'line drawing of ships', figure 12b, site 204, p 57. The site at Jabal al-Jussasiyah, south of Fuwairit in Qatar has some 900 figures and compositions which have been painstakingly investigated by the Danish archaeologist Hans Kapel in 1974; boat carvings are shown in plan cut into the rock face and in elevation as line drawings, see Kapel 1983: 1-126 and Appendix, also Facey (1987): 199-222.

3 A *baghla* from Lingeh on the Iranian coast of the Gulf could carry 500 tons of cargo, see Lorimer 1986, I, iib: 2322.

but without the ornate transom stern (there is a c 1830 model of this type in the Science Museum in London). It was designed to be a fast dhow for piratical activities. I have not come across this type in any account or report.

Of all the ocean-going dhows the *baghla* had the largest tonnage. Rowand's (Lorimer 1986, I, iib: 2326–7) classification of dimensions of vesssels in the 1900s shows the *baghla* as the heaviest cargo vessel. I saw a large *baghla* named *Al Hashemi II* under construction in May 1998. Husain Marafie planned the building of this craft to commemorate the memory of his great-grandfather who, little more than a century ago, built a *baghla* naming it *Al Hashemi*. The construction of *Al Hashemi II* was under the supervision of Muhammed Jasim al-Masqati (nicknamed Abu Mubarak)[4] and the Indian master builder V. K. Narayanan from Beypore, with some 140 carpenters working on site. *Al Hashemi II* is considered to be the world's largest wooden sailing vessel, with a length of over 269 feet, a width of 60 feet and weighing over 600 tons[5] (illus. 9). By the 1940s the *baghla* had become smaller and the largest cargo capacity was 400 tons, with lengths varying from 100 to 140 feet.[6]

9

The *baghla Al Hashemi II* with its richly ornamented carved transom stern, elaborated with foliar scrolls, Kuwait

4 Interviewed on 4 May 1998. Al-Masqati, now in his eighties, was in his younger days a *nākhōda*. For many years he was mentor to Husain Marafie. He volunteered to assume the office of the Project Adviser of *Al Hashemi II*. Some 175 skilled and unskilled workers were involved in the construction of this *baghla*.

5 Large *baghla*s recorded by Hawkins (1977: 84–5) were: a) *Mahamoodia* from Lingeh (1890s) length 112 feet, beam 28 feet 9 inches, depth 18 feet, register 516 tons; b) *Mahamoodia* from Bahrain (undated) length 105 feet, beam 27 feet, depth 16 feet 5 inches, register 413 tons.

6 A statistical table compiled by LeBaron Bowen (1949: 101) based on Hornell's study (1942: 11-40) in the 1940s shows the *baghla*'s gradual decline in cargo capacity. The *būm*, as we shall see further below, had a higher cargo capacity.

The term *baghla* or *bghala* (pl *bghāla*) takes different written forms among western travellers and writers.[7] That the sixteenth-century Portuguese hull-design style played an influential role in the construction method of this vessel, has gained a wider acceptance among maritime historians. A different theory on the origins of the craft comes from the maritime historian Hikoichi Yajima (1976: 22–3): he argues that the massive square stern and the quarter projection richly ornamented with carving, may have been influenced by Chinese junks which anchored at south Indian ports close to the end of the thirteenth century. Several Chinese immigrants called Chīnī-Bachaghān, accompanied by their carpenters, settled in these ports. They were engaged in trading and repairing of junks initially but probably with time were employed in the construction of Indian and Arab vessels. Yajima claims that some of the traditional shipbuilding techniques in the area went through several alterations with the introduction of Chinese nautical techniques. If this is so then the *baghla* may predate the Portuguese influence by at least a century. Interestingly enough, almost contemporary with the Portuguese era in the Gulf and Indian Ocean, we find transport *baghla*s recorded by the Egyptian Mamlūk historian al-Maqrīzī (d 845/1442), most probably in reference to a Red Sea type (1911–24, IV: 10),[8] which ran to the harbours of west India and Sri Lanka.

The Arabic term *baghla* seems to have become confused with the Anglo-Indian name *bungalow*, *buggalow* or even *budgero* found on the west coast of India. This nomenclature was also applied to an Indian type, the *pagell*, which the Dutchman and factor of the East India Company, Peter Floris, saw in one of the west Indian harbours in 1611 (*The Voyage* 1934: 14). Political Agent Arnold Wilson (1928: 225), writing about the British in India in the late nineteenth century, noted that in the navy *baghla*s were called in official documents *bugles* or *buggalows*. Another bit of confusion is the interference of the Indian and Arabic nomenclature with the Persian name *bajra*. The names may be related phonetically but whether these dhows shared similar structural features is another issue. Information about the *bajra* is sketchy. According to Grant Colesworthy (as quoted by Hill 1958: 214), the craft was a pleasure boat 'having more pretensions to comfort than speed' with a high stern and flattish rounded bottom, frequently used up and down the

7 Burton 1964, I: 178, fn 2; also see Edye 1835: 12–13 and Yule and Burnell 1994: 123. Written forms noted are *baggala* or *buggala*, *bagalā*, *baglā*, *buglah* and *budgerow*.

8 Two important sources that throw light on ship types during the Ayyūbid (564–650/1169–1252) and Mamlūk (648–922/1250–1517) periods are those by al-Maqrīzī: the first *Al-Mawāʿiẓ wa l-iʿtibār fī dhikr al-khiṭaṭ wa l-āthār*, deals generally with Egyptian history and topographically with Fusṭāt, Cairo and Alexandria, the second *Al-Sulūk li-maʿrifat al-mulūk* is exclusively on the Ayyūbid and Mamlūk periods until al-Maqrīzī's death, see Agius 1998: 185–7.

principal towns of the Ganges. It was large, fully decked with a cabin and the smallest type was half decked. The *bajra* was the type which the East India Company's employees travelled on, as Hill (ibid, 213) understood it. It was called the European *budgerow*.[9] However, the lack of references to these names and their hull design is frustrating. I therefore brought this inquiry to a halt.

My next step was to look at the possibility of linking the name *baghla* and its hull design with another Indian name and ship type. I do not believe, as is generally claimed by Gulf Arabs, that the name *baghla*, which means 'mule', has its etymological origins in Arabic. Although the prototype *baghla* looks remote from any type discussed so far, I am of the view that the *baghla* could be a development of the Indian dhow *pahala*, both from a design and phonological perspective, for the following reason: it is often pointed out in technical sources, that similarities exist between the *baghla* and the *kūtiyya* but there is rarely any mention of the features which the *kūtiyya* shares with the *pahala*,[10] a ship type (details of which will be given later) that was found from Bombay to Calicut. My contention is that the Arabic name *baghla* derived from *pahala* but its hull design was always associated with the *kūtiyya* because of its popularity among Arab shipwrights. We know historically that Arab shipowners from the Gulf went to the south-west Indian coast, had ships built there then sailed them across to the Arabian Gulf (Dale 1997: 182), and that the *baghla* and *ghanja* were some of the most common types built. Diachronically, the phonological development from *pahala* to *baghla* took place as follows: i) bilabial /p/ is foreign to Arabic and it is automatically switched to a bilabial occlusive /b/, ii) a laryngeal /h/ is possible in Arabic and it can alternate with a uvular fricative /gh/, thus /p/a/h/ala became at some time */b/a/gh/ala (which some Gulf Arabs currently pronounce) and then *baghla*. Semantically, Arabs found the term *baghla* culturally convenient as the word means 'female mule', ie a beast of burden. Also, in the view of some Arab mariners, female names semiotically represent a craft which is large and heavy such as the *baghla*, *ghanja* and *kūtiyya*.

The Suri *ghanja*

The *ghanja* (pl *ghanjāt*) used to be built at Sur; it was similar to the Kuwaiti *baghla*; though its design is near identical to the Indian *kūtiyya*, as will be

9 That it is phonetically related to *bazara*, a Bengali boat recorded in the European documents, with Portuguese *pajeres* giving the Anglo-Indian *buggalow* is open to question, see Hill 1958: 204, 214 for a detailed study.

10 It is possible that the Indian term may have a Portuguese connection with the word *baxel*, a generic name for any kind of ocean-going vessel as listed in Cobarruvias' Spanish dictionary of 1611, see OED 1982, I: 1160.

illustrated below. Distinguished by a square galleon-shape stern with a high poop and the rails on the poop extending aft of transom, the *ghanja* had the port windows and the stern painted with blue and white decorations. Colourful as the Indian, Chinese and South Asian native craft were (Yajima 1976: 23–4), it must be said that their carving was not as elaborate as that on the *baghla*. Characteristic of the *ghanja* was the distinctive bollard figurehead with an iron ring on the stemhead (*gubēt*). A typical *ghanja* was two-masted (illus. 10), but some were three-masted as the 1920 photographs show (Facey 1979: 122). The earlier *ghanja*s mentioned by Hunter (1877: 83–4) were smaller with a weight of from 50 to 70 tons, identical to the ones recorded in Lorimer's chronicles which are said to have carried 20 to 80 tons of cargo and with a crew of from 15 to 20 men (1986, I, iib: 2322). These were probably what the Suris called *shwēʿi*, the main difference from the *ghanja* being that they did not have a bollard figurehead. Larger *ghanja*s were some 70 to 100 feet long with 70 to 200 tons register, the beam from 18 to 24 feet and the depth from 8½ to 11½ feet (Hornell 1942: 17). The last *ghanja* to be built in Sur was *Feth el-Kheir* in 1952 by Mohammed bin Khamis Ali al-Shaqa al-Arbi. Its length was 90 to 100 feet with a weight from 120 to 150 tons.

10
The *ghanja*: painting by Rabee (1995) in the Mina of Sur, Oman

The origin of the name of *ghanja* is not clear. The popular belief is that it is linked to the holy Indian river, the Ganja. The name *ganjo* or *gunjo* often registered on Indian dhows, could have become directly involved with the dhow nomenclature, hence the Arabic name *ghanja*. It is pronounced *ghanye* or *ghinye* in Sur, *ghanche* or *khanche* in Bahrain and *gancha* or *ghancha* in Kuwait. Written variations are *qanja*, *ghancha*,[11] and *khansha*; Dickson (1949: 475) identifies the latter with the Suri dialect. Speaking to Ahmed Salih Husain al-Hamash,[12] a shipwright from Khor Fakkan, about the close similarities of the *ghanja* and *baghla*, he said that he worked as a dhow-builder for 40 years and he could make the distinction very clearly, but in general, he remarked, locals tend to attach one name not another purely because it came down to them from their ancestors and not for any technical reason. '*Ghanye* [as he pronounced it] is made in Sur, in Kuwait they call it *baghla*, here in Khor Fakkan we call it *kūtiyye* like the Indians do', he concluded – a good example of a vessel, the nomenclature of which varied as it anchored in different ports of the Gulf.

Indo-Pakistani designed dhows

The *kūtiyya* (pl *kuwātī* or *kūtiyyāt*) was, until fairly recently, built in Kuwait and Bahrain and still is in Bushehr on the other side of the Gulf. In all respects it resembles the *baghla* or *ghanja*. As mentioned earlier, the name *baghla* often replaces the name *kūtiyya* in the Gulf language of the dhow because of the similarity.[13] The stemhead motif is mainly what differentiates a *kūtiyya* from a *baghla*; it is like a parrot's head pointing backwards unlike the *baghla*'s plain knob. Facing inboard, mariners believe that the bird is in a position to ward off evil spirits giving protection to the vessel and its crew. The *kūtiyya* is used mainly as a cargo craft and is considered to be a fast-sailing vessel. On some of the older *kūtiyya*, like the one I saw in Dubai port, you find false stern galleries with a flat and plain transom stern. They are some sort of modern Gulf Arab adaptation.[14] Also found in Dubai is the Indian-design, *wāhan*, another modern adaptation of the *kūtiyya*, described as the giant of the Indian Ocean (Prins 1972–4: 159).

11 Not to be confused with the Ottoman Turkish *qanja* which was used by the sultan on the Bosphorus, described by Dozy (1967, II: 409) as being a 'gondole, galiote, long bateau couvert'. Landberg (1920-42, III: 2381-2) quoting Jal connects it with the Nile. It is a light, narrow and swift boat, about 30 to 40 feet long. Its keel is curved from the fore to the middle, one mast; larger boats carry two masts with lateen sails. Equipped for 6 to 10 rowers, some *qanja*s were decked, others not. The decked *qanja*s had one or two cabins fitted on the aft deck.

12 Interviewed on 17 April 1996.

13 Also, in the Maldive Islands, Hawkins (1977: 92) tells us that an Indian *kotia* (GA *kūtiyya*) was called *buggalow*.

14 The Kuwaiti dhow-builder, Khalil bin Rashid (interviewed on 16 January 1985) informed me that the *kūtiyya* is sometimes styled *dangiyya* if the ship is double-ended. It has some similar features to the *būm*; see section on 'The *būm* family' below, p 66.

When I visited the boatyards in Doha (Kuwait) in January 1985, I was shown several *kūtiyya*s (or as sometimes pronounced there 'kūtiyye') which, though they looked very similar to the *baghla*s, were all Indian designed, my Pakistani and Indian informants told me. It was only after a few visits on the deck of these vessels, where I was served several cups of *chāy* (tea), that the real name *brīch* or *ibrīch* was revealed, the Indian native type belonging to Karachi and the Kutch Madvani coast. Two skippers told me that a common *brīch* has a cargo weight of 200 tons and is between 40 and 80 feet long. In the past it used to carry one or two masts and was heavily rigged with lateen sails. Two builders I spoke to in Dubai in April 1996 referred to the craft as *ibrīch bākistānī*, and in Qatar they were called *kalikut ibrīj*. The *brīch* that I saw under construction in the Deira boatyard of Obaid Jumaa bin Suloom in Dubai was one of the largest I had ever seen – 130 feet long taking up to 900 tons of cargo weight (illus. 11).

11
The *brīch* in the boatyard, Dubai, United Arab Emirates

The word *kūtiyya* is Hindi and it could have originated from Gujarat (Yajima 1976: 24) or Sri Lanka (Yule and Burnell 1994: 265), recorded in the sixteenth and seventeenth centuries as *cotia* (or *kotia*). Moore (1925: 76) and Serjeant (1974: 135) think that the Arab *kūtiyya* or Indian *cotia* might be identified with the medieval *qiṭʿa* (pl *aqṭāʿ*, *qiṭaʿ* or *qaṭāʾiʿ*). Essentially, *qiṭʿa* was a common term for a galley and it is generally associated with the Mediterranean craft, reference to which is found in medieval historical works (Kindermann 1934: 82). We find in the chronicles of Bāfqīh al-Shaḥrī, mention of Frankish (Portuguese) *qiṭʿas* which were seen on the Arabian coast west of Mukalla in the sixteenth century (Shihāb 1987: 54–5). The question is whether the *qiṭʿa* is a reference to a particular type of galley or, in the absence of any nomenclature, it means specifically 'a piece of the fleet', in other words, any type of vessel. More facts need to be corroborated if a link between *kūtiyya* and *qiṭʿa* is to be proven. The linguistic link is always difficult to establish, though technically it has been shown that the *kūtiyya*'s hull design and (often) rounded stern so characteristic of this ship, is but another modified survival of a sixteenth century trading vessel.

Two other Indo-Pakistani designed dhows, *padão* (or *padow*) and *pattamar*, are similar to the *kūtiyya*. They were trading vessels and were seen in Dubai by Hornell (1946: 206) in the 1940s and by Hawkins (1977: 49) in the 1970s. None of the shipwrights and carpenters in the Gulf could give me details about these types though like other Indo-Pakistani vessels they were called by Arabs *lanchāt hindiyya* (Indian launches) and regularly plied in the Gulf. Much of the *padão*'s hull planks were 'almost completely hidden by the bamboo and split palm screens' (Hawkins 1977: 105); it had a cargo weight of from 30 to 60 tons, carried two masts and the stem had a long projection with a parrot's head facing forward at the top, and a delicate painted foliation on the transom. The *pattamar* was a distinctive type of coaster the design of which was mainly Indian,[15] but influenced by European and Arab contacts and its cargo weight was 60 to 180 tons. It was distinguished by the 'great sheer fore and aft, the long curving grab overhang of the bow' (Hornell 1946: 206) and its full rounded stern was like the Indian and Arab *kūtiyya*. Both the poop and the transom stern were decorated with stars and painted portholes.

To conclude, the *padão* and *pattamar* have a lot in common with the Indian *kotia* or *cotia* (and the Arab adaptation *kūtiyya*) which is, so it seems, the forerunner of the sister types, the *baghla* and *ghanja*. The handsome carving on the arched transom of these craft was of great craftsmanship, but in the 1950s and 1960s, as the work that this involved became a financial burden on shipowners, carving was replaced by picture galleries. The increased contact between Oman and the English East India Company in the eighteenth century must have brought new ideas to Arab hull designs. The English had at this time built dockyards at Bombay to construct European

15 Molesworth's dictionary *Maráthi and English*, volumes I-IV (Bombay 1857; second edition) lists *patamārī*, 'a sort of swift-sailing vessel', see Yule and Burnell 1994: 687.

vessels and to make Indian-design dhows, as the demand for Indian products increased. The Omanis joined this boom trade and it was perhaps at this time that Indian shipwrights were contracted to produce for Arab clients, large trading vessels like the *baghla* and the *ghanja*. Before long an Arab 'type' was standardized, cross-fertilized with European and Indian ideas, and we then find this craft being constructed in Mutrah, Sur and Kuwait during the nineteenth and until the mid twentieth century.

War vessels and slavers

The *dāw*, *ghurāb* and *battīl* were designed as ocean-going merchant ships and operated in time of conflict as war vessels or privateers, having a low freeboard and guns mounted on poop and forecastle. During the pearling season these well-armed ships patrolled on the sea nearby to protect the pearling fleet from pirates. Some were purposely designed as naval ships with high castles erected at bow and stern to give a better field of fire and also to provide a defence against boarders entering by the waist. Renowned for their speed, these three types of vessel served as slavers in the latter years of the nineteenth century, between the east coast of Africa and the Gulf, the slave market being in Muslim lands.

The war dāw

The Perso-Arab or Indian *dāw* vessel was until comparatively recent times seen anchored in the ports of Kuwait, Bahrain, Dubai, Mutrah, Raysut and the Red Sea. It was manufactured in Cochin on the Malabar coast 'most perfectly in the European style', John Edye wrote (1835: 11) (illus. 12). It appears for the first time in Ḥasan Tāj al-Dīn's (d 1139/1727) account of the history of the Maldive Islands (1982–4, I: 116), but information on its size and function is lacking. In later reports the craft is generally described as, 'an old-fashioned vessel of Arab build, with a long grab stem, ie rising at a long slope from the water, and about as long as the keel' (Yule and Burnell 1994: 314), being smaller than the *baghla* and *ghanja* but, like them, having a high stern and poop projecting considerably over the rudder. It was a cargo vessel, single-masted, lateen-rigged, with 10 to 12 ports, some 90 feet in length, 20 feet wide, with a depth of 11 feet and of 150 to 200 tons burden.[16] These craft were common in the late eighteenth century carrying coffee and spices but they were very much sought by merchants to ferry Muslim pilgrims during

16 The Jabal al-Jussasiyah ship (Kapel 1983: site 204, p 57; also Appendix, p 25) was identified as a *dāw* by Norbert Weismann in a personal communication (16 January 2000) but as *baghla* by Kapel (ibid, 118). The similarities are such that it is difficult to mark one from the other.

the pilgrimage season. It was a surprise to find an engraving of a *dāw* high up on the wall of a 150-year-old house in Marbat that once belonged to a frankincense merchant and the owner of many ships (illus. 13).

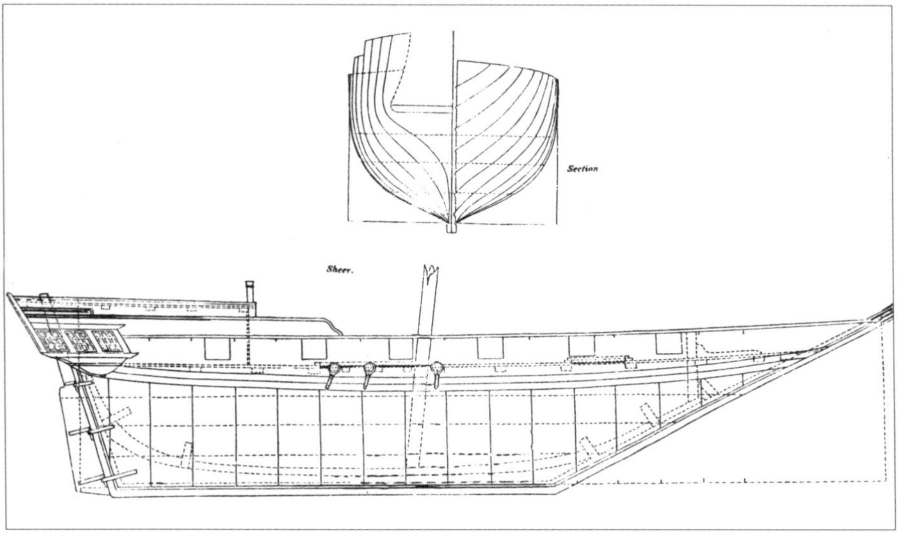

12
Plan of the *dāw* according to Edye (1835, Plate XI)

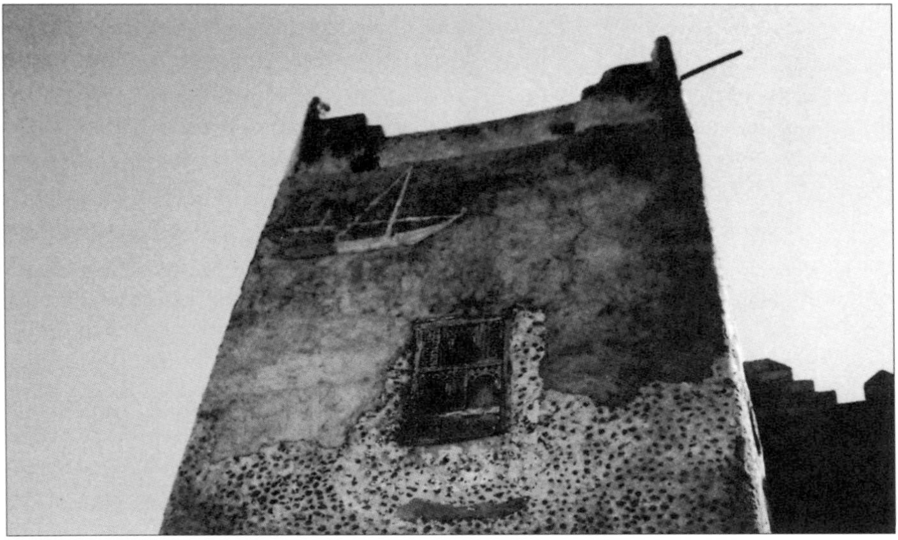

13
A *dāw* engraved on the tower wall of a rich merchant house, Marbat, Dhofar (Oman)

The *dāw* also functioned as a war vessel or privateer. The sheikh of Ras al Khaimah, Ṣaqr bin Rashīd Al-Maṭar, had a large fleet of warships and the *dāw* was one type recorded in 1761 as having been used as a transport ship for troops and provisions.[17] At the time of the Khedive Muḥammad ʿAlī (1183–1266/1769–1849), *dāw*s often transported soldiers from one coast of the Red Sea to the other (al-Nakhīlī 1974: 45). But the *dāw*s in the Arabian/Persian Gulf were mainly fighting vessels, as the British Gombroon Diaries from 1761 to 1808 show.[18] In one document there is mention of '5 large cruising dows'[19] which probably acted as patrol ships in the area. Writing on Oman and Zanzibar at the turn of the twentieth century, Moritz, quoted by Kindermann (1934: 26), reported to have seen armed merchant *dāw*s which he described as being large-bottomed with 16 guns if they were decked, carrying more than 100 tons of cargo, and they travelled with a square sail. The *dāw* was too heavy to make use of oars and was high enough in the water to cope with the heavy seas.

A medieval reference to a ship called *daww* could be linked with the present type under discussion. It is mentioned by the classical Arabic lexicographer al-Azharī who suggests a Fārsī origin (Lane 1984, I: 928), though no description of it is given. For the name *daww*[20] (or present day *dāw*), the

17 CDRAD/British Archives GD, G/29/13, 6 October 1761.

18 CDRAD/British Archives GD, G/29/13, 7 December 1761, 'fighting doughs'; GD, G/29/21, 7 November 1782, 'armed dows'; GD, G/29/23, 1 July 1797, 'certain dows . . . with evil intention'; GD – SPDD, no 232 fols 5669–70, M. 215–6 (10 May 1808), 'dows in operation'.

19 GD – SPDD, no 232 fols 5669–70, M. 215–6 (14 April 1808).

20 I found an almost similar name, *zaww*, recorded by the historian al-Ṭabarī in the fourth/tenth century signifying a small river-boat for crossing the River Tigris (1965, XI, iii: 682, 1168) which, as far as type and function, has little to do with the *zaww* mentioned 300 years later by the geographer Yāqūt (d 626/1228). He described the craft as a huge vessel but with no clue as to its location (1866-73, II: 960). In terms of ship type, Kindermann (1934: 36) suggests that the Arab *zaww* came from Fārsī term *zawd*, 'swift', however there is nothing to suggest a Persian boat with that name. My curiosity about the name is on a phonological level because initial position alveolar spirant /z/ is possibly shifted to alveolar occlusive /d/, thus changing **zaw* to **daw*. The matter, however, gets complicated with Ibn Baṭṭūṭa's reference to a medium-sized Chinese vessel called *zaw* (1994, IV: 813-4), which looks curiously similar to the terms discussed above. Most likely these terms developed independently of each other. One possibility, however, is that the old established name Arabic(-Fārsī) *zaww* was absorbed from Chinese, based on the fact that Chinese shipbuilders were established on the south-west Indian coast. Ibn Baṭṭūṭa's description of the Chinese trade activity and their presence in the south Indian coast at the end of the seventh/thirteenth and beginning of the eighth/fourteenth century is quite remarkable. Note Ibn Baṭṭūṭa's term *zaw* has been identified as Chinese *sao* or *seou* as suggested by C. Defrémery and B. R. Sanguinetti, see Ibn Baṭṭūṭa 1968, IV: 91 and

anthropologist Adriaan H. J. Prins (1965: 79) thinks that the origin may be found in the Fārsī *dawh*, signifying a small ship, though no source is given to justify his assertion. Another source in the historical search of the name can be sought in the travel account of the Russian Athanasius Nikitin who says that around 1470 he shipped his horses in a *tava* ([?] *dava*) which sailed across the Indian Ocean to Muscat in ten days (Yule and Burnell 1994: 315); this does suggest that the ship was rather large to only be carrying horses. Based on the graphemic representations of both the Fārsī *daw(h)*, the Indian (?) *tava*, and the Marāthī form of *dāo* and *dāva* for 'ship', we note the following phonological correspondences: dental sounds /d/ and /t/ and labials /w/ and /v/ are generally interchangeable, which could be the clue to the origins of the present Perso-Arab or Indian *dāw*. What is not clear is how the east African name *dau* (or *dow*) discussed earlier (Chapter 3) came about. Two types of the east African flat-bottomed *dau* were noted by Prins (1965: 79); the rib-constructed dhow, the so-called *dau la mataruma* and the short-keeled nail dhow, otherwise called the *dau la msomari*. They were used for laying traps and other fishing activity, common among the Bajuni of northern Kenya and southern Somalia. Is the vessel an independent Swahili development, and a ship type which was succeeded in a modified design by the Lamu *mtepe*,[21] or is it a development of the Persian *dawh*? The word relation is possible but the design connection is not definitive.

The Indian Ocean ghurāb

Another war vessel was the *ghurāb* (pl *aghriba* or *ghirbān*), which had a low and sharp projecting prow and a square stern like that of a galley, two or three masts, weighed from 150 to 300 tons, and was very broad in proportion to its length. There has often been mention of this vessel in connection with India after the arrival of the Portuguese there. In the mid-eighteenth century this craft was known as the (Dutch) *goerab*, *gourab*, *gorab* or *grab*[22] and the

sao or *tsʾao*, see Kindermann 1934: 36, though, according to Hess, *tsʾao* is more accurate in the context (ibid).

21 The *mtepe* was a large sewn vessel common on the east African coast. It became extinct by the beginning of the nineteenth century. It was described by Hawkins (1977: 20) as being 50 feet in length with 'a monstrous beak-like projection', having a flower pattern on either side of the decorated sternpost. A model of this craft is to be found at the Fort Jesus Museum in Mombasa, also in the Science Museum, London (in storage). Another type mentioned was the sewn-hulled *dau la metpe*, almost the same size as its predecessor though the stemhead was not as high (ibid).

22 CDRAD/Dutch Archives, VOC 2680, OB 1747, 10 fols 43-4, 34, fol 365; VOC 2996 Kharg, November 1759, fol 20; VOC 9101 Masqat, 8 March 1758, fol 15; VOC 1913 Bandar Abbas, 2 April 1717, fol 29; VOC 2748, 1741, fol 87; VOC 2680, 1741, fol 44; VOC 2546, fols 1804-6.

(English) *ghorâb* (Hyde 1767, I: 97), *grabb* or *grab* (Toreen 1771: 205). The *ghurāb* served as a corsair ship and the British popularized its name by calling it *grab*, referring to 'grab(bing) all that passed the sea' as it was believed to do (Yule and Burnell 1994: 392). The English East India Company employed *ghurāb*s, one of which carried 18 guns around 1754 (ibid). It has been suggested that this war vessel was probably built in Muscat. The Imam of Muscat, Aḥmad bin Saʿīd (1154–88/1741–75) on 8 March 1758, 'equipped *ghurāb*s with men, ammunition and weapons to go to Mombasa . . . in order to quell a rebellious uprising against his rule'.[23]

The word *ghurāb* sounds Arabic, meaning as it does, 'crow'. Other names of ship types in the medieval period seemingly had names of birds such as *ḥamāma* (dove), 'transport ship' and *ṭayra* (big bird), 'swift boat', as we are informed by the geographer al-Muqaddasī (Agius 1997: 324, 328), but there is nothing to point out why such names were given to vessels in the first place. The word *ghurāb* may have originated from Fārsī *gharāb*, an old-fashioned term for 'launch' used in official documents (Prins 1972–4: 157). The several Iranian sailors I met in Doha, Qatar and Dubai called any vessel, new or old, *gurāb*. In Umm al Quwain the term *ghayrab* and *ghrayb* (the Arabic pattern denotes a diminutive), perhaps a smaller version of the *ghurāb*, cropped up in the course of my conversation with the shipwright Ibrahim Khamis Bu Haroon[24] who said that it was a general term used by the local fishermen. Both terms were not heard of by any of the informants I spoke to except in Dubai, where Saif Mohammed bil-Qaizi (who proudly said that he belonged to the ancient tribe of Banū Īyās),[25] an experienced shipwright at the Deira boatyard, told me that *ghayrab*s were built there and at one time they were stitched, resembling the *baqqāra* (a double-ender with a very sharp-pointed bow) but smaller, with the stempost pointing further forward.

If the Fārsī origin is not accepted then it would be interesting to find out what connection there might be between the Mediterranean *ghurāb* and the one used in the Gulf or Indian Ocean. There is enough evidence to show that the Mediterranean craft was both a merchant and a war galley, and several accounts report *ghurāb* as a pirate vessel used by Frankish corsairs. Christian and Muslim diplomats employed *ghurāb*s to discuss peace and to draw up treaties concerning trade and safety.[26] Of all the ship types that the Mamlūk historian al-Maqrīzī mentions, the *ghurāb* was certainly considered one of the

23 CDRAD/Dutch Archives, VOC 9101 Masqat, 8 March 1758, fol 15.
24 Interviewed on 16 April 1996.
25 Interviewed on 15 April 1996.
26 Al-Nuwayrī l-Iskandarānī, KLI (no 738) MS 2335, fol 254r; fol 239v.

most important galleys that was known at the time (Agius 1998: 185–97). The problem is that we have little indication as to how this Mediterranean *ghurāb* looked. Moreover, the reference to Christian and Muslim *ghurābs* by Muslim chroniclers complicates the issue as to whether the term is Arabic, Latin or Greek in origin. Were the Christian and Muslim *ghurābs* identical? All that we are told is that the Muslim type was much smaller.

It is possible that the Indian Ocean Arabic name developed from the Mediterranean nomenclature: *ghurāb*, the galley that sailed in the Indian Ocean during the sixteenth century as attested by the Hadrami chronicles (Serjeant 1974: 44, 62, 67). There is no record of the name having appeared earlier in the Indian Ocean area and its mention by Ibn Baṭṭūṭa in a Mediterranean context is significant. On his visit to Qandahār[27] in South India in 1343, he wrote that he embarked on a ship called a *ʿukayrī*, belonging to Ibrāhīm, one of the principal Muslims in the court of the sultan of Qandahār, Jālansī. He said that this boat resembled very much a Mediterranean *ghurāb*,[28] only that the latter was a broader vessel equipped with 60 oars and 'covered with a roof during battle in order to protect the rowers from arrows and stones' (1968, IV: 59; 1994, IV: 800). Ibn Baṭṭūṭa was very familiar with Indian Ocean and Gulf vessels; the detail which he comes up with concerning such craft compared with Mediterranean ships is quite remarkable.

The pirate vessel renowned for speed: battīl

The *battīl* (pl *batātīl*) operated as a pirate ship, a coastal trading vessel in times of war, and occasionally as a pearling vessel. A document dated 1797 makes reference to one or two fighting *patill*s (Ar *battīl*s) which probably belonged to Shaykh Ṣaqr bin Rashīd Al-Maṭar of Ras al Khaimah, the sheikh of the Qawāsim Arabs.[29] As late as the beginning of the twentieth century, Bent (1900: 8) speaks of fine war-*battīl*s. It may be added that the *battīl*, renowned as it was for its speed, became very popular among slave traders as it sat low in the water[30] and could easily defend or attack aggressors that patrolled the Arabian Sea and the Arabian/Persian Gulf.

A double-ended craft, the *battīl* had a long overhanging, fiddle-headed bow, a high sternpost often called by Arabs the *fashīn* (a false sternpost), and

27 The name Qandahār is an arabicization of the Indian Gandhar. It is now a fishing village at the mouth of the Dhandar River (Ibn Baṭṭūṭa 1994, IV: 799, fn 10).

28 H. A. R. Gibb translates *ghurāb* as English *grab* (Ibn Baṭṭūṭa 1994, IV: 800).

29 CDRAD/British Archives GD, C/29/23, 7 October 1797.

30 Although it is true that a *battīl* had little freeboard, Tom Vosmer told me in a personal communication (21 April 2000) that this was a disadvantage in battle.

double forward-leaning masts. From the keel, which was about one third the length of the vessel, the after part rose upwards forming a thin stern-board, towering over the poop. The line drawing at the Jabal al-Jussasiyah shows clear evidence of the *battīl* type with seven nearly-round-bladed oars on one side (illus. 14), and the characteristics of the bow shape and the high stern with its rudder in place. The drawing shows a triangular and a lateen sail which were probably used in combination, for different winds.[31] The cargo weight of this craft varied from 15 to 60 tons, some from 100 to 200 tons (Miles 1994: 412). The *battīl* was decked but apparently, so I was told, this was not common. Speed was this vessel's main feature, which made it the most desired fighting craft among Arab ships. The craft came in various sizes. In Chapter 5 we discuss similar smaller vessels or boats based on the same larger type of *battīl*, the prototype of which was probably a stitched vessel with a curved keel, a *fashīn* and a raking stempost, such as the small *battīl* of the Musandam Peninsula and the *baqqāra* and *shāḥūf* of the Al-Batinah coast of Oman and Ras al Khaimah in the east of the Emirates.

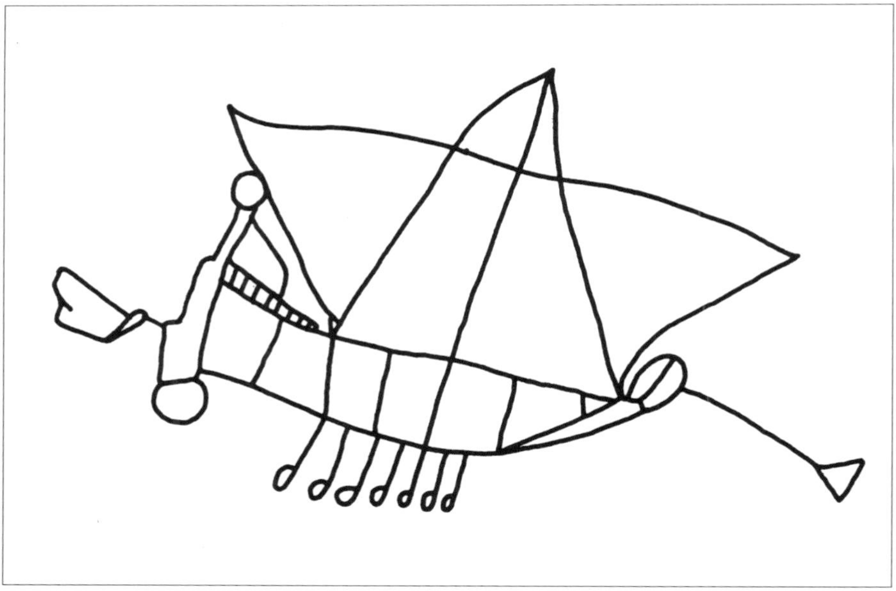

14

The *battīl*: line drawing at Jabal al-Jussasiyah, north-east Qatar (Kapel 1983, Figure 9, site 421)

31 Kapel 1983: Figure 9, 'line drawings of ships; and of animals', site 421, p 52; also Appendix, p 53.

I spoke to the shipwright Mohammed Khamis Bu Haroon at al-Butteen boatyard in Abu Dhabi,[32] who recollected his grandfather talking about a cargo *battīl* carrying up to 200 passengers. I gathered from other interviewees that only three *battīl*s, in Kuwait, Dubai and Lengeh on the Iranian coast, were recorded to have existed in the 1930s and 1940s.[33] During my early field trip to Doha (Qatar) in April 1992, I spoke to the master-builder Yousef Al Majid,[34] who at the time was building a 90-foot-long *battīl*, which was to become a model of craftsmanship. I was surprised to see the plans for this craft – usually, Arab shipwrights do not rely on such things but use the accuracy of their eye[35] (illus. 15).

15
Master builder Yousef Al Majid with the plans and model of the *battīl* (interviewed by the author 18 April 1992, Doha, Qatar)

The origins of the Arabic *battīl* are obscure, not only the name but also its hull design. The north-west Indian *batella* described in the mid nineteenth century as having 'a square flat stern, and a long *grab*-like head' (Yule and

32 Interviewed on 16 April 1996.

33 See Dickson 1949: 478-9; the Kuwaiti *battīl*, he reports, had its bow and stem altered on 3 May 1937 to adapt to a fast sailing *būm*.

34 Interviewed on 18 April 1992.

35 A report on the building of this *battīl* was recorded in detail by Muḥammad ʿAlī ʿAbdallāh, see *Taqrīr binā' safīnat battīl fī Qaṭar*, volumes I-III (Doha: Markaz al-Turāth al-Shaʿabī li-Duwal al-Khalīj al-ʿArabiyya, 1987).

Burnell 1994: 72), is difficult to relate to the Gulf *battīl*. The Indian *batella*s are reminiscent of the Portuguese *caravel*s as are the *baghla* and *ghanja*. Hornell (1942: 33) reported that the *batella* was a cargo boat of 40 to 100 tons' register which ran between Cambay and Bombay. He claimed that the name *batella* was of Portuguese origin, *batelha* or *batel*, 'a small boat', and he was of the opinion that the Arabic *battīl* was too. Both names were adopted on the Gujarat coast.[36]

Summing up the importance of the war vessels in the Gulf and Oman one is struck at the role each one played at a time when European powers were seeking dominance over the sea trade in the Indian Ocean, and Arab tribes were settling on the coasts for economic security. India's vast resources of timber provided an advantage for its inhabitants and for Arabs, enabling the building of swift sailing vessels, such as the *dāw*, *ghurāb* and *battīl*. They were cargo vessels but also privateers with guns, operating in time of war against enemy trading during the pearling season or, in the days of slave trade, defending against raids by British cruisers, probably in the Red Sea, around East Africa, the Arabian/Persian Gulf and the west coast of India. The *battīl* survived during the first half of the twentieth century as a pearler when the industry was at its height, bringing prosperity to the north of the Gulf and the Arabian littoral.

The *būm* family

Often what is known in the West today as a dhow actually refers to the Kuwaiti *būm*. One of the finest ship types in the maritime history of the Gulf, the *būm* (pl *abwām*) is distinguished by its straight, sharp-pointed stemhead (known in Kuwait as *ṣāṭūr*), usually painted black and white. Kuwait has been known since the early part of the twentieth century for building this craft (Dickson 1949: 474-5). Though used mainly for trading, some were used for pearl diving and they were numerous at that time in the ports of Muscat, Ras al Khaimah, Abu Dhabi, Bahrain, and Bushehr on the Iranian coast. The *būm* superseded the ornately decorated square-sterned high-pooped *baghla*, and was smaller, as Hess remarked on his visit to Kuwait in the first decade of the twentieth century (Kindermann 1934: 13). In the days of sail the *būm* had two masts (illus. 16), the main mast was raked forward and the mizzen was vertical; some of the larger *būm*s had three masts. An ordinary rudder and wheel were used on Arab *būm*s; Hornell (1942: 23) had seen some in the late 1930s with a primitive rudder-gear fitting. Apart from the iron fittings

36 Other details such as the Indian clinker-built *patela* being cognate of *batella* (or *batela*) but distinct types and whether *patela* is derived from Hindi *patila* (or *paṭelā*) are found in Hill 1958: 212-3; see also Hornell 1946: 200-2.

16
A *būm* passing the Pillar Rock, near Muscat, Oman
(oil painting by John Whale, courtesy of the artist)

below the waterline, the rest was connected to the rudderpost by means of coir rope lashings, as were the Omani *baqqāra* and the *badan* at one time (see Chapter 5). According to Prins (1972–4: 159), the *būm* was a development from the large square-sterned *baghla*. The *baghla* took longer to build, was expensive to run, heavy, and not a fast craft at all whereas the *būm*, smaller as it was, proved to be cost-effective. It was lighter, with a better cargo space, and with its pointed stern was a much faster ocean-going vessel.

An experienced sailor, now retired, Yusuf bin Abdalla bin Yusuf Al-Farisi[37] from Harat al-Sheikh near Sohar, travelled on *būms* to Kuwait, Bahrain and Bombay for over thirty years. He recalled travelling on a large ocean-going *būm* with six sails carrying a weight of some 400 tons and having a crew of 40. It is not surprising that he travelled on such a large *būm*; one Iranian *būm* which Villiers (1948b: 413) saw in 1939 at Mombasa, was over 400 tons and there was in fact one Kuwaiti *būm* of more than 500 tons, called *The Light of the Earth and Sea*, which was one of the largest dhows to be built on the Malabar coast in the 1940s. It was built over a period of six months by the Kuwaiti master-shipwrights Mohamed Thwaini and Salim bin Rashid,

37 Interviewed on 28 November 1996.

assisted by more than a hundred Indian carpenters. However, it did not live up to expectations and saw only the beginning of its existence; on its first voyage it foundered causing great financial loss to the dhow owners and the merchants, both of whom probably never recovered from the tragedy (Villiers 1952: 86–7).

The commonest types of *būm* range in weight from 60 to 200 tons with the length varying from 36 to 120 feet. The *būm* named *al-Muhallab*, outside the National Museum of Kuwait, was constructed in 1997 under the supervison of the master-builder Ali bin Jasim al-Sabbagha, together with the help of 10 Kuwaitis and 14 Indian builders. The keel is 66 feet long, the width 28 feet, and the vessel is 15 feet high with a weight capacity of 225 tons (or 3000 sacks of dates). The main mast (*ʿōd*) is 66 feet high and the mizen mast (*ghulamī*) 48 feet. The present *al-Muhallab* is a replica of the one built in 1973 by Mohammed bin Abdullah for two merchants Thunayyan and Mohammed al-Ghanem,[38] and it was razed to the ground by Iraqi forces in 1990.

The smaller *būm* was manufactured in Sur in the 1970s of a standard tonnage of from 60 to 120 tons with one mast, and diesel-engined. It was not uncommon to see a *būm* being built on the west Indian coast: Yajima (1976: 20–21) records in his study on Omani *būms* that the 120 to 150-ton vessels were built in Calicut, a traditional dhow-building yard in South India. Of course, this was the obvious choice, as building materials largely came from India and also, perhaps more relevant, the forties were difficult years for the Gulf economy. It was essential for Arab shipwrights to hire Indian carpenters to build their dhows because they were practically the only skilled men in Kuwait or Oman who could do the job. On my visit to Kuwait in May 1998, I met master-builder Muhammed Jasim al-Masqati[39] and his Indian partner V. K. Narayanan who, in Calicut in 1979, supervised the building of the *būm* named *Mohammedi II*, using authentic drawings of *Mohammedi I*, constructed in 1915–16 and historically the largest *būm* at 130 feet long, 33 feet wide and with a cargo capacity of 415 tons. Some of the teak used in 1979 was 200 years old and iron nails from 3 to 30 inches long were manufactured in Kuwait. It was a multi-million Kuwaiti dinar project sponsored by Husain Marafie.

The Kuwaiti maritime historian Yacoub Al-Hijji[40] told me that in 1939 alone there were as many as 150 large Kuwaiti *būms* trading with Karachi,

38 See *Kuwait* 42 (1997): 4-5; also al-Ḥijjī 1988: 335-7; 1997: 16. In December 1958 Johnstone and Muir (1964: 299) made measurements on the original *al-Muhallab*, which was lying at the time in Kuwait harbour.

39 Interviewed on 5 May 1998.

40 Interviewed on 5 May 1998. As stated in my 'Note' at the beginning of the book, all names of interviewees are written according to the state's transliteration system; hence

Bombay, Mukalla, Aden and Zanzibar. It was an impressive scene to see many of these *būms* with other dhows, crowding the waterfront, almost touching one another. One *būm* that Al-Hijji accidentally discovered had survived in the waters of Hamriya, near Dubai. This was the *Fateh-el-Khair* (CA *Fatḥ al-Khayr*, lit 'The Gate of Wealth'), a deep-water sailing dhow built in 1938. Thunayyan al-Ghanem commissioned its construction and asked Ali Abdul Rasool to design and build it under the supervision of the master-builder Ahmed bin Salman who was assisted by 18 carpenters. *Fateh-el-Khair* is 95 feet long, 27 feet wide with 226 tonnage and can sail up to 13 knots. I saw it on display in 1998 at the Exhibition of Kuwaiti Sailing Ships in Doha.

The most common of the medium-sized *būms* served as cargo vessels carrying mangrove wood from East Africa and teak from India. Some, called by Kuwaitis *būm al-qaṭṭāᶜ* or simply *qaṭṭāᶜa*,[41] transported rocks or stone, cement, iron, camels and lorries to Gulf ports. The water transport was often called in Kuwait *būm al-māʾ*. Tanker dhows shipped water from Shatt al Arab near Basra to reservoirs in Kuwait until the early 1950s when a distillation plant was installed at Shuwaikh (Hawkins 1977: 40). Neither the *būm al-qaṭṭāᶜ* nor the *būm al-māʾ* exceeded 100 tons weight and both were sturdy enough to cope with the winds and waves (al-Ḥijjī 1988: 41).

The origins of the name *būm* (written also *boom* or *bhum*) still remain a mystery.[42] I could not locate the name in any literature, nor, indeed, in any Arabic dictionaries. Yajima's (1976: 22) assertion of *būm* coming from Chinese *bo* or *po* (the latter originating from a Malay or other south-Asian word), a seagoing vessel, seems far-fetched. It is tempting to accept what is commonly believed, that the Arabic name of the ship represents the bird

Al-Hijji follows that order except when I am referring to his works, I use the Library of Congress system – al-Ḥijjī (1988, 1997).

41 The term does not represent a ship type as such but only a descriptive functionary word for 'crossing', ie ocean-going. However, there is a medieval name of a ship type called *qaṭāᶜ* (pl *qaṭāʾiᶜ*) mentioned in connection with the Portuguese in Mukalla and Shihr by Bāfqīh al-Shiḥrī (Shihāb 1987: 54–5), a type identified by Moore (1925: 76) as similar to the Indian *kotia* or *cotia* (Ar *kūtiyya*). The name could also be functionary as the modern usage. It was recorded by Ibn Mājid (Tibbetts 1981: 138) though Serjeant doubts its existence in his time and thinks it is probably a Mediterranean craft (1963: 135) which, according to Muslim sources, appeared from the fifth/eleventh to the seventh/thirteenth centuries as *qiṭᶜa* or *qiṭᶜ* (pl *aqṭāᶜ*), a general classificatory term for a Mediterranean galley synonymous to *markab*, see Agius 1998: 187.

42 In the *Taʾrīkh al-mustabṣir* of Ibn Mujāwir (d 690/1291) we come across the word *būmāt* (1954: 124) in the plural form though this is not clear because in other places in the text we encounter *burm* and *burmāt*, in which case the copyists would have added an /r/ (ibid, 299). The term *burma* (lit. 'pot') is a boat type listed by al-Muqaddasī (1906, III: 32), which probably is a round ship; see Agius 1997: 313.

'owl'. Although in the medieval period we do have a few examples of bird names given to ship types such as *ḥamāma* (dove), 'transport ship' and *ṭayra* (big bird), 'swift boat', as listed by al-Muqaddasī (Agius 1997: 324, 328), and the *ghurāb* (crow) 'galley' discussed earlier, it is not culturally acceptable among Arabs to have a name of ill omen such as the owl, attached to a ship.

It has often been said that the *būm* has retained its hull shape from the pre-Portuguese period, thereby showing similarities with the seventh/thirteenth century ship of al-Ḥarīrī (d 515/1121–2) illustrated in the *Maqāmāt*.[43] The illustration shows the belly-shape of the hull, and a rudder attached to the sternpost. A feature of this medieval ship is the high, straight bow angled at 45 degrees which is also seen on the modern *būm*. It is certainly intriguing that the *būm* carries a bowsprit which is believed to be a remnant of ancient ships. The projecting spar over the stern 'provide[d] the means of staying a fore-topmast' (Kemp 1992: 102–3). Pictorial evidence, argues Muir (1955: 358), cannot be taken as conclusive; we may find clues as to how things looked at the time, but a lot of artistic licence should be taken into consideration. In the case of the al-Ḥarīrī ship, he is right to question the artist's knowledge of the sea before making comparisons with modern traditional craft. The similarities are accidental because the hull design of a modern *būm* is a Kuwaiti adaptation going back to the earlier part of the twentieth century.[44] However, in terms of hull design, the *būm* is an adaptation of an ancestral Indian-built vessel, the *dhangi* (see below), which was, I am told by my Kuwaiti sources, probably introduced to Kuwait in the eighteenth century. There may be, in spite of Muir's reservations, some credence to the theory that the *dhangi* could be a descendant of the medieval types of ship shown in al-Ḥarīrī's *Maqāmāt* and al-Ṣūfī's *Ṣuwar al-kawākib* (Nicolle 1989: 173–4). It is worth noting the similarity of horizontal bow timbers in *dhangi*s and al-Ḥarīrī's vessel.

The ancestral Indo-Pakistani vessel

The Kuwaiti double-ended *dangī* (pl *danākī*), sometimes called *dangilī*, was a two-masted vessel, decked just abaft and it weighed from 60 to 200 tons; the stem was slightly curved and, like the *kūtiyya*, had a bird's head with the beak pointing aft at the stemhead, a feature the Kuwaitis adopted. It had a raked stern, more rakish lines than the *būm* and a long rudder with a tiller. The

43 It is an Iraqi double-ended passenger boat which clearly shows planks stitched together, the foremast rigged with small square sails, a four-pointed iron grapnel anchor and a line of merchant faces looking out of portholes: BN, MS Arabe 6094.

44 The first time a *būm* was recorded was on 6 December 1903 by the Swiss traveller Johann Ludwig Burckhardt, one of the most distinguished visitors to Arabia, see CDRAD/Dutch Archives (Burckhardt bibl no 4.009) 1906, p 1.

older Indo-Pakistani *dhangi* type held the rudder stock 'four feet above the sternpost and the tiller', the purpose of which, Hawkins (1977: 105) remarks, was that if the vessel had a bulky cargo stacked high on deck the helmsman could steer it from an elevated position by tilting the tiller as needed. Captain Jenour (1791: 36) on his voyage to India wrote that the Indian *dhangi* (written in the text as 'dinggee') was the 'most clumsy, inconvenient, unmanageable thing' he had ever seen; in spite of this, the craft seemed to have been an exceptionally fast sailer.[45] Hornell (1946: 199–200) sees the *dangī* essentially as a Perso-Arab ship type but, as he noted, adopted by Indian shipbuilders and owned by them in the ports of Sind and Kutch. The shipwrights I spoke to at Doha (Kuwait)[46] could not confirm the report entirely; their memories of this craft relied on what they heard from their fathers and grandfathers, chiefly that the *dangī* built on the Indian coast between Karachi and Calicut was, as far they were concerned, the Arab *būm*. In terms of hull design, the *būm* has much in common with the old established Indo-Pakistani *dhangi* and it is safe to assume that the latter has been ancestral to the *būm* of Kuwait. However, this divorced itself from the *dhangi* and adopted some features of its own, at a time when Kuwaiti shipowners and shipwrights were visiting the south-west Indian coast in the late nineteenth century. The Arabic name was symbolic, and chosen to represent a new beginning in the making of the craft.

Some Kuwaiti and Bahraini sailors I spoke to referred to a dhow called *dangiyya* (pl *danāgī*) which they claimed to be identical to *dangī*. We learn from the interviews Tibbetts (1981: 48) conducted with Gulf shipbuilders that the *dangī* built in Sur, which Omanis called *ṣūr* or *ṣūriyya*, was actually known as the *dangiyya*, a one-masted vessel with a low bow and a high poop (illus. 17). In Jayakar's (1889: 662) Omani word list, it appears as 'a kind of boat, dinghy', which suggests a different type, or a smaller version of the large *dangī* or *dangiyya*; al-Dujaylī (1912: 98), speaking about Iraqi vessels, lists *dangiyya* as 'a large sailing ship' specifically used in Basra.[47] Possibly also linked

45 The Indian *nauri* was another vessel resembling the *būm* and the *dangī*. It was built on the Kathiawar coast: its stemhead ornament contained a curved parrot-head with a crest like the *kūtiyya* and the steering gear was slightly different from its sister dhows, see Hornell 1946: 200. The *nauri* was a trade ship which frequented the Gulf ports at one time. It was described as the medieval Hanseatic cog, the thirteenth and fourteenth-century seagoing ship of England: 'In the cog one sees the straight raking stem and sternpost, the rudder hung on the sternpost, the deck set low in the ship and even the high extension of the stemhead' (Howarth 1977: 23–4).

46 Interviewed Khalil bin Rashid and Hassan Abd al-Rasool on 14 February 1985.

47 The name is recorded as *digniyya* in which the letters /g/ and /n/ have been switched for *dingiyya*, see Kindermann 1934: 29.

17
The *dangiyya* according to Pâris (1841, Plate 4)

phonetically with *dangiyya* but not in design is the Tigris *dāneg* (pl *dawāneg*), called by some Iraqis *ʿāniyya*, made of teak, up to 13 feet long and used as a ferry boat seating 6 to 10 passengers. The description that Ritter (1919: 138) gives of this *dāneg* is more accurate: '[an] asphalt boat on the Tigris, with a particularly high stern and a load-bearing capacity of 10 *ṭghār*'.[48] This is phonetically identical perhaps to *dānūq* (pl *dawānīj*), 'a small and narrow boat for fishing and pleasure' which Kuwaitis used in the 1920s (Kindermann 1934: 29).

The *dangī–trānkī* connection

The Arabic term *dangī* comes from Hindi *ḍēṅgā* or *ḍōṅgā*, a large boat, sloop, or coasting vessel, now applied to a small sailing boat on the west coast of India.[49] In what way can we justify Hornell's (1946: 200) claim that this craft is the lineal descendant of the Hormuz undecked sewn ship (with one mast

48 An Iraqi weight equalling 2000 kilograms, in Basra 1537 kilograms (Wehr 1966: 561).

49 Originally *ḍēṅgā* or *ḍōṅgā* was a native Indian boat similar to a canoe, of different sizes and shapes; the diminutive is the Anglo-Indian *dinghy* (and other variations of spellings *dingey*, *dingy*, *dingee*, *dinghee*), or small wherry boat which comes from Hindi *ḍēṅgī* or *ḍiṅgī* (OED 1982, I: 731).

and one rudder) which was described in Marco Polo's memoirs (*Travels* 1982: 52)? Information on the ship's design is lacking and we have no other source to verify Hornell's assumption. Perhaps the Arabic/Fārsī and Hindi nomenclature is connected with the vessels termed *terraquin* in Portuguese documents[50] and *trankey* (*tranki*, *tranky* or *tranquin*) in Dutch documents,[51] the latter having references to the craft being a cargo ship,[52] and a transport ship for soldiers.[53] The *terraquin*s were large war vessels; one letter mentioned '110 well-manned' ships furnished with war ammunition.[54] The Omanis, renowned for their sailing skills, had a good number of these craft, which they used to lay siege to the island of Diu, in Gujarat (Ibn Razīk 1871: 88). From the British Gombroon Diaries we know definitely that *trankey*s were war vessels belonging to Arabs, namely the Julfar coastal community.[55]

We find the Arabic name *trānkī* in a few modern travellers' accounts: it was a large trading dhow that plied between the west Indian coast and Mocha in the Red Sea, a double-ended, undecked vessel of large dimensions with a weight varying between 70 to 100 tons; Miles (1994: 413) noted that it was very long and wide, with a low stempost and very high stern, similar in some way to the *badan* (see Chapter 5); the smaller type were compared to the *baghla* and were used regularly by Omani Arabs sailing from Jeddah to Basra.[56] One source tells us that parts of the *trānkī* were sewn together, planks first, which were then fastened to the ribs; the flexibility of the planks when sailing gave these *trānkī*s some advantages over those fastened by nails (Chesney 1850, II: 645–6). The wood for building this vesssel was local and Hornell (1942: 32) did not think it was a particularly beautiful craft.

The word *trānkī* may have been a general word for any open, double-ended vessel. The attempt by Yule and Burnell (1994: 937) to link the word to the Portuguese *trincador*, 'a sort of flat-bottomed coasting vessel with a high stern' or to the English *trinquart*, 'a herring-boat used in the English channel',

50 CDRAD/Portuguese Archives, AHU, Conselho Ultramarino, COD. 501, fols 238-40v [1645]; 169-70v [1646].

51 CDRAD/Dutch Archives, VOC 2680, OB 1747, 77 (fol 825); ARA/Aanw no 1889-23b (fol 8); VOC 2584 Persia Part 2, 1741, fols 2109-17, 2133-6, 2228-40; VOC 1913 Bandar Abbas, 1717, fol 50; VOC 2748, 1741, fol 87; VOC 2546, 1741, fol 33; VOC 2546, fols 403-5, fol 1434.

52 CDRAD/Dutch Archives, VOC 2680, OB 1747, 77 (fol 825); VOC 1913 Bandar Abbas 1717, fol 50.

53 CDRAD/Dutch Archives, VOC 2584 Persia Part 2, 1741, fols 2109-17.

54 CDRAD/Dutch Archives, VOC 2546, fols 403-5, 1434.

55 CDRAD/British Archives, GD, G/29/17, 31 December 1751 and 5 August 1760; GD, G/29/13, 16 October 1761.

56 CDRAD/Dutch Archives, translation of Niebuhr's *Description of Arabia* (1774: 8). Niebuhr lists *tranki* and *tarad* (sv *ṭarrād*) as the same boat.

is tenuous. Hornell's (1942: 32) attempt, though, to derive the Arab *trānkī* from Indian *dhangi* is worth considering. We have here two issues: a) the possibility of Hindi /ḍ/ and /g/ in *ḍēṅgā* producing a trilled sound /tr/ and a velar /k/ to realize the word *trānkī*, and b) that *trānkī* or **tarānkī* is a separate Indian term related to the verb *táran*, 'to cross over, swim';[57] both are possible. Nonetheless, the theory that the Arabic term derives from the Fārsī *trānkeh* (a small undecked double-ended craft used for pearl-fishing)[58] and detached from any Indian influence, presents a stronger case.

The sister chāla

Finally, in the *būm* family, there was what was commonly known by Kuwaitis and Bahrainis as the *chāla* (pl *chāchīl* or *chāshīl*), a double-ended fully decked craft, with a peculiar stemhead and pointed stern similar to the *būm* though smaller (al-Ḥijjī 1988: 46) and with projecting quarter strakes. The craft was built in Kuwait and Bahrain but also, I was told, by Emiratis in Sharjah; I could not confirm this from any other Gulf Arabs.[59] Muhamed Saeed al-Balushi,[60] a Qatari folklorist, informed me that in Oman the *chāla* served as a transport ship, carrying coral rocks for house-building (because no other building material was available). Occasionally it functioned as a ferry boat. In the Emirates it was used for pearl-diving and short-distance trade. Different phonetic variations in Kuwait and Bahrain are *tashshāla* or *tashshāle* with plural *tashāshīl* or *tashāyil* and in Sharjah *chyāla*, *tishāla* or *tishshāle*. The origin of the word *chāla* could be linked to Hindi.[61]

To conclude, the twentieth-century double-ended *būm* replaced the giant *baghla* and *ghanja* of the nineteenth century and became the principal ocean-going trading vessel of the Gulf. The common structure of the three

57 Verb derivation is provided by Captain Stafford Bettersworth Haines in his report about Dhofar published in 'Memoir of the South and East Coasts of Arabic', *Journal of the Royal Geographical Society* (1845), see Ward 1987: 478, 488.

58 OED 1982, II: 3377; in connection with pearl-fishing, *trānke* means in Fārsī 'the basket that the diver hangs around his neck to collect pearls' (interview with Al-Hijji in Kuwait, 5 May 1998).

59 A ship related to the *chāla* was the *būgāʿa* (or *bugāʿa*), according to the historian Abd al-Rahman Musamih whom I met on my visit to Bahrain (interviewed on 21 April 1991). He said that it was a harbour boat which could carry heavy cargo. The nomenclature attached to this craft is a functionary term which seems to have been known by Bahraini locals as the flat-bottomed cargo ship but has no classificatory name of its own.

60 Interviewed on 23 April 1992.

61 A reference to a *jāla* in Fārsī, 'a raft made of leathern bottles' (Steingass 1977: 350) sounds a totally different type.

types was their narrow beam and deep keel, with their sheer rising to a high poop. The *būm* was a successful design, more economical than the *baghla* and much faster: it was modelled after the Indian-built *dhangī*, the latter probably related to the seventeenth and eighteenth century Perso-Arab *trānkī*, recorded so often in European chronicles and reports. Travel accounts of this century often mention the hundreds of *būm*s that lay at anchor in the ports of Kuwait, Bahrain, Doha (Qatar), Dubai, Mutrah and Sur, preparing for voyages to India and East Africa. Today, the majestic *būm*, albeit not Arab, still plies between the waters of Dubai and the shore of Iran, and some sail beyond the Straits of Hormuz.

5
FISHING AND PEARLING DHOWS

ونبكيها لما نراها

wa-nabkī-hā lammā narā-hā
'. . . and we cry over [the *baggāras*] when we see them'

(Saeed Haddad, an Emirati poet from Kalba)[1]

The versatile craft

The most common fishing craft in the northern Gulf and Oman were the *sanbūq*, *shūʿī*, *jālbūt* and the *badan*. They were extremely versatile. The *badan* was the most distinctive craft of Oman, renowned not only for fishing but for coastal trading. The *sanbūq*, *shūʿī* and *jālbūt* also served as traders and cargo carriers but for many years they were the Gulf pearling vessels and turned the area into a vibrant commercial artery. Of these vessels the *shūʿī* has today become the universal fishing dhow of the Arabian Gulf and Oman, distinguished by its simplicity and elegance.

The *sanbūq* family

During visits to the Gulf countries over many years, I was always under the impression that there was only one type of fishing *sanbūq* (commonly pronounced *sanbūk*),[2] but in fact there are a number of variations in design. The type known in the northern Gulf is the one featured by a low, curved, scimitar-shaped stempiece. The vessel is also recognized by its high square stern which looks like the shape of a shield (Hawkins 1977: 60) and is embellished with flower and petal carvings. Almost identical is the Omani *sanbūq*, not used nowadays, which I saw beached on the shores of Al-Batinah; this type had a much higher and narrower stern and fishermen told me that it had no decoration. Nonetheless, the Suri *sanbūq*s I saw had blue and white decoration on the stern.

From the pictures I saw of pearling *sanbūqs* in the northern Gulf, I noticed that they had a short keel. This puzzled me until I met some dhow-builders repairing an old *sanbūq* on my visit to Doha (Qatar),[3] and asked them

1 Interviewed on 17 April 1996. The poet laments the abandoned dhows on the beach.

2 The phonetic realization of /q/ in *sanbūq* among Gulf Arabs becomes rather a voiceless velar stop /k/. I am adopting the name *sanbūq* (with a /q/) throughout as this is the conventional writing of it in modern standard Arabic sources.

3 I have only tape-recordings of these people; unfortunately, I lost some of my field notes which contained names of seamen interviewed on 21 April 1992.

the reason. They believed that the short keel made the dhow suitable for use in shallow waters where the oyster beds were laid; one of them made the interesting remark that it was a perfect design for the quick and frequent pulling around with oars, thus increasing the speed with the least paddle action. This is true, because the Red Sea *sanbūq*s with a sharper keel, seem to be less manoeuvrable in shallow waters. In my last field trip to Kuwait I asked the boat researcher Yacoub Al-Hijji[4] about the *sanbūq*'s curved stemhead, much of which lies underwater. From his response it appears that it was designed that way to make it more hydrodynamic, in contrast to the Yemeni type which has a less pronounced curve, making it a slower vessel.

There was another type of *sanbūq*, a double-ended vessel. Mohammed Abdallah Al Saqar,[5] a one-time dhow-builder in Bahrain, recalled that when he was young, Bahrainis prided themselves on their double-ended *sanbūq*s: the square-sterned type was a later adaptation he said, which became popular with the rest of the Gulf states only in the last fifty years. The double-ended type was found in the south-west of Oman in the Dhofar region though it has been identified as a Yemeni or Red Sea craft. Hawkins (1977: 76) however, remarked that at one time Adenis in particular were using the transom-stern vessel and only recently did they replace it with the double-ended type.

I found one double-ended *sanbūq* lying on the beach and not in use (illus. 18), in Sadh on the Dhofari coast; the local seamen informed me that it was the only one left in the whole area as many dhows were being replaced by fibreglass boats called *ṭarrāda*s. My guide Salem Amer Nassib Al-Amri, a graduate in archaeology from Moscow, took me to see two wrecked stitched *sanbūq*s[6] in Taqa, east of Salalah. The elegance of these boats struck me, abandoned in a cemetery as they were, I thought perhaps it was the safest place for them. Of course the wear and tear of the elements is gradually affecting the wood and in less than a decade these stitched *sanbūq*s will be gone; they are the relics of the fishing *sanbūq ẓufārī* (ie *sanbūq* of Dhofar) or the *sanbūq mukhayyaṭ* (stitched *sanbūq*) as recorded by earlier travellers (ʿAbdallāh 1987, III: 75). Folkard and Crauford (quoted by Donaldson 1979: 80) noted that this fishing *sanbūq* bears a resemblance to the *masula* surf boat of India,[7] both stem and sternposts 'are straight and raked at approximately the

4 Interviewed on 5 May 1998; see note 40 (Chapter 4)

5 Interviewed on 22 April 1991.

6 The Dhofaris, in general, pronounce a voiceless retracted velar plosive /k/ representing the classical Arabic voiced uvular plosive /q/; thus *sanbūk*.

7 Details about a Madras *masula* stitched boat is found in Edye 1835: 8-9 and Plate VI, Mookerji 1912: 236 and a partial design of it in Hornell 1920: 174; see also Kentley 1985: 303–17.

18
A small double-ended *sanbūq* in Sadh, Dhofar (Oman)

same angle'.[8] Basheer Saeed Rabee,[9] a *nākhōda* in his sixties, from Marbat east of Salalah, told me that often *sanbūq ẓufārī*s were small coastal boats that carried from 5 to 10 passengers: 'we called them here *kambārī* or *kumbārī*',[10] he concluded, though Saeed Masaud Muhammed Al-Mashini, Director of the

8 Donaldson (2000: 17) has seen the *sanbūq ẓufārī* in Salalah during his research there in 1977. When I visited the Dhofari coast in November 1996, however, I saw no stitched *sanbūq* except the wrecked ones mentioned above.

9 Interviewed on 16 April 1996.

10 The medieval Arabic version is *qanbar*, *kunbār*, *qinbār* (Dozy 1967, II: 408) or *qunbār*; the word originally an Arabic or Fārsī term *qinnab* 'cannabis, or hemp', it is the sort of flax 'of which are made ropes and the like' (al-Zabīdī 1968, IV: 81), hence the word came to represent the boat stitched from the *ḥibāl al-qinnab* 'the ropes of hemp', see Lane's (1984, II: 2566) detailed description of this term though the nomenclature *qanbar* (and its variants) is a local Dhofari term: it was used by Ibn Baṭṭūṭa (1968: IV: 827) in the context of the Maldives.

Heritage Department in Salalah,[11] believes that *dhawākī*, a local *jabbāliyya* word,[12] is a more accurate term as it means 'boats employed during the *rabīʿ* fishing season' (July to September, ie the monsoon season) – known locally as the *ṣirb*.[13] The *kambārī* (illus. 19a) was constructed of imported mango wood from Malabar, the planks of which were stitched together (illus. 19b) with local coconut fibre threads, and most of the older fishermen I spoke to in Raysut recalled how wooden pegs were fitted in prepared drilled holes in the planks so as to securely tighten the threads to them. The pegs were made from local wood (*ḥfūt*), brought down from the mountains to the coast on donkey or camel-back; the wood was dried for almost twelve months before it was cut and carved. I was informed that the drier the wood, the more it held the wooden planks tight and secure. Tar was spread on the planks and the stitched areas to hold them firmly and to keep the water out. Al-Mashini remarked that the hull, mast and rudder, were generally constructed of *nārjīl* wood (the coconut tree), and the rope was *nārjīl* too. For other parts like the ribs, the Dhofaris used wood from local trees such as the *arīr* and the *athab*,[14] and the oars were carved out from the wood of the *kilīt* tree; the stem- and sternpost were thicker than the planks of the hull. Double-ended stitched *sanbūq*s were built so as to resist the toughest storms of the Indian Ocean. The stitched planks were covered with fish-liver oil; the sewn construction made them supple and flexible in surf and these lasted longer than nailed planks which were stiff and broke easily.[15] The *kambārī* was found from Aden all along the coast of Yemen, Hadhramaut and Dhofar. Fishermen from Raysut always sailed on the *sanbūq*: Saeed Saleem Jaafari[16] recalled stitched *sanbūq*s operating by the rope system like the *badan* and *baqqāra* (see later section); they were equipped with oars and also operated by sails, using

11 Interviewed on 18 November 1996; also author spelt in the Library of Congress system al-Maʿshīnī (1992), see note 40 (Chapter 4).

12 Arabic (s) *ḍāqiya*, (pl) *ḍawāqī*; a common feature in several Arabian dialects is the shift from classical Arabic /ḍ/ (voiced alveo-dental plosive) to dialectal /dh/ (voiced interdental fricative) as is the case in Dhofar.

13 Al-Mashini, however, pointed out to me that the *dhawākī* is precisely a term to indicate the fishing season of sardines during the months of October to mid-December; culturally and linguistically the term extended to mean the sewn boats.

14 In modern standard Arabic *ʿaṭab*, see al-Maʿshīnī 1992: 95. Note the voiceless alveolar plosive /ṭ/ of *ʿaṭab* is realised in Dhofari /th/, a voiceless interdental fricative.

15 Nailed dhows are also covered in fish oil. During construction, to make the planks more pliable, Bahraini builders applied old date syrup and then warmed them. This was a common practice: Tom Vosmer told me in a personal communication (27 April 2000) that on constructing the stitched dhow named *Sohar* (Severin 1982) the carpenters partly applied this method.

16 Interviewed on 19 November 1996.

19A
The *kambārī* with sewn planks, Taqa, Dhofar (Oman)

19B
The inside of the *kambārī* with stitch patterns around the planks, Taqa, Dhofar (Oman)

20
The *sanbūq*'s stemhead in Marbat, Dhofar (Oman)

the lateen and the square sail. The craft generally ranged from 24 to 40 feet in length with an average crew of 4 to 8 fishermen and were usually employed for coastal fishing of *ʿūma* (sardine), caught mainly for use as animal fodder and manure.[17]

Some of the stemheads of old Dhofari *sanbūq*s that I saw in Marbat, Sadh and Raysut in November 1996 were decorated with a symbol on each side consisting of a crescent with a star, on top of a pair of horns pointing upwards. Some carry an oculus with a white circle over a blue background and the tip painted white as on the *sanbūq* shown here (illus. 20). In Sadh and Raysut I saw a few *sanbūq*s with Qurʾānic verses or invocatory prayers and the name of the boat engraved on the stern, a custom carried out in Dhofar and Hadhramaut, I was told. The Adeni-type *sanbūq* has curved panels running along the length of the quarter strakes; the transom's panels are decorated with cut-outs of different shapes, and others are painted with stars and crescents. You find the upper strakes at the stern are painted blue or terracotta colours with black, yellow, or white borderings. An oculus consisting of a star and crescent symbol is found on the stemhead. I have not seen an Adeni

17 *ʿŪma* or *ʿōma* is a kind of sardine, caught in enormous numbers all around the Omani coast down to the Dhofar region on the Arabian Sea. The *barriyya* is also caught: it is a small fish like whitebait, dried in the sun and used as animal fodder.

sanbūq during my stay in Dhofar but was told that these dhows occasionally were seen in Raysut.

While I was staying in the town of Sur in December 1996, dhow-builders told me that up until the late 1950s the *sanbūq* was one of the most common fishing and pearling boats being built there and in Kuwait. The builders described it as a fairly large vessel, a piece of information which confirms what Ritter (1919: 137) found in Basra and the Gulf in the 1900s.[18] From reports about Gulf *sanbūq*s in the past I gathered that Kuwaitis built the large *sanbūq* on the model of the *baghla* while Suri shipwrights used the *ghanja* design, except that those built to the latter design had no ornaments. The *sanbūq* that Von Neimans saw in 1858 looked 'disproportionately broad and elevated', the triangular sail spread so wide that it covered the whole length of the vessel (Yule and Burnell 1994: 788). What a beautiful scene it must have been for onlookers to see the fishing *sanbūq*s gliding on the sea with their spread lateen sails as they approached the shore loaded with their catches, one hour before the *maghrib* prayers. Both the larger and medium-sized *sanbūq*s were rigged with two masts, the smaller vessels had a mizen. Their size ranged from the smaller craft of 30 tons, to the larger ones of 200 tons, and which had a length of over 70 feet. The few *sanbūq*s I saw under construction in Kuwait and Dubai from 1985 to 1995 were the smaller type of some 50 tons. The Hadrami *sanbūq* was described as a large boat from 80 to 180 tons and the Zanzibari craft was small with two masts (De Landberg, 1920–42, III: 1985). Richard Burton (1964, I: 178) in 1855 observed small and medium-sized *sanbūq*s in the Red Sea varying from 15 to 50 tons; he described one as being 400 *ardeb*s (50 tons) with narrow, wedge-like bows, and carrying two masts, raked imminently forward.

The *sanbūq* of today and the origins of the name

The earliest mention of *sanbūq* comes from Buzurg b Shahriyār, a storyteller who collected accounts reported to him by Omani, Persian and Indian seamen. In one of these stories he narrated how a sailor sailed on a *sanbūq* from Sarīra (presumably Sarbuza in Sumatra)[19] to China. There is enough

18 Ritter visited Iraq some time after Kāẓim al-Dujaylī published his articles on Iraqi vessels and boats in the *Lughat al-ʿArab* (1912a: 93-103; 1912b: 152-5; 1912c: 198-205). In his article 'Mesopotamische Studien 1. Arabische Flussfahrzeuge auf Euphrat und Tigris' in *Der Islam* (1919: 121-43), Ritter generally re-examines and updates al-Dujaylī's findings.

19 There is a long discussion on the name Sarīra, which Devic (see al-Rāmhurmuzī 1883-6: 247–8) understands to be Sarbuza, basing his information on a story related by Buzurg b Shahriyār earlier (p 176). He states that Sarbuza is situated at the extremity of the island of Lameri in the south of Sumatra, being on the route from Oman to China.

evidence to suggest from the medieval accounts that the *sanbūq* was then a small boat, known at the time in the Indian Ocean on the coast around Calicut. Ibn Baṭṭūṭa (1995, II: 280, 374, 383) embarked on a small *ṣunbūq* (pl *ṣanābiq*, as recorded by him) on his voyages from Basra to Ubulla (10 miles), in Maqdashaw (Mogadishu),[20] in Ẓafār (Dhafār) on the southern coast of Arabia,[21] in ʿAydhāb on the Red Sea, and on the Arabian coast, between 732/1331 and 733/1332. From his writings, I learnt that he would generally never use the name of a ship type unless it was part of the natives' register. We can therefore infer from the above that the medieval *ṣunbūq* was a common craft around the Indian Ocean, the Gulf and the Arabian Sea, and known to many locals.

Writing in the ninth/fifteenth century al-Maqrīzī (1270/1853, II: 180) reported that Aḥmad b Ṭūlūn (fl 254–70/868–84) had a whole fleet of *sanbūq*s which sailed the Mediterranean and the Red Sea. The question here is whether the term *sanbūq* existed in Ibn Ṭūlūn's times, ie almost seven hundred years earlier than al-Maqrīzī's report? There is no record that the Ṭūlūnids had used *sanbūq*s. In connection with the tenth/sixteenth century we often find mention of a Yemenite *sanbūq* by al-Nuwayrī l-Iskandarānī (al-Nakhīlī 1974: 70) which, according to the lexicographer al-Zabīdī (d 1205/1790–1), was a particular type built only on the Yemeni coast. The Portuguese record in their chronicles as having seen this vessel in the Arabian Sea and the Indian Ocean on several occasions: Gaspar Correa, writing about the voyages in 1498 and 1516 of Vasco da Gama (d 1524) along the coast to Mozambique, came across Moorish *zambuk*s, as he called them (*Three Voyages* 1869: 75–84), and Ludovico di Varthema (fl sixteenth century) is the only one to describe the boat (recorded as *zambuco*, *cambuco* or *sambuco*)[22] as 'a flat-bottomed vessel' (*The Travels of Ludovico di Varthema* 1863: 154). Indeed, this information is still meagre and it does not tell us much about how the rest of the vesssel was shaped. The original design of the medieval *sanbūq* is different to how we know it today. The square-sterned *sanbūq* was perhaps a later development; it has been likened in design to the sixteenth century Portuguese *caravel*. Howarth (1977: 36) notes that, above the square stern, there are two planks which form a curved extension just like the European

20 H. A. R. Gibb notes that Mogadishu was a fourth/tenth century trading colony founded by the Arabs from the Persian Gulf, most of whom came from al-Ḥasā tribal group, see Ibn Baṭṭūṭa 1995, II: 374, fn 47.

21 Ẓafār is the old town which is part of what is today Salalah. There is a high ridge named Jabal Qara where the summer monsoon rains pour heavily on the area covered with tropical vegetation.

22 Several references are also found in *Hobson-Jobson* (Yule and Burnell 1994: 788).

ship; nowadays these planks simply stick out like wings and are quite visible on *shūʿīs* (see section below).

The name of this craft is found written in different forms.[23] The most common dialectal usage recorded in my interviews was *sanbūk* and the plural *sanābīk*,[24] very rarely *sambūk*, and only in Qatar did I hear *sambūg*.[25] In classical Arabic, al-Zabīdī, quoting al-Ṣaghānī, claims that the nomenclature *sunbūq* is Yemeni because it is being built locally;[26] but there is no evidence to support this assumption. Oddly enough in the seventeenth century al-Khafājī (d 1069/1658–9) lists the name as a relatively new term belonging to the people of Ḥijāz (1865: 118). As a lexicographer he was not aware that the term already existed, indeed Ibn Baṭṭūṭa mentions it in his diaries about 300 years earlier in connection with the Red Sea and the Indian Ocean.

Several authors attempted to derive the name from Fārsī[27] through middle Persian **sambūk*, resulting in various spellings in classical Arabic literature and lexica such as *sunbuk*, *sunbūk* or *ṣunbūq*.[28] The original name, however could be traced back to Sanskrit *çambūka*,[29] a source that came in contact with Malay *sampan*[30] (Kindermann 1934: 43) or Chinese *sanpan* (Yajima 1976: 24). We find, furthermore, that the name was commonly known in the Red Sea with cognates such as the Mehri, Hadrami, and Amharric *sambūq*, and the Tigré *sembuk*.[31] I think the Greek *sambūke* (Anāstās al-Kirmilī 1900: 68) came about because of its contacts with the Semitic type and nomenclature, which in their turn, because of the trade contacts between the Red Sea, the Persian Gulf and the Indian Ocean, absorbed the Indo-European, middle Persian and Sanskrit names. We can therefore conclude that this craft is historically a universal type assuming different names, and that it was an Indian Ocean type (of different sizes) found in

23 Examples are: *sunbūq* (pl *sanābīq*) (Hārūn *et al.* 1960-1, I: 455), *sunbuk* (pl *sanābik*), *sunbūk* (pl *sanābīk*) (Wehr 1966: 434) and others *sunbūk* or *sambūk* (pl *sanābīk*), *sanbūq* (pl *sanābīq*), *ṣunbuq* or *ṣunbūq* (pl *ṣanābīq* or *ṣanābiq*), see De Landberg 1920-42, III: 1985-6.

24 I heard in Raysut two unusual plurals, *sanbakīn* and *snōbek*.

25 Though the fronting and affrication of the velar stop /g/ is a common feature generally among the Gulf Arabs, this phoneme does not feature with the medieval Arabic *ṣunbūq* (and other variants) except with the Qatari 'sambūg' (note voiced alveolar nasal /n/ shifting to voiced bilabial nasal /m/, common with this word).

26 Al-Zabīdī (1989, XXV: 468) defines *sunbūq* as a small *zawraq* (boat) which in the context of Yemen and the Red Sea is larger than an ordinary ship's working boat.

27 See al-Jawālīqī 1969: 177-9, Tabrīzī 1982, II: 1170; also Glidden 1942: 71.

28 See footnote 22.

29 See Yule and Burnell 1994: 789.

30 *Sampan* is a small boat or skiff which was adopted on the Indian coast known to the Portuguese (Yule and Burnell 1994: 789).

31 Other details in De Landberg 1920-42, III: 1985-6, fn 1 and Glidden 1942: 71.

the waters of the Red Sea and in an ocean stretching from East Africa to the seas of the Malay Archipelago and China.[32]

The *sanbūq* sister-types

A sister-type we find in the Yemen and the Red Sea today is the open double-ended *zārūk*[33] with a sharp, pointed stem and stern and which has a gentle curve from the keel upward. The rudder, observed Howarth (1977: 47), is fixed to the boat by two loops of line, the lower one tied to the sternpost through a hole, the second one passing through a hole in the rudder and extending to the gunwale. The *zārūk* is generally two-masted, the smaller size vessels having one, or two which lean heavily forward. Because *zārūk*s were swift sailers in any wind they were used as slavers until the 1930s, carrying their cargos from Ethiopia to the Arabian coast of the Red Sea.

A similar dhow to the Adeni *sanbūq* is the *sakūna* 'with an exceptionally long and deep stemhead' and devoid of ornamentation (Hawkins 1977: 73); there is no record of this type having been seen about the Arabian Sea or the Gulf.

The *zaʿīma* (pl *zaʿāyim*) is another sister-type. The name is commonly used in Hadhramaut and Yemen as a general term for a sailing boat, though Shihāb (1987: 119) classifies it as a special ship type of Aden and the Red Sea. It is a large double-ended craft with a curved scimitar-styled stem like the *sanbūq*, a slightly raked stern, and decked fore and aft with matting: two masts (or one if the craft is small) are inclined forward. Weighing from 2 to 12 tons the *zaʿīma* is steered manually by a tiller or the rope system (see below). Hawkins' (1977: 76, 78–9) comments on the *zārūk-zaʿīma* distinction are of interest and show the difficulties which the researcher comes across in the search for boat typology.

You do not hear Emiratis speaking of the *sanbūq* as much as the *samʿa* (*sumʿa* as pronounced in Sharjah) or *ṣamʿa* (pl *samʿāt*). The only striking difference I could find between these two types was that the *samʿa*'s stempost looked shorter and less curved than the *sanbūq* and its head was painted white and black. Older seamen in Abu Dhabi recalled this type, the *samʿa*, in the 1940s and 1950s, as a pearler and occasionally as an ocean-going vessel that sailed to India and East Africa.

I inquired about a dhow within the *sanbūq* family called an *abūbūz*, and often mentioned in maritime literature. Almost everyone I spoke to had not the faintest idea what it was. However, the shipbuilder Rashid bin

32 For more information on *sanbūq*s, see also Jewell 1969.

33 Not to be confused with the Musandam *zārūka* or *zawraka* which is a double ender with a short stem and a high stern, see below.

Khadim bin Ali of Liwa (Oman)[34] informed me that it was at one time used in Majis, Saham and Khabura on the Al-Batinah coast but could not remember any details of the craft. It seems it was a 'distinctively Suri craft', according to Facey (1979: 134), though the seamen at Sur whom I met on my 1996 December trip could not confirm this, they thought it was of Kuwaiti origin; I found no other Gulf person to support their claim. I understand from some builders that two features found in the *abūbūz* were remarkably different from the *sanbūq*: they were the rounded stern incorporating designs of European sailing ships (Hawkins 1977: 88), and on the tip of the forward end of the vessel, one of the builders told me, you find a simple decoration as you would see on *būm*s. The name *abūbūz* is unusual and its origins are difficult to trace. I gathered from my informants that this craft had not been built for the past twenty or thirty years.

Similar to the *sanbūq* hull design is what was called the *dūba* (pl *dawābī*, *adwāb*, *dawabāt*), a large double-ended craft which transported cargo from the shore to a vessel at anchor nearby. The length of the *dūba* was some 80 feet and for a long time it served as a cargo vessel for many Gulf ports including Kuwait, Abu Dhabi, Dubai and Muscat. In Dubai I was told that it also functioned as a pearl-diving boat. The *dūba* vessels I saw lying on the beach in Salalah, Raysut and Sadh in Dhofar were large and had fallen out of use. I discussed this boat with Abd al-Amir Abdallah Hussein,[35] a shipbuilder near Manamah in Bahrain, who said that the *dūba* he recalled when he was young was a huge boat and flat-bottomed. The impression I got was that he was talking of a barge, the absence of a keel permitting it to operate effectively in shallow water and to remain upright when beached. This could be similar to the Iraqi *dūba* (pl *duwab*)[36] which made trips from Baghdad to Basra and which was called *bārj* by al-Dujaylī (1912b: 152); it is possible that it also made trips to Kuwait and Bahrain.

Some of my older informants in Raysut remembered in their youth a small and medium-sized type of *sanbūq* called *qaṭīra* (pl *qaṭāʾir*) or *katīreh* (as I heard it in Kuwait, Bahrain and Qatar),[37] the transom of which was like a *dangī* (illus. 21). It was known to the Egyptian historian al-Jabartī (d 1237/1821–2) around the year 1811 as a boat or barge (as quoted by Kindermann 1934: 83).

34 Interviewed on 30 November 1996.

35 Interviewed on 25 April 1991.

36 The Ottoman *dawba* (pl *duwab*), a war vessel, used on the river Nile (al-Nakhīlī 1974: 49) is perhaps related to this.

37 Other transcriptions given by Hawkins (1977: 81) are: *khatira* as the fourteen-foot type he saw in Ma'alla in 1972 and *gatira* that Alan Moore's correspondent recorded in 1918 at Port Sudan.

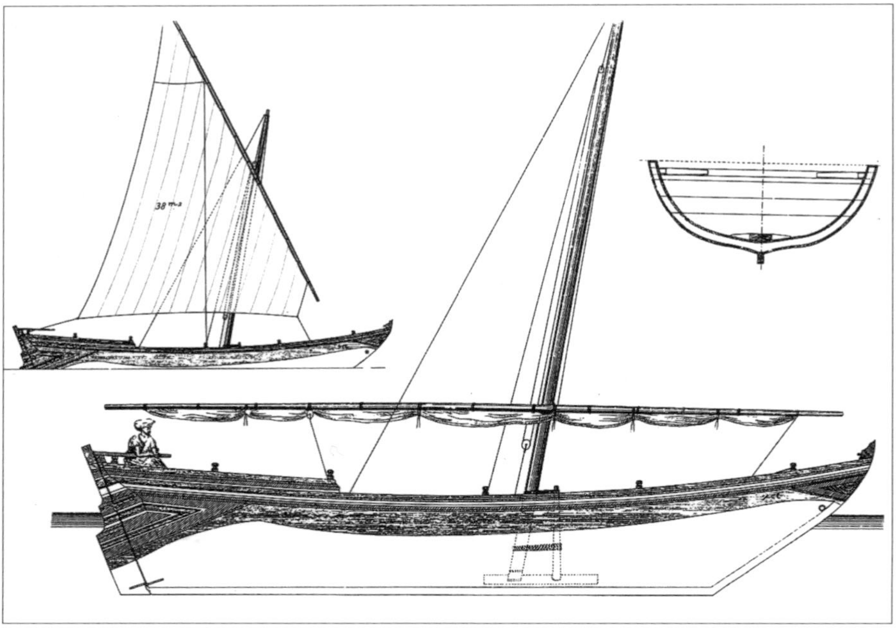

21
The Indian-built *qaṭīra*, 1879 (Pâris 1975, no. 56)

Hunter (1877: 83), Moore (1920: 133) and Serjeant (1974: 133) report to have heard the term in Sudan, where it represented a sailing ship.

The *qaṭīra* was generally a coastal boat which, though associated with the Red Sea, seems to have had its origins in the west Indian coast, the name being traced to Hindi *catur* or *kaṭōrā* and described originally as a small war vessel with oars (Glidden 1942: 72).[38] We encounter the name *catur* (also recorded *chaturi*) as witnessed in the sixteenth and seventeenth centuries by Ludovico di Varthema and the Jesuit missionary Francis Xavier (d 1552) in their travels to India (Yule and Burnell 1994: 175), but there is no mention of it having been a war vessel. Jal (1840, II: 259), quoting Witsen says it was a double-ended Calcutta vessel curved at the back, from 60 to 80 feet long, using both sails and oars.

38 Burton's assertion that the Malabarian *catur* (which he described as a light rowing vessel originating from Arabic *qaṭīra*) is the English *cutter* has, as Yule and Burnell (1994: 175) contended, no real foundations. OED (1982, I: 634) rejects any connection between the Indian *catur* and the English term *cutter* even though OED, as Yule and Burnell (1994: 175) argued, has no references to *cutter* earlier than 1745. The etymology given by Johnson, 'a nimble boat that cuts the water' (OED 1982, I: 634) is no more convincing.

The universal fishing dhow of the Gulf and Oman

The *shūʿī* (pl *shawāʿī* or *shwāʿ*), correctly referred to by the Gulf seamen as the sister of the *sanbūq*, is almost identical, the difference being the shape of the stemhead: the *shūʿī* has a straight stem ending in a double curve while the *sanbūq*'s stem is cut off in a single concave curve. The tip of the *shūʿī*'s stemhead is usually painted blue. It has a transom stern with projecting quarter strakes which look like wooden fins (illus. 22). I noticed that the Emiratī *shūʿī* now has a platform attached to the fins on which fishtraps are carried, an adaptation that allows more space in the undecked middle part of the craft for better storage of fish and for the men to move about (illus. 23). One is struck by the beauty of the *shūʿī*s as they approach the shore laden with nets and fish. They are the 'most charming and elegant of all Arab dhows', Howarth (1977: 38) wrote.

22
The projecting strakes of the *shūʿī* that look like wooden fins, Ajman, United Arab Emirates

23
Returning from a day's catch with fishtraps attached to the fins of a *shūʿī*, Dubai Creek, United Arab Emirates

The vessel is 15 to 20 feet long, about 5 tons, and carries a crew of 6 to 10 fishermen. The *shūʿī*s I saw in the fishing town of Al-Khor, Qatar in 1992 were all Emirati, constructed in Dubai, Ajman and Ras al Khaimah, or so Ahmed Muhammed Munhadi of Al-Khor[39] informed me. In a third trip to the Emirates in 1998, practically all the boatyards I went to had *shūʿī*s being constructed. In Sur, Oman, it is the only craft being built and is called specifically *shūʿi sammāk* (fishing *shūʿī*) (illus. 24).

Not recorded anywhere, nor turning up in any of my interviews, is Prins' (1972–4: 163) assertion that a *shūʿī* in Kuwait was traditionally known to be a double-ended fishing vessel. None of my informants could confirm this piece of information. Nonetheless, it could be that Prins' data came from information about an Iraqi coastal *shuwayʿī* (a dimunitive form), similar to the double-ended *chāla* (or *tashshāla*, as described in Chapter 4) or the *muhayla* (Iraqi *muhēle*), used in southern Iraq to transport dates, so I was informed in Bahrain. It may be that the ocean-going cargo-*shūʿī* which Ritter (1919: 137) reports having seen in the Arabian/Persian Gulf earlier this century could have been a double-ended craft designed to cope with rough seas and strong winds.

39 Interviewed on 20 April 1992.

24
The *shūʿī sammāk* in Sur, Oman

The Kuwaiti development in the design of a *jalbūt-shuāy* recorded by Prins (1972–4: 163), was an amalgamation of features such as the stem of the *shūʿī* and square stern of the *jālbūt* (which will be discussed in the next section). This is probably what Bahrainis used to call *ṣinkīrī* or *ṣinqīrī* (al-Shamlān 1990: 110), a pearler which, according to the historian Abd al-Rahman Musamih,[40] was used during the pearling boom years, all over the Gulf. I have not come across this word anywhere in my reading nor have I heard it in the course of my interviews. The Bahraini boat-builders claim to have invented the *jalbūt-shuāy* which they now call *bānūsh* (see Chapter 3), a type rarely exceeding 15 tons, which prevailed in Kuwait and which was often referred to by Kuwaitis as a *shūʿī ghawwāṣ* (pearling craft). It had one or sometimes two masts with a large platform over the poop for the skipper to sleep on. An alternative name for a *shūʿī* in the Emirates today is *lanch* (as we have explained in Chapter 3) and, sad to say, other dhow types are assuming this name all over the Gulf.

We find several ways of how the word *shūʿī* was recorded in written sources: *say*, *saiyah*, *shewe*, *shewee*, *shuʾai*, *shuʿai*, *shuai*, *shuāi* and *shuʾa*.[41] One phonetic plural variant I heard in Al-Khor was *shwāʿī*, and in Sharjah and

40 Interviewed on 20 April 1991.

41 See Moore 1925: 123; Howarth 1977: 38; Facey 1979: 132; Prados 1997: 193.

Ajman, *shwāʿ*. There is a possibility that the name came from a type of tree called *shūʿ*, described by Ibn Manẓūr (d 711/1311–2) as the 'ben tree, a species of moringa', a kind that grows tall and straight and its wood is soft (1955–6, IV: 2360). I could not locate this tree anywhere in the Gulf or on the south Arabian coast.

The *jālbūt* of the north

The *jālbūt* (pl *jalābīt*) was a typical coastal dhow used mainly in the northern Gulf: it was recognized by its prominent upright stem and transom stern, these features pointing to European influence in the design (illus. 25). Single-masted, it had a rudder and tiller, and was propelled by oars and sails; by the 1970s it was engine-powered. In general open-hulled, some were decked, 20 to 100 feet long and ranging in size up to 25 tons or more. Essentially, there were two types, one of which was a larger vessel carrying a small boat on board; sailors used this for small errands when the ship was at anchor near the shore, or as a lifeboat in emergencies. The large type of *jālbūt* had a multi-purpose function as a pearler, fishing vessel, cargo and ferry boat, in Kuwait, Bahrain and the Gulf's Saudi coast. It plied in and around the Gulf ports such as Basra, Kuwait, Bushehr, Qatar, Dubai and Muscat, and was often referred to, according to Ibrahim Khamis Bu Haroon from Umm al Quwain,[42] as *jālbūt ʿūd*. Times have changed and the modern *jālbūt* which is built in Abu Dhabi and Umm al Quwain and comes in different sizes, is designed for racing and called *jālbūt lis-sibāq*.

25
The *jālbūt* in the Amiriyya, Doha, Qatar

42 Interviewed on 16 April 1996.

The name is variously pronounced: in Kuwait, Bahrain and Qatar as *jālibūt*, *jalbūt*; as *yālbūt* in Ajman and Ras al Khaimah; as *yālbūt* in Abu Dhabi, and *gālbūt* in Sur. Consequently, these phonetic variants give rise to different western transcriptions.[43] The plural is generally *jalābīt* but in Bahrain and Qatar I heard *jawālbīt*.

Tracing the name *jālbūt*

The *jālbūt*, historically, appears in several western travel accounts at the turn of the twentieth century; there is no record of it earlier. Two German boat researchers, Ritter and Hess, are probably the earliest to describe this craft: Ritter (1919: 137) gives '*ğālibōṭ* . . . the lifeboat of a steamer on the Euphrates and Tigris' and Hess, quoted by Kindermann (1934: 20), has '*dzālbût*, a small rowing boat'. The Arab (Lebanese) traveller, Amīn al-Riḥānī who visited Iraq and the Arabian Gulf in the twenties is perhaps the first one to come close to the present description of a *jālbūt*; he did not usually give much space to describing ships in his diary but the *jālbūt* was indeed an exception. What I found interesting was his comment on the name of this craft: 'it is called thus only in Bahrain [my underlining]' (al-Riḥānī 1960, II: 29, fn 2),[44] which suggests that either there were phonetic variants elsewhere in the Gulf or that the same type was called by different names, something that occurred occasionally during my fieldwork.

Tracing the name and origins of *jālbūt* remains a labyrinthine puzzle. First of all, it needs to be said that the term is unknown in classical and modern standard Arabic. I started my search into the medieval Arabic *jalba*[45] in Arabic literary works to see if, because of its common radicals, /j/, /l/ and /b/, there was any connection with *jālbūt*. I could not find information as to exactly which type it was except that, according to the travellers Ibn Jubayr (d 614/1217–18) and Ibn Baṭṭūṭa, and the historian al-Maqrīzī,[46] it was a light passenger boat found in the Red Sea. According to Ibn Jubayr (1907: 70–1), it was a wooden boat of light construction and (like other ship types) its planks were stitched together with coconut fibre thread called *qunbār*, caulked with flakes of wood from the date palm, and smeared with *samn* (castor oil) or *kirsh* (shark oil) – this was to make the wood soft because of the numerous coral

43 The most common are: *jalbuti*, *jaliboot* (Hornell 1942: 16), *jalbaut*, *jalibut* (Prins 1965: 75-7) and *jalbut* (Hawkins 1977: 135).

44 He gives *jalbūt*, which perhaps means that historically this term was pronounced with a short /a/ in contrast with today's long vowel /ā/ – *jālbūt*.

45 Also rendered *jilabah* (presumably *jilāba(h)* with a long vowel on the first /a/), see Ibn Jubayr 1952: 65.

46 Ibn Jubayr 1907: 70-1; Ibn Baṭṭūṭa 1968, II: 158 and 1995, II: 361, fn 6; al-Nakhīlī 1974: 28, fn 82-86.

reefs. In addition to this, al-Nuwayrī l-Iskandarānī reports in the eighth/fourteenth century that a *jalba* in the Indian Ocean carried seven mats made of coconut fibre (*qunbār*) and linen.[47] It is listed as *jalaba* by Mookerji (1912: 227), a maritime historian, denoting an Indian boat of the seventeenth century.

It would appear from the above that the craft belonged both to the Red Sea and Indian Ocean. I thought that the name could also be linked phonetically with the sixteenth century Portuguese *gelba* or *gelva* of the Red Sea and the Indian Ocean, but the lack of sources giving details as to what type of vessel it was, brought my investigation to a dead end. I therefore decided to resort to oral history and see if I could come up with something more concrete. I interviewed a number of elderly people in the Gulf and Oman, particularly shipwrights and *nākhōda*s, asking them if they had ever heard anything relating to the name and design of this medieval craft. The name *kalbā* or *galbā* crept up occasionally in our conversations though no one could tell me what it was except that it was used by the Gulf Arabs up until fairly recent times. Prins' (1972–4: 159) information on this craft was useful. He says it is a Dubai post-war design of Indo-Pakistani origin, a straight-stemmed transom dhow with a long keel. But in the early part of the twentieth century Miles (1994: 414) heard the name *kalbā* in Oman and he described the boat as being 'of peculiar architecture'. I am not sure what he meant by that but, significantly, he mentioned it in the context of a warship. This was the clue I was looking for. One craft is an Indian *gallevat*, 'a kind of galley' (Yule and Burnell 1994: 361) and the other a Perso-Arab *gallivat* (with almost identical spelling except for the middle vowel), known as 'a war vessel', both related to the late medieval period and also possibly linked to a prototype Persian **galabat* mentioned by Prins.[48] If there were any link between the early Arabic *jalba* and the latter names, the absence of the final position /t/ in Arabic (Indian and Portuguese) might explain its presence in Fārsī, because Prins (1965: 76) interestingly remarks that the final /t/ is a Fārsī phonological feature, often found in noun borrowings from Arabic.

Late medieval war vessels mentioned in connection with the Arabian/Persian Gulf and the Indian Ocean are: *galliot*[49] (or *galeota*) and *gallouet* (or

47 Al-Nuwayrī l-Iskandarānī, KLI (no 667) MS II 359/60, fols 127r and 127v.

48 The reader is referred to Yule and Burnell (1994: 361-3) for a discussion on the etymology of *gallevat* giving all possible derivations put forward by contemporary writers of the nineteenth century; also of interest is Prins' comments on the origins of the Swahili *jalbuti*, his views on the names *jalba* and *jālbūt* and their representation of 'almost-convergence on both sides of Arabia' (1965: 75-7 and in particular his diagram 1 [A and B]).

49 A *galliot* is 'a small galley rowed by sixteen or twenty oars, with a single mast and sail, used in the 17th and 18th centuries to chase and capture enemy ships' (Kemp 1992: 336); not to be confused with *galion* or *galleon*, a larger vessel of a later period.

gallivat) mentioned in the Portuguese documents,[50] and *gallivat*, *gallowet* or *gallouet* in the Dutch.[51] What needs to be noted here is the fact that these names of ship types are found in the context of local Arab and Persian war vessels of the time (ie seventeenth and eighteenth centuries). Following this inquiry further, it is clear from the British Gombroon Diaries that the war *gallivat*[52] was prevalent in the Arabian/Persian Gulf waters during the eighteenth century particularly from 1746 to 1774. Some letters point specifically to '*gallivat*s belonging to the Persians',[53] though one refers to '30 *gallivat*s from the [Arab] shaikh of Julfar',[54] which could have been war vessels captured from the Persians. A letter from Shāh Karīm Khān (then Persian ally to the British) to Henry Moore, Agent of Basra, requests him to order 'the prohibition of the said *gallivat*s acting offensively against the British',[55] which explains the political and economic upheaval these and other vessels caused in the area. Niebuhr (1774, II: 186) in his travels to the Gulf around the same time tells us that he heard Bahrainis talking about a vessel called *galwet*, graphemically similar to the *gallouet* found in the Portuguese documents. The names are identical to the *gallivat* of the Dutch and English documents, and phonetically this makes sense because Europeans recording the name may have heard a labiodental fricative /v/ for a bilabial /w/.

The first time we find a description of this craft is in 1763 from Robert Orme (quoted by Yule and Burnell 1994: 363), who writes: 'The *gallevat*s are large rowboats, built like the *grab* [ie *ghurāb*], but of familiar dimensions, the largest rarely exceeding 70 tons; they have two masts . . . they have 40 or 50 stout oars, and may be rowed four miles an hour'. After this date I could not trace the name in any travel or maritime literature. The description of Orme's *gallivat* is one of a small galley because it is likened to a *ghurāb*. It is quite probable that when the Perso-Indian *gallivat* did not function anymore as a war vessel in the nineteenth century, it became a popular coastal boat on the west Indian and the Arabian/Persian Gulf coasts, and the British

50 CDRAD/Portuguese Archives, AHG, Moncões, liv, fols 9-11v, no 6 [1640].

51 CDRAD/Dutch Archives, VOC 3184, 1766, 7 (fol 8), 11 (fol 17), 12 (fol 18), 27 (fol 51), 33 (fol 61); ARA/Aanw. no 1889-23b fol 6; VOC 2864, letter no 1 to Isaak Sweers in Amsterdam 1756; VOC 2996 Kharg, November 1759, fols 8-9; VOC 2996 Kharg, November 1759, fols 10-11; VOC 9101 Masqat, 8 March 1758, fol 15.

52 CDRAD/British Archives, GD, G/29/7, 24 December 1746; GD, G/29/12, 24 July 1760; GD, G/29/13, 6 October 1761, 12 October 1761 and 7 December 1761; GD, G/29/14, 14 November 1761; GD, G/29/5, 17 March 1769; GD Secretariat Inward Letter Book, vol 13, 18 November 1756.

53 CDRAD/British Archives, GD, G/29/17, 31 December 1751; GD, G/29/17, 5 August 1760; GD, G/29/20, 12 March 1772; GD, G/29/13, 16 October 1761.

54 CDRAD/British Archives, GD, G/29/14, 18 November 1761.

55 CDRAD/British Archives, GD, G/29/21, 10 February 1774.

stationed there conveniently called it 'jolly-boat' (a multifunctional boat), by which time the Arabs were calling it *jālbūt*[56] (or other phonetic variants I heard: *yālbūt* and *gālbūt*). Rowand's survey in Lorimer's *Gazetteer* (1986, I, iib: 2325–6) defines *jālbūt* at the beginning of the twentieth century as 'a small square-sterned passenger-carrying craft, from 20 to 30 feet long . . . has one mast with usual sails and fittings, and bowsprit and jib-stay sail . . . it is steered with a rudder and tiller, and carries a crew of from 4 to 6 men'. He wrote of the possibility that the name is derived from the English *jolly-boat* and many writers (Arab and non-Arab) have ever since, in their technical description of dhows, accepted this theory.[57] I believe that the English term was superimposed on an earlier nomenclature used in India or the Arabian/Persian Gulf which was probably *gallivat* or *gallevat*, and that the British nicknamed the Perso-Arab or Indian vessel 'jolly-boat' because phonetically it sounded close to the local name.[58] This is a case where a cross-fertilization of name and design from different sources has occurred over the centuries, evolving into a single name which is today known by Arabs as *jālbūt*.

Cross-features of *jālbūt* and *sanbūq* – the *jahāzī*

The ocean-going sailing coaster of Lamu, the *jahāzī* (sometimes *jihāzī*),[59] seen by Prins (1965: 75) on the Iranian coast of the Gulf and the east African coast in the fifties and sixties, has similar features with the *sanbūq* because of its slightly curved stem, but in Hawkins' words (1977: 79), it is 'more uncouth or rougher build'. Or it can be compared with the *jālbūt* (or *jalbuti* as it is known in Swahili) of East Africa.[60] On the *jahāzī* of Zanzibar and the

56 Rowand noted the name *jālī* used simultaneously with *jālbūt*, see Lorimer 1986, I, iib: 2325-6. I have not seen any other reference to this. One may speculate that *jālī* and the name *bōṭ* or *bōt* for 'boat' (borrowed from Hindi *pōtī*) were separate terms becoming ultimately *jālbūt*. Note *bōt* (pl *bawātī*) was recorded by al-Dujaylī (1912a: 98); and according to Ritter (1919: 137) it was 'the name of a type of a sailing vessel in Basra and the Persian Gulf'. One other possibility put forward by Hawkins (1977: 89) is Hindi *jāl* 'net' and *pōt(i)*, 'boat' giving Arabic *jālbūt* meaning 'net-boat'.

57 Hawley (1995: 191) derives the Arabic term from a Portuguese *jalbuta* but gives no description. The name is rather dubious; I could not place its occurrence in a Portuguese dictionary or documents related to India and the Arabian/Persian Gulf.

58 Kemp (1992: 434) relates no connection between the English repertoire and the Arabic *jālbūt* or the Indian *gallevat*. Regarding the origin of the English word *jolly-boat* he says it is 'possibly from the Dutch and German *jolle*, Swedish *jol* a small bark or boat though this may be the derivation of the English *yawl*, or possibly a perversion of *gellywatte*, a small ship's boat generally of the 18th and 19th centuries, used for a variety of purposes . . .'

59 The Swahili *jahazi* is pronounced with short vowels. I list it here with long vowels, *jahāzī* as known among Gulf Arabs and south Arabians.

60 Older people in Mombasa, Tumbatu, Zanzibar call *jahāzī* by the name *buti* (see Prins 1965: 75), probably influenced by the Omani term. Caroline Sassoon's detailed drawings

neighbouring coast, a circular ring-oculus is painted on the moustache of the bows; the Red Sea *jahāzī* has a white circle oculus painted on each side of the stitched projection. The proto-*jahāzī* was a craft with slightly different bows and a somewhat curved cutwater. Omani fishermen and boat-makers in Mutrah used to see numerous Zanzibari *jahāzī*s in their youth: they were described as sturdy and were, reputedly, good vessels. They called on Khasab (Musandam), an old commercial sea port which, until three decades ago, was the hub of the frankincense and myrrh trade in the northern Gulf, so I am told by my Omani and Emirati informants.

An attempt was made to trace the word *jahāzī* to Arabic but I could not place it in any classical or modern Arabic dictionary: the word sounds like Arabic because of its tri-consonantal radicals /j/, /h/, and /z/, and could derive from *jihāz* meaning 'equipment or fittings' and also meaning 'tackle or rigging', according to Kindermann (1934: 21). Suʿād Māhir (1967: 338) classifies it as of Fārsī origin but gives no sources to support her claim. The earliest mention of a *jahāzī* comes from al-Idrīsī (d 561/1165), as a trading vessel (Dozy 1967, I: 228), but we have no knowledge as to its location. Two sources lead us to believe that this craft could be either Arab or Indian: a reference to a boat called *jase* is made by Friar Odoric in 1321 (*Cathay* 1866, II: 113) on his journey to Tana in India in which he said he could find 'no nail therein', meaning that the boat was stitched (a common feature that emerges in several medieval Arabic and western sources). The other reference is by Ibn Mājid in the ninth/fifteenth century (Tibbetts 1981: 261) but gives no details.[61] I have not come across any other reference either in the medieval or the more recent sources, except for the Zanzibari type, cherished by the many old Arab seamen I have spoken to. The east African *jahazi* functions these days as a transport vessel and a ferry boat.[62]

Another type of craft designed on the model of *jahāzī* and *sanbūq* was a *māshuwwa* (pl *mawāshī*), a cargo and fishing vessel which, at the turn of

of a Lamu and Zanzibari *jahazi* (Swahili spelling) would be of interest to the reader (1970: 185–6, Figures 3–6).

61 It is suggested by Tibbetts that *jihāz* could be interpreted in the context as fleet or expedition. I am not sure whether this is correct. It is more probable that Ibn Mājid was writing about a type of ship; see also Serjeant 1974: 136.

62 Susan Beckerley in an Oxford workshop on 'Ships and the development of maritime technology across the Indian Ocean' held in May 1998 at St Antony's College told me that some east African *jahazi*s still transport mangrove poles, traditionally known for domestic building, to Arabia. For the most part of the twentieth century, hundreds of Arab dhows used to sail from Lamu or the delta of the Rufiji River in the months of April and May laden with mangrove poles. I was told by several people in Sur, once a centre for mangrove-pole distribution to the Gulf, that apart from being excellent beams for a house they served as firewood.

the nineteenth century, was very common on the Arabian coast from Ras al Khaimah to Kuwait, and on the Iranian coast from Bushehr to Jashk (Lorimer 1986, I, iib: 2325). It was square-sterned and broad-beamed, decked fore and aft and had a single mast: the larger type, some 40 feet long, was steered by a rudder, the smaller one by a tiller. The Suri racing *māshuwwa* of today is designed, I am told, on similar lines to the earlier version of the *jahāzī* known to the local boat-builders, but with some adaptations to accomodate 24 rowers. I came across motorized *māshuwwa*s in Khasab, primarily used as fishing vessels but some as cargo boats and a few functioned as passenger boats. The Zanzibari *mashua* (Swahili spelling as recorded by Prins 1965: 77) is similar in design to the *jahāzī*, and carries about 10 tons' weight. It is an all-purpose boat,[63] and unlike the Gulf *māshuwwa*, it has on either side of the stempost an oculus on a triangular patch painted green. The word *māshuwwa* is of Indian origin.[64]

To sum up, the *sanbūq* and its sister-types are similar because of a common ancestry. While it is certainly true that some look like a miniature of a late sixteenth century European *caravel* with a quarter deck and rails running on either side over the stern, one may ask whether this is really a design which owes its origins to Portuguese influence, or is there any Yemenite or Indian trace which pre-dates the coming of the Europeans?

The traditional craft of Trucial Oman

My trips to Khor Fakkan and Kalba in April 1996 and the Musandam Peninsula of Oman in November of the same year led me to some of the most handsome and well-preserved traditional wooden fishing craft I have ever seen in the Gulf. These are the *badan* and *battīl*, recognizable by their stem and stern pieces sewn to the hull planking. Also striking about these craft and another type called *baqqāra*, is the rudder, fitted to the sternpost, and which was at one time manipulated with ropes from aft-pointing tillers.

The badan

The *badan* (pl *badana* or *bdāna*) was found all along the north and south eastern coast of Oman. Rowand (Lorimer 1986, I, iib: 2325), in the early twentieth century, records the *badan* belonging to not only Oman but the Arabian/Persian Gulf and Kindermann (1934: 6) includes Aden; this

63 Prins (1965: 78) reports that the Zanzibari *mashua*s are utilized by the east African communities for different purposes; the Bajun for shark fishing, the Wa-amu for ferrying pilgrims, the Mafia for line fishing, and the Malindi for laying traps.

64 For Indian cognates, see C. W. Mitman, 'Catalogue of the watercraft collection in the United States National Museum', *Smithsonian Institution Bulletin*, 127 (1923): 264–6.

information was questioned by many shipwrights I spoke to. Donaldson (1979: 77) rightly queried the source of this information and says: 'that it was used [his underlining] over this whole coast is not in question, though whether it was constructed over so extensive a stretch can be doubted'. The craft was still being built until some twenty years ago in Sur and Umm al Quwain. It served as a coastal trading vessel but was mainly used for fishing and could take up to 12 rowers. Carvel-built, the boat is double-ended and double-keeled with a long slim hull having a sharp needle-nose stem and high unswept sternpost about ten to twelve feet above the ground (illus. 26). The double keel is slightly curved up at each end, so that the stem and stern barely touch the surface of the water (Miles 1994: 412). Richard Burton (quoted by Hornell 1942: 29) evocatively described the *badan* as being 'long, narrow, quoin-shaped craft, with towering sternpost and powerful rudder like the candal fin of some monstrous fish'. I had never seen a *badan* before until one afternoon in November 1996 before the *maghrib* prayers while I was sitting on the beach at Al-Hail near Muscat enjoying a peaceful sunset; to my left on the shore, at a distance of 50 feet, I spotted some boats shimmering in the golden rays of the setting sun. They looked unfamiliar to other traditional boats I had seen so far. The old fisherman sitting next to me mending his fishing nets under a *ʿarīsh* (an open hut made of palm-tree branches), seeing me rather puzzled, explained. 'They are old *badan*s. None of them is now being used, they are relics of the past', he commented, something all too frequently heard from the older men during my field trip in Oman. As they lay there, canted over on their sides, they resembled nothing so much as a row of daggers, glittering in the sun. The *badan*'s unusual features reminded me of what Hawkins (1977: 82) described over two decades ago as an, 'odd yet distinctive dhow'. But is it a remnant from Arabia's past as he claims? I looked closely at the sternpost which has a piece of timber extended in a tall pointed manner, almost looking like a secondary sternpost. A long rudder is hung to this extension which is held together by horizontal batters. What struck me about these craft was that they were sewn between the hull planking and the stem and sternpost, while on the rest of the hull, the planks were nailed to the ribs throughout. After taking a closer look at the sewn parts I could see clearly how the teakwood planks were drilled with holes and stitched together with coiled cords of coconut fibre called *qunbār* or *qinbār*,[65] as mentioned earlier (illus. 27). All planks of the *badan* were originally sewn with coconut fibre and by the time Miles (1994: 413) visited Oman in the late nineteenth century, the *badan*'s planks were nailed. However, George Bertram

65 Tim Severin (1982: 23) remarked that one finds the same stitch pattern with knots and fastenings on other types of boats on the Malabar coast of India.

(1948: 8) saw stitched *badan*s on the Al-Batinah coast as late as the 1940s. The *badan* carried one lofty mast, was rigged, and some had bowsprits.[66]

26
The *badan* in Udhayba near Muscat, Oman

27
***Badan* showing the hull planking stitched to the sternpost, Al-Hail near Muscat, Oman**

66 Suʿād Māhir's (1967: 333) claim that the 'Indian Ocean' (she means Omani) *badan* is what Iraqis call *balam* or *zawraq* is incorrect. Iraqi and Gulf *balam* is canoe-shaped and the *zawraq* is a small boat, both of which have hull features different from the *badan*'s.

The *badan*'s rudder (like that of the *sanbūq*, *baqqāra* and *battīl*) was operated by the rope steering system; the Omanis call the whole mechanism *sukkān bil-ḥibāl* (a rudder with ropes). I had read about this,[67] and also spoke to a number of seamen about it, each time with the hope of getting further details. One November morning in 1996 I went with my guide Salem from Salalah to Raysut to meet an old sailor, Raghab Khamis,[68] an experienced *sukkūnī* (steersman) of a *sanbūq*. The old man was keen to explain how the steering gear worked. He got up and gave a performance to all of us sitting round him, showing every detail he could remember. It was so clear that since then I have never needed to ask anyone else about it. Essentially, the mechanism works with a small rudder hung way below the waterline, the purpose of which was to provide extra stability when sailing, and when the vessel was beached the rudder was easily dismantled. It was held with lashings passed through holes instead of by gudgeon and pintle. It was controlled by two lines, both of which passed from a hole in the after-edge to each side of the gunwale. The *sukkūnī* sat at the stern deck; he tied each piece of the rope to his right and left big toes and by hauling on one tackle and slacking on the other, pulled the lower side of the rudder right or left as needed.

Pâris'[69] distinction between *badan ṣayyād*, 'the fishing *badan*' and *badan safar*, 'the seagoing trading *badan*'[70] at the beginning of the nineteenth century, does not appear anywhere in the contemporary or late travellers' accounts but it is clear from my Omani informants that the *badan* always had this dual function (illus. 28). When I was in Dhofar I asked a number of fishermen on the beach of Raysut[71] about their recollections of *badan*s. The older men recalled having seen cargo *badan*s anchoring at the port, having come from Muscat. One of the men, Saeed Saleem Jaafari, told me that he always travelled on *badan*s to East Africa. 'These were the large type of *badan*s', he said. 'They sailed to Aden, Mukalla, Soqotra and Somalia; of course, there were the smaller fishing *badan*s but these were found on the east side of the

67 Balbi in 1580 (quoted by Slot 1991: 91); see Pâris 1841: Plate 5, Figures 3-7; Moore 1925: 123; Hornell 1942: 29-30; Johnstone and Muir 1962: 62; LeBaron Bowen 1963: 30-4; Muir 1965: 358; LeBaron Bowen 1966: 35, 51, 111–12.

68 Interviewed on 19 November 1996.

69 François Edmond Pâris is renowned for his detailed plans of ship construction around the world in two of his works: *Essai sur la construction navale des peuples extra européens* (Paris: Arthur Bertrand, 1841) and *Souvenirs de plans ou dessins de navires et de bateaux anciens ou modernes existants ou disparus*, Parts I-III (Grenoble: Quatre Seigneurs 1975; first published 1882).

70 Recorded by Pâris *beden seyad* and *beden safar* (1841: Plates 9 and 7).

71 Sabi Khamis, Saeed Saleem Jaafari, Musallam Saeed Ahmad, Muhad Ali Amer, Mubashir Khamis Ragab, Hafiz Awad and Raghab Khamis, interviewed on 19 November 1996.

28
The *beden seyad* (Ar. *badan ṣayyād*) according to Pâris (1841, Plate 9)

Omani coast of the Indian Ocean'. I then spoke to some other old fishermen in their sixties and seventies at Al-Hail and Udhaiba near Muscat and they told me that in their youth a *badan* carried two sails if it were a cargo or transport vessel; otherwise oars were preferable with fishing *badan*s. The number of rowers depended on the length of the boat. I understood that typically there were 12 rowers (6 on each side) on a boat, though Donaldson (1979: 79) remarks that there were up to 28 rowers on the Al-Batinah fishing boat.

Several fishermen I interviewed on the south eastern coast of Oman spoke with nostalgia of the *badan* of some forty years ago.[72] They mentioned how it sailed with amazing rapidity often with one mast, carrying a large spread of sail. In a favourable western wind, a *badan* with one sail could reach Muscat from Tiwi in one day, or two or three days of rowing if no wind was blowing. These figures varied of course depending on the size of the vessel and the number of rowers. The larger *badan*s were decked. The ones abandoned at Al-Hail were lined with the remains of bamboo matting or date sticks laid athwart. Some vessels were 30 to 40 feet long and carried

72 Interviewed Khilfan Rashid Suweid al-Shuaybi, Khalfan Said Helit Farraji, Frish Said Helit Ferraji in Qalhat on 26 March 1998; Khalfan Salim al-Maghrebi, Ali Sunnah Isa al-Muqaini, Said bin Masud Musallam al-Salti in Tiwi on 31 March 1998.

a weight of some 10 tons. The smaller *badan* was half-decked or open, no longer than 20 feet, and could carry some 5 to 7 tons. I was told by several seamen[73] that most of these craft were built at one time in Sur, and Quriyat near Muscat. Local builders in Tiwi used wood from *qaraṭ*, *sidir* and *ghaff* trees which grew in abundance in the *wādī*s (valleys) (illus. 29a and 29b). The sheikh of Masirah, Abdullah bin Khalifa bin Khamis Al Majally,[74] informed me that *badan*s were the most common craft that were built at the island's number of shipyards. During my visit there, I was extremely fortunate in being able to inspect the only *badan* on the island. It was in the south-west at a place called Sfaik, a once famous port; a 77-foot-long *badan*, beached upright, supported by wooden props, and had been built by the sheikh's father. Some of the large vessels often had two sails and with a favourable wind, I am told that it took one day from Masirah to reach the town of Sur. The same journey time was recorded by Ibn Baṭṭūṭa: 'We continued our voyage [from Masirah Island] for a day [my underlining] and came to the roadstead of a large village on the seashore called Ṣūr' (1995, II: 394).

29A
The wood from *qaraṭ* trees is used to build parts of a dhow

73 Interviewed Mubarak Salim al-Muqaini, Yaqub Ali Sulaiman al-Gaddani in Fins on 1 April 1998; Rashid Hamid Salim al-Harbi, Nasser bin Hamad bin Salim al-Harbi in Ras al-Hadd on 13 April 1998; Mohammad Humeid bin Abd Allah al-Amiri, Ali bin Salim bin Salim al-Amiri in Khor Gharama on 13 April 1998.

74 Interviewed on 4 April 1998.

29B
The wood from *sidir* trees is used to build parts of a dhow

Today, you do not see any *badan*s. In ān interview with an old fisherman from Seeb,[75] he lamented the days of the *badan* but was glad that those days of hardship and toil were gone. He exclaimed: 'why use wooden boats at all? They are a nuisance to us; fibreglass boats are faster, lighter and easy to look after'. Prins (1972–4: 159) remarked that the *bedēn* (his transcription)[76] belonging to Muscat was different from the type found in Bandar Abbas in Iran but he did not state what the differences were. The Omani craft is now somewhat modified to fit the features of a racing boat, taking up to 16 rowers, while the Iranian version (which I have not seen) may still have some of the early features found in the abandoned boats I saw at Al-Hail. A variety of *badan* but larger is, *ʿuwaysī* (some say *ʿuwaysiyya* or *ʿuwaysiyye* in Masirah) with a lower stempost, long-remembered by the sailors on the Al-Batinah coast and Masirah Island. It was an ocean-going vessel with two masts and it traded with East Africa; remnants of it can be seen lying on the beach between Saham and Sohar.

I have recorded several alternatives for the word *badan*, all along the Omani and Emirati coast: the majority of seamen say *badan*, *badani*, *bedani* or

75 Interviewed Salim Mubarak Al-Furi on 12 November 1996.

76 The way Prins transcribed *bedēn* (with a long /ē/) is Fārsī, which could be a Bandar Abbas term. Those of the Omani seamen I interviewed who said *beden*, pronounced it with a final short /e/.

bedayni, the last three being less frequent and inconsistent to a point that I could not establish any particular pattern. In Sur, sailors and fishermen spoke of *bdeini* and in Sharjah, *beden*. The plural for some was *badana* or *badānāt* in Raysut, and *bdāna* in Al-Hail. One intriguing piece of my research on the origin of this word was what the historian Abd al-Rahman Musamih from Bahrain[77] told me: *badan* is an Arabic term which stands for the trunk of a tree cut into several planks from which the ship is made, hence the name. There may be some truth in this. In fact the word *badan*, according to Ibn Manẓūr (nd, I: 233), does mean 'wood (coll)' or 'forest' but with no reference to any ship. It is tempting to believe the word is Arabic because of its three-consonantal base but an earlier Semitic origin or possibly Fārsī or Hindi connections should not be ruled out.[78]

The baqqāra *and its sister* shāḥūf

Another relic of the past, the *baqqāra* (pl *baqāqīr*), generally pronounced as *baggāra* (pl *bagāgīr*),[79] was used until the 1950s for pearl-diving. It has some hybrid features of the *badan* but with a very raked stem. It was from 30 to 60 feet long with a crew of 10 to 15 men and carried a cargo of from 10 to 30 tons. It used to be operated by the rope steering system as mentioned earlier. I could not find any suitable clues as to the origin of the word. It was known also in Umm al Quwain and Ajman as *baggārī*, and in Bahrain as *bachchāra* (pl *bachāchīr*). The *baqqāra* was commonly used for fishing and sometimes for transporting goods from one port to another in the Musandam Peninsula and the Al-Batinaḥ. It was also noted for the transportation of stone as well as being used as a passenger ferry boat (al-Nakhīlī 1974: 17). Rowand (Lorimer 1986, I: iib: 2323), in his report on sea craft of the Gulf at the beginning of the twentieth century, stated that the Iranian *baqqāra*s had only one mast while the Arab *baqqāra*s (probably larger) had two. But Ahmed Muhammed Munhadi,[80] in his late seventies, from Qatar, remembered the *baqqāra* with a single leaning mast, used in Marbat as a vessel for long distance fishing. The craft belonged to all the Gulf ports: Kuwait, Bahrain, Abu Dhabi and Muscat on the Arabian coast, and Bandar-e Lengeh, Bandar Abbas, and Qishm on the Iranian coast. I doubt Facey's (1987: 200) identification of a *baqqāra* carved

77 Interviewed on 20 April 1991.

78 Shihāb (1987: 53) claims this vessel was known under a different medieval name. Could it be the *trānkī* mentioned by the travellers and explorers of the eighteenth and nineteenth centuries, Miles asks (1994: 413)? Both *badan* and *trānkī* have similar features such as the low stempost and a very high stern, but what about the hull design?

79 Hardly ever pronounced with a /q/ voiced or voiceless uvular plosive.

80 Interviewed on 20 April 1992.

on the rocks at Jabal al-Jussasiyah as c AD 1000–1200 is correct.[81] I have not come across any mention of the name *baqqāra* earlier than the eighteenth century Dutch documents, and nineteenth century India Office records.[82]

Some of the north Omani seamen[83] told me in 1996 that they had recently seen cargo and fishing *baqqāra*s making trips from the Musandam Peninsula down to the Al-Batinah coast but Suri informants[84] denied this information, saying that no Arab *baqqāra*s were seen these days. I remember on a *battīl* trip in Qatar in 1992, two Iranian merchant sailors, Mohamed Ali Ahmed al-Farsi and Salim Majid Jabri,[85] pointing out to me two Iranian *baqqāra*s entering the port of Doha, and commenting on the fact that you only see these types coming from the shores of Iran. The Omani seamen of the Al-Batinah coast were right then, only what they saw were Iranian *baqqāra*s. The older men in Sohar recalled with nostalgia the *baqqāra*s and *badan*s they had owned and spoke of them as being excellent fishing boats. They recounted stories of their catch after a long day on the open sea, bringing back an abundance of *ʿūma* or *ʿōma* (sardine) and *barriyya* (whitebait). The only *baqqāra*s I saw were those beached and abandoned in Kalba on the east Emirati coast. They were laid on their side far away from the shore, their prows pointing to the sea. The planks of the hulls were bleached grey and starting to break up after being exposed for such a long time to the intense heat of the sun. My guide Saeed Haddad from Kalba,[86] a poet and historian, looked at them sadly and holding his right hand on the gunwale, said: 'wa-nabkī-hā lammā narā-hā' (we cry over them [ie the *baggāra*s] when we see them). The breaking of the waves seemed to echo Saeed's words. Looking at these craft one can only reflect on what a proud heritage the Gulf Arabs had for thousands of years.

Baqqāra is an odd term and localized to Oman or the Iranian littoral of the Gulf. Many of my Arab informants said that the word was related to the

81 See Kapel 1983, Figure 10 'line drawing of a ship', Site no 422, Appendix p 53. N. Weismann in a personal communication (16 January 2000) holds that line drawings of a *baqqāra* are found in Sites nos 421 (f) and (g).

82 CDRAD/Dutch Archives, VOC 3184, 7 (fol 8), 11 (fol 17), 12 (fol 18), 27 (fol 51) and 33 (fol 61), year 1766, recorded as *bagaar* or *baqara* and listed with *gallowet* and *batil*; also IOR – SRBG vol 24, fol 474, year 1856 [?], *buggarah*.

83 Interviewed Abdalla bin Fadil bin Abdalla Al-Shizawi, Ibrahim Muhammed Ali Al-Nawfali in Sohar on 28 November 1996; Ibrahim Abd Alrahman Al-Kumishki in Harat al-Sabara on 28 November 1996.

84 Interviewed Muhammad bin Salim Al-Araimi on 2 December 1996; Khamis Nasir Al-Sinani, Sami Hilal Muhammad Ibrahim Mukhaimi on 3 December 1996.

85 Interviewed on 22 April 1992.

86 Interviewed on 17 April 1996.

Arabic-speaking nomads of Sudan but this connection is far-fetched and has no foundation. It is possible that the origins go back to Fārsī.

The word *baqqāra* hardly figured in my meetings with Kuwaitis, Bahrainis and Qataris.[87] It was only when I left Dubai to travel north east of the Emirates to Ajman that newer names of types started to emerge, namely *baqqāra*, *shāḥūf* and *zārūka* (on the latter name see section below). The *shāḥūf* (pl *shawāḥīf*) is a double-ended fishing craft belonging to the east Emirati and north Omani coasts (illus. 30). It is like a *baqqāra*, though smaller, with a pointed stemhead and a long upright sternpost. It varies from 12 to 25 feet in length, is rowed by 4 to 6 men and in the past was operated by both sails and oars. A carving of a *shāḥūf* at the Jabal al-Jussasiyah site in Qatar shows the main features of this craft but without mast and rudder.[88] An experienced boat-maker from Ajman, Ibrahim Rashid Shattaf[89] explained that the stempost of these craft (ie the *baqqāra*, *shāḥūf* and *zārūka*) is pointed as it gives the boat better manoeuvrability when facing the waves. One sees the *shāḥūf* nowadays, being employed for net and line fishing, but in the old days it was also used for pearl-diving. Most of the *shāḥūf*s I saw in Liwa on the Al-Batinah coast had their sternpost cut off to fit an engine, with extended top sides of the square-shaped stern looking like wooden fins.

30
The *shāḥūf* in Umm al Quwain, United Arab Emirates

87 One type of *baqqāra* I could not identify on the Arabian Gulf is the *kishtī*, a fishing vessel which Shihāb (1987: 124) claims to be still in use in the Gulf.

88 Identified by the boat researcher N. Weismann in a private communication (4 August 1998), see Kapel 1983: Site no 421, Appendix, p 53.

89 Interviewed on 16 April 1996.

The *zārūka* and *battīl* of the fjords in the Musandam Peninsula

On the Al-Batinah coast I heard fishermen talking about a *zārūka* (pl *zarārīk*) but had never seen one until I visited the Musandam Peninsula in November 1996. The *zārūka* (also *zārūk* or *zawraka*) is associated with the general type found among the Musandam vessels, a double-ender of about 50 feet in length on the waterline. It has a stern-piece in the shape of a stylized dog's head. The tonnage of the small *zārūka* is about half that of the larger one and carries a crew of up to 20 men. It functions as a light transport boat but is used mainly for fishing. In former days it was a pearler. I heard that the *zārūka* was commonly used in the fishing village of Kumzar at the foot of the mountains by the Straits of Hormuz in the Musandam Peninsula (illus. 31). The fishermen there use it exclusively for fishing on the neighbouring coast. On the head of the stempost is a piece of goatskin with the fore or back paws hanging which, I am told, acts against the evil eye.

The difference between a *baqqāra* and *zārūka* bothered me for some time because they are almost identical in design but have a different nomenclature. I put the question over and over again to my informants[90] but no one could explain why. I remember one fisherman in Sohar said in utter exasperation: 'a large *baggāra* cannot be anything else but a *baggāra* and a small *zārūka* is a *zārūka*'. The *zārūka*s I examined in Khasab and Kumzar certainly looked much smaller than the large and broad *baqqāra*s that I had seen left on the beach in Kalba. I also noticed that the *zārūka* has a higher sternpost which looked not much different from that of the *battīl*, as will be shown later. As a matter of fact the younger fishermen called it *battīl*.

31
The *zārūka* in Kumzar, Musandam Peninsula (Oman)

90 Interviewed Yusuf bin Abdalla bin Yusuf Al-Farsi in Harat al-Shaikh on 28 November 1996; Ibrahim Muhammed Ali Al-Nawfali in Sohar and Darwish Abdalla Saeed Al-Zaabi in Saham on 29 November 1996.

A confusion of designs and terms comes with a boat by the name of *garookuh* which the nineteenth century French maritime historian Pâris drew during his sojourn in Muscat (illus. 32). Its name certainly sounds very similar to *zārūk*(*a*). Its construction or design, with 'a false sternpost and rudder control', argues Hornell (1942: 27), conforms with that of a common *badan* of the Omani coast from which he gives three important deviations in design: the *badan* has an upright stern, an open waist, and the mast is vertical, compared to Pâris's *garookuh* which has a grab form of bow, is fully decked fore and aft, and has a raked mast. He calls the *garookuh* a hybrid between a *zārūka* and a *badan*. So here we have a boat with a name that phonetically sounds like *zārūka* but is not similar in design to it. Interestingly, the older seamen in Musandam referred sometimes to the *zārūka* as *zaʿīma*. They were talking of a southern Arabian type,[91] because the *zaʿīma* used in Oman at one time was a rectangular coracle (see Chapter 6).

32
The *garookuh* according to Pâris (1841, Plate 6)

It was in the village of Kumzar that I found the most primitive of traditional boats. To reach Kumzar you have either to go through the mountain paths overlooking the deep fjords (*khawr*s), or by sea. I boarded a *lanch* with a number of other passengers one morning at the Mina in Khasab and headed for Kumzar, the village where *zārūka*s and *battīl*s are made. The first thing I saw after pulling the *lanch* onto the shore was a decorated *battīl*. Ribbons with cowrie shells (*bakkī*s) were wrapped around the tall stern

91 The *zaʿīma* is a Red Sea or Yemeni type known as a barque or a small ship. The word has different spellings which suggest various pronunciations in the Red Sea, Somalia, Yemen and Hadhramaut, see Kindermann 1934: 34.

fins (*fashīn*) of one boat while a goatskin was dressed in the pointed stemhead of another (illus. 33 and 34). A tassel of shells, called *zanzūr*, was strung together and hung from the tip of the pointing stempost. 'It is a marriage celebration', said Abdallah bin Ali Mohammed Al-Kumzari; '*battīl*s are our life', he continued, 'we decorate them as a sign of rejoicing with everyone in the community'.[92]

33
Cowrie shells wrapped around the tall stern fins of a *battīl bahwī* in Kumzar, Musandam Peninsula (Oman)

92 Interviewed on 24 November 1996.

34
The goatskin on the *battīl kārib*'s stemhead in Kumzar, Musandam Peninsula (Oman)

The *battīl* (pl *batātīl*) is unique to the Musandam Peninsula; it is a double-ended fishing vessel distinguished by its low pointed prow, high sternpost and projections. There are in a *battīl*, as Bertram Thomas observed (Ward 1987: 467), hybrid features of the Omani *badan* coastal craft with its high stern and the long stempost, so characteristic of the Kuwaiti *būm*. Three other sub-names are given to this craft: *selek* (or *kārib*), for the largest craft, *bahwī* for the medium and *faydar* (a rowing boat) for the smallest. The *selek* used to sail to Abu Dhabi and Muscat I am told, but today all types are confined to coastal, mainly seine fishing. The large and medium *battīl*s are decked fore and aft and a mast is located in the middle of the undecked part. The *battīl bahwī* appears similar to the *battīl selek* but has features of the extinct *battīl* described earlier in Chapter 4. All three sizes are shell-built; the main keel stretches to almost half the boat and a second one links the first with the sternpost. At one time all parts of the *battīl* were sewn together, Salih Zaid Mohammed Jumaa Al-Kumzari,[93] a boat-builder, explained, 'but this practice came to an end some three or four decades ago'. The frames are fastened to the planking with iron nails, but the stem and sternpost timbers are stitched to the ends of the planks, a method applied to the *badan* and *baqqāra*, as we pointed out earlier. I was shown how the headknee is sewn to the stem of the bow. The builder drills holes about two inches from the edge of two pieces of wood, positioning the holes opposite each other, then: a) stitches with the use of a steel needle, in diagonal pattern from right to left,

93 Interviewed on 25 November 1996.

first downwards and then, b) upwards, crossing the first stitching pattern; c) the builder then sews the holes which are facing each other, starting from the top, down to the bottom and d) finally, in order to secure both pieces of timber tightly, he hammers wooden pegs in, through holes, already prepared, between each cross stitch (see diagram 1).

When this is completed, fish-liver oil is spread over the stitched parts to strengthen the structure. The builder showed me how the athwartship timbers are sewn to the side of the hull, locking the sides together, a technique, apparently still used for some types of boat in south and south-east Asia. The projecting beams, about four in all, are used by the fishermen to grab and pull the vessel onto the shore or into the water. However, as will be shown in Chapter 7, the projecting beams serve to lock the sides of the hull. Salih Zaid pointed out how pulling and pushing the *battīl* may cause damage to the hood ends of planks, 'if these ends were nailed they would be difficult to replace'; he continued, 'it would mean having to start over again; stitching the hood ends, therefore, is more practical and economical'. Normally, boats are drawn up onto the beach on moveable runners, otherwise the keel is damaged if bounced on the sand; boats can easily get damaged when left rolling in the surf and bouncing on the sand.

On the raised foredeck the wood is carved to give it a pleasing decoration, and is surmounted by a pair of carved wooden horns called *kalb* (or *chalb*), which are used to secure mooring lines. Also, you find four long narrow timbers (only two on the *bahwī*), a pair on each side, fastened to the lower end of the sternpost to protect the rudder (*sukkān*). What was curious to see was the tiller, not fastened atop, but attached to the aft side of the rudder. A system of ropes and levers are connected to the tiller as you would see on the *badan*. The rudder is hung from tall stern-fins (the so-called *fashīn*); I am not sure what their original purpose was.

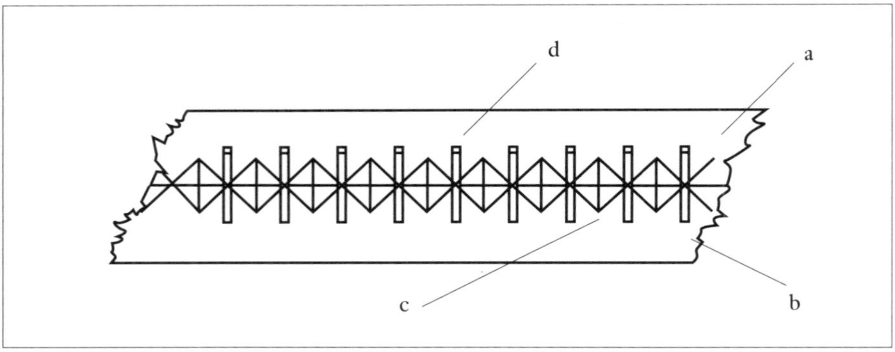

Diagram 1

The Arabic word *battīl* is probably related to the Indian term *batel*, a small boat on the west coast of India totally different in type to the *battīl* but rather similar to an Arab *sanbūq*. Indian *batel*s, though frail to the eye, were soundly and sturdily constructed. The Arabic term could also be directly connected with the Portuguese *batel* or *batelha* (a small boat), although the Hindī *pāṭ* (a board, plank) seems more likely to be its origin, independent of any Indo-European cognates (eg medieval Latin *batellus*, *batus*, *battus*, Spanish *batel*, Italian *battello* etc.).[94] The square stern and the surviving poop of the Indian *batel*, Hornell (1946: 201) remarked, is a remnant of the small Portuguese vessel used in coastal trade during the sixteenth and seventeenth centuries.

The *balam* of Basra and Kuwait

The trading vessel called *balam* (pl *ablām* or *blām*) bears some resemblance to the *baqqāra*. I gathered some information on this type from Kuwaiti seamen in 1985. There were essentially two types[95] which sailed between Basra and Kuwait: the *balam* *ʿashārī*, which served as a passenger boat or lighter (light cargo boat), was some 50 feet long carrying 20 passengers, and the *balam naṣārī*, a freighter, fishing or pearling vessel, about the same length, 40 to 50 feet long.[96] There was another type of *naṣārī* called *baṭīra* (or *batīra*) (Shihab 1987: 121), which no shipwright I interviewed could describe. The information I have about it comes from Hawkins (1977: 135) who describes it (transcribed as *butaira*) as a high sided double-ended dhow with a swept back stemhead, and which sailed in the Gulf. It had a manually operated tiller with one mast made of bamboo, a broad beam and was slow sailing. According to Rowand (Lorimer 1986, I, iib: 830), both the *ʿashārī* and *naṣārī* were recorded as having been built in Kuwait at the beginning of the twentieth century. But old Kuwaiti builders told me that the craft were built in both Basra and Kuwait and were described as almost flat-bottomed and without a keel; the *naṣārī* was designed to take two outboard engines. The craft used on the Iraqi rivers were generally poled along the bank and when sailed, a rudder was attached to the stern. The *naṣārī* took different names: it was known in

94 For details on the Indo-European cognates of 'boat', see OED 1982, I: 1700.

95 Another type mentioned by Rowand (Lorimer 1986, I, iib: 830) was the *ʿarāgiyya*, a large cargo boat, some 60 feet long and carrying 50 tons of load. Mainly found on the Euphrates and Hindiyya, the term *ʿarāgiyya* represents the collective name of the neighbouring river port ʿRāg, though the term is loosely used to denote any Euphrates boat.

96 One other piece of information given by Captain Shakespeare was that the *ʿashārī* type was 20 feet long but useless for transport. The *naṣārī* was much sturdier as a cargo boat, see CDRAD-IOR, R/15/55/5 (1913).

Lower Iraq as *muhayla*, in Bushire as *belem* (a Fārsī usage), and as *baqqāra* in Kuwait. Dickson (1949: 475) commented in the memoirs of his days in Kuwait, that the *naṣārī*, badly constructed as it was, resembled the *būm* in the hull except that the stemhead was straight. Kuwaiti shipwrights[97] were surprised to hear about the *naṣārī*'s shabby construction; they seemed to think that the craft was solidly built of teak. The Kuwaiti *balam* was also known as *balam fūdrī* with two sharp ends (al-Ḥijjī 1988: 43). The *balams* I saw under construction in Qatar in April 1992 were all designed as long and narrow double-ended racing boats taking 36 oarsmen. The word *balam* may be traced back to Hindi (**valam*) according to al-Dujaylī (1912a: 97), probably related to the Tamil Nadu *vallam*, a fishing boat, or to Dravidian (Hornell 1942: 33–4). Of interest is the classical Greek πλοῖον,[98] 'a floating vessel', referred to generally as 'a ship', but also known by the historians Thucydides (d c 400 BC) and Herodotus (d c 430 BC) as a 'small craft; fishing boat' (Liddell and Scott 1953: 1422). The word therefore is a general term for 'ship', applied by Indo-European languages.

It may be said, therefore, that in appearance the *balam* can be considered a rather ordinary vessel with no particular distinguishing features in spite of having some resemblance to the *baqqāra*. The *badan*, *baqqāra*, *battīl* and *shāḥūf* however, stand out as handsome examples of a seafaring heritage;[99] more perhaps than any other wooden watercraft in the Gulf they retain features that suggest types of a distant past, pre-dating Portuguese influence. The fact that one often finds them in isolated communities should ensure their survival.

97 Interviewed Khalil bin Rashid and Hassan Abd al-Rasool on 14 February 1985.

98 Transcribed *ploion*; the two pairs of contrastive sounds, initial /b/ (or /v/) /p/ and final /m/-/n/ are interchangeable and suggest a common Indo-European origin.

99 Norman Weismann is conducting a research on the *battīl* family, reconstructing the proto-type and pointing out to similarities that exist among the *shāḥūf*, *zārūka*, *baqqāra* and *battīl*, characteristics of which are the false stern post, the decorated stem part and the bent keel, the latter suggests that at one time these boats were sewn together (private communication 21 September 1999).

6
Ships' Boats, Canoes and Rafts

تمنيت من حبي علية اننا
على رمث في البحر ليس لنا وفر

In my love for ʿUlayya, I wished that
we were on board a raft on the sea,
without any wealth.[1]

(Abū Ṣakhr al-Hudhalī,
second half of the first/seventh century)

Ships' boats

The Gulf boats, the *keter*, *qalṣ* and *māshuwwa* are typical of coastal boats or lifeboats found on larger dhows. They are open, without any decking and, until quite recent times, they were propelled by oars and sometimes by a small lugsail; today, many such boats are operated by an outboard engine.

The *keter* (or *kitr*) served as a lifeboat for large ships; it was about 18 to 20 feet long and could carry up to six people. Kuwaiti boat-makers and sailors employ the term *ketīre* which they describe as a rowing boat, not to be confused with the small *sanbūq*-type called *qaṭīra* as discussed earlier in Chapter 5. Abd al-Amir Abdallah Hussein,[2] a dhow-builder from Bahrain recalled his father speaking of a *keter* likened to a *balam fūdrī* with two sharp pointed ends. The *keter* was generally associated in Bahrain with the *nākhōda*, who in the pearling days was ferried from one dhow to another or to and from the shore. Another type, perhaps related to the *keter* is what is called *kīt*, a small boat, some 15 feet long carrying up to 6 passengers and of Indian origin in which the *ṭawwāsh* (the pearl merchant) used to go from one dhow to the other in mid sea or to sail to different ports from the main harbour (illus. 35). I heard this term in Al-Khor (Qatar) and also Ajman, where the locals tend to say *kēt*.

Anywhere I travelled in the Gulf, seamen were familiar with the name *qalṣ* (pl *qulūṣ*), a lifeboat. Bahraini builders refer to it poetically as 'the son or daughter of a big ship'; it is operated by oars or poles and carries up to 20 people, and can also be used to transport passengers or to carry cargo to and

1 'Tamannaytu min ḥubb-ī ʿUlayyata anna-nā/ʿalā ramathin fī l-baḥri laysa la-nā wafru' (translation by Montgomery 1997: 195).
2 Interviewed on 25 April 1991.

35
The *kīt* was often used by the pearl merchant, Kuwait

from the ship (al-Shamlān 1990: 110). Pearling dhows carried a very small *qalṣ* for the use of the *ṭawwāsh* and the *nākhōda*. It is pronounced 'jals' in Bahrain. In Qatar the *galṣ* or *gals* (or even *galsh*) with plural *gulūṣ* or *gulūs* is a racing boat often referred to as *galṣ lis-sibāg*, a type built by Yousef Al Majid in Doha, Qatar.[3] I saw several of them in his boatyard at Amiriyya, the hull design being similar to the small *qalṣ*; some were 52 feet long and designed for 60 rowers, others were 25 feet for 20 rowers and the smallest was 14 feet long and could take 8 rowers.

Kuwaitis and Bahrainis often speak of the *māshuwwa* (pl *mawāshī*) as the *būm*'s lifeboat, a small open-ended craft about 24 feet long and 9 feet wide (illus. 36). It had eight oars and was used by the sailors as a ferry or cargo boat. This craft is different from the *jahāzī-māshuwwa*-type of the *sanbūq* family we saw in Chapter 5. The *māshuwwa* lifeboat is a more inclusive term referring to any small boat in the Gulf. However, the seamen I spoke to kept interchanging its name with *kīt* and *qalṣ* to a point where I was not sure which was which. Admittedly, the boats almost all look identical and have similar functions. I was told that as a pastime, merchants used to build *māshuwwa*s during their long, often boring journeys, from the Gulf to the west

3 Interviewed on 19 April 1992.

36
A *māshuwwa*, the *būm*'s lifeboat, Kuwait

Indian or east African coast (ʿUthmān 1990: 157). In East Africa we find Zanzibari *mashua*s (as recorded by Prins 1965: 77), which carry an oculus on either side of the bow and sometimes on the stern. *Māshuwwa*s are also found on the north-west Indian coast where they are used mainly for fishing and small cargo transport; they are essentially of Arab design and build, known by the Indian name *machwa*, but of two varieties: Hornell (1946: 202–3) reports one as having a transom stern while the other, very prevalent as far south as Bombay, was 'lean in the quarters and terminated sharply in a greatly raked sternpost' (with some differences in the hull construction among the Gujarati *machwa*s). The term is of Hindi origin, *machū* or *machwā* (Jayakar 1889: 821) though Marcel Devic (al-Rāmhurmuzī 1883–6: 203) quoting De Vries, speaks of a Chinese boat with the name *mauchua*.[4] I have no information to verify the authenticity of the Chinese name and its relation to the Indian provenance.

Although the above-mentioned boats were designed primarily as lifeboats, they were also employed for other purposes. When carried onboard trading

4 'De Vries parle bien d'une petite barque chinoise, qu'il nomme *mauchua*, mais nous ne savons pas quel est le bateau qu'il veut indiquer par ce nom' (sv *m.ṭyāl*).

and piratical dhows, they were used mainly for ship-to-ship communication at sea, as was also the case in pearling days. The *keter*, *qalṣ* and *māshuwwa* are the most common of all coastal boats or lifeboats. They are suspended from davits when at sea and not stowed inboard. As to how stable these craft were in case of danger, I obtained no information. I understand, however, from my informants that these boats were under constant review and experiment. The *māshuwwa* was perhaps the only type that was preferred, because of its buoyancy and robustness of construction.

Canoes, rafts and waterskins

The early craft in the Gulf and the Arabian Sea which were made from materials most ready to hand, are: the rough *balam* and *hūrī* dug-out canoes, the *shāsha* made of date-palm branches, and the *ramath* constructed of logs tied together. These craft were sturdy and seaworthy and offer an intriguing insight into the past.

The dug-out balam

Balam (pl *ablām* or *balāmī*) is a dug-out canoe, round bottomed and without decking. The name may be related to the *balam* we discussed in Chapter 5 but is obviously a different type. Often found in the Gulf on large ocean-going vessels, it was used to ferry the crew and passengers to and from the shore. The canoe comes from Bombay and Malabar and is employed directly without any additions though sometimes a number of thwarts are fitted. The *balam*s dubbed out of mango tree trunks are of lesser quality than the ones dug out from more durable trees.[5] They are very common in Basra and the name came to denote, by extension, any double-ended canoe-shaped river boat whatever the tonnage (Hornell 1942: 31). The *balam*s in southern Iraq described by Thesiger (1967: 47, 221) were flat-bottomed, carvel-built and roomy, some 30 feet long, with high sides and the prow and stern carved and decorated. *Balam*s are sometimes punted or sailed. The Iraqis call the man who operates a row-boat, *ballām* (Woodhead and Beene 1967: 43).

During my stay in Bahrain in April 1991 I visited the fishing village Malikiyah[6] and saw a dug-out fishing *balam* made from teak, which looked like a flat-bottomed rectangular box, decked over at the ends; no oars but a

5 Hornell (1942: 31) mentions several trees that produce long lasting *balam* canoes: *Calophyllum inophyllum* (a genus of beautiful evergreen, leathery-leaved tropical red tree from which the timber is valuable for building purposes), *Astocarpus lakoocha*, *Adina caordifolia* and *Terminalia*.

6 Locals say Mālchiyya; one phonological change that affects a large group of eastern Arabian dialects is the fronting and affrication of the velar stop /k/ to alveolar affricate /ch/, see Holes 1987: 32.

khaṭra (punting pole) made of bamboo was used, its length between four and five feet. The Bahraini *balam* is often referred to by the locals as *māshuwweh*, a term used in Bushehr and Ganaveh on the Iranian coast (Prins 1972–4: 161). The name *ballam* (or *vallam*) is used on the Tinnevelly coast of India, and the Iraqi name quoted in Lorimer's *Gazetteer* (1986, II B: 830) is also *ballam* (double /l/), while I have heard all around the Gulf, *balam* (one /l/), and the plural in Umm al Quwain *balāmī*. The Fārsī version is *belem*.

The traditional hūrī *of Arab seamen*

Perhaps the most common of primitive dug-outs used in many parts of the Gulf, the Arabian Sea and the Red Sea is the *hūrī* (pl *hawārī*): the canoe, made of mango from the Malabar coast and imported from Bombay and Calicut ready hollowed, is known as the *hūrī ḥafar* (CA *ḥafar*, 'to carve') in south-east Oman. It is about 15 feet long. The sight of a dug-out *hūrī* always caught the attention of western travellers and many were they who described it as a passenger boat in a harbour, carrying one or two persons. In Qatar, I was told that a pearl merchant was often ferried from one pearling dhow to another in a *hūrī*. Today, you still see the odd passenger *hūrī* being used here and there in the Gulf and Oman. During my fieldwork in Sur I often came across fishermen embarking on *hūrī*s to get to their dhows from the shore when the tide was in. In general, the narrow hull of this craft copes well with the surf, but I was told in Mutrah of one or two incidents being reported every year, of *hūrī*s capsizing. To give them stability some *hūrī*s have stone or gravel as ballast.[7] Instead of oars these canoes have paddles, thrust into the water like 'diggers do their spade into the earth', as Wilson (1954: 21) described them.

The many *hūrī*s in Oman that I examined, particularly in the Seeb, Sidab and Mutrah areas, in Sohar, Saham, and in al-Radah on the Al-Batinah coast, were the fishing type with some features added to them (illus. 37). They are used for both line and net fishing. My guide Hamad Saeed Hamad al-Breiki from al-Radah,[8] a folklorist, explained how a dug-out canoe cannot be used other than as a coastal passenger boat. 'If it serves as a fishing boat', he continued, 'then the builder needs to strengthen the prow, and adds a gunwale carving the inside of the hull in rib-shaped relief' (illus. 38). This type is called *hūrī manshūr* (CA *nashara*, 'to saw apart'). The builder fits

7 On the question of stability I heard in Muscat a proverb not very complimentary about the people of Sur: *lā ta'min ṣūrī wa-lā tarkab hūrī*, 'do not trust a Sūrī as much as you would not ride a *hūrī*', in other words the people of Sur are as unreliable as an unstable *hūrī*.

8 Interviewed on 29 November 1996.

37
A fishing *hūrī* in Sidab near Muscat, Oman

38
Fishing *hūrīs*: the inside of the hull is carved with ribs, Sur, Oman

an engine near the rear and shapes a *karwa* (a semi-oval design at the bottom of the stern) to fit a shaft and propeller. The hulls are kept oiled with fish oil and are normally hauled out of the water on to the beach when not in use. In the days of sail, a short mast carrying a small settee sail was fixed, and to the curved stern, a rudder was hung by gudgeon and pintle (Hornell 1942: 30). In Salalah fishermen use local wood[9] to build the ribs of the *hūrī*.

For net fishing, in south-east Oman the fishermen preferred to construct a large *hūrī* using the traditional shell-construction method (ie planks first, after laying the keel, bow and stern; see Chapter 7). The length of these *hūrī*s varied from 15 to 30 feet, carrying 4 to 8 seamen. The longest type of *hūrī* (25 to 40 feet) I saw was in Masirah in April 1998; it was built locally, and used for line and net fishing. This type also served at one time to ferry passengers to and from the laden dhows that anchored in the port of Sur, or was used by smaller traders who called on the shores of the neighbouring villages. The Bahraini *hūrī* is a boat 10 to 20 feet long which carries up to 10 passengers. I came across the name *beylī* which is close to the *hūrī* family-type but wider and bigger. Rashid Obeid Al Shouq, a *rāwī* 'storyteller',[10] heard from some old seamen that this boat was in past times used in the Emirates for fishing, and ferrying passengers from one side to the other of the Dubai port.

The *hūrī* is mentioned by travellers in connection with both the Red and the Arabian Seas. The name is from Hindi *hōṛī*, originally coming from Sanskrit *hoḍa*[11] (Glidden 1942: 72). An Indian *hody* was reported by Hornell (1920: 148) as being 22 to 40 feet in length and up to 6 tons in weight. It was a copy of the *toni*[12] in Bombay, a dug-out canoe built up of planks and having the stem and the sternposts curved; a rudder is fixed to the stern by lashings or iron gudgeons. The link of *hūrī* with Chinese *hu*, 'floating boat', as proposed by Yajima (1976: 29), seems rather dubious. The most common plural of *hūrī* that I heard was *hawārī* and in Oman, *hewārī*; other plurals are: Mehri, *hōwárīt* or *hāwérīt* and Hadrami, *hawáriye* (Jahn 1902: 272).

The Omani shāsha

If we were to trace the origins of small open boats in the Gulf, we would find the *shāsha* (pl *shāshāt* or *shūsh*) to be the most primitive type, in which paddles

9 In Dhofar I am told by the Director of National Heritage (Salalah) that the locals use wood mainly from *athab* and *arīr* trees which grow in the valleys and hills of the region.

10 Interviewed on 18 April 1996.

11 Note Urdu *hōdzī* (Badger 1889: 824); also Soqoṭrī *hóri*; see Vollers 1896: 651.

12 This must be the *doney* (or *dhony*) that Yule and Burnell (1994: 323) list as a native dug-out craft from south India, the word originating from Tamil *tōṉi* or Sanskrit *droṇa*, a wooden vessel. A *doni* described by John Edye (1835: 13) is a totally different type. It is a huge vessel of 'ark-like' form about 70 feet long, 20 feet broad and 12 feet deep.

were the motive force. It is about 10 feet long and belongs to the east Emirates and northern Oman, but was also seen at the turn of the nineteenth century in Qishm and Bandar Abbas on the Iranian coast of the Gulf (Lorimer 1986, I, iib: 2326). The nomenclature is not found in classical Arabic lexica nor in modern Arabic dictionaries. I think the origin of this word can be found in the Arabic word *shīsh*, 'a sort of dates' (al-Zabīdī 1977, XVII: 240), from which root came the word *shāsha*, to signify a canoe made from *jarīd saʿaf*, ie the central spines of the leaves of the date palm tree. The *shāsha* is bound together with coir to form a point at bow and stern. On top of the base, palm bark, coconut fibres, and the bulbous ends of palm branches ensure buoyancy so that the boat floats like a raft. As early as the mid nineteenth century W. M. Pengelley (1860: 31–2) noted how fishermen could use the *shāsha* in rough weather because of the flexibility of its construction. Fishermen in Sohar[13] during my visit there were very enthusiastic about showing me these beach boats: 'It is a small canoe', one of them said, 'but it is good with big fish and unlike wooden boats it copes well with surfing and is more resilient than an iron-fastened boat'. It takes one to two days to construct.[14] What is striking about this boat is that it is economical. It requires very little labour, costs practically nothing and it is made from one tree, the palm; all locally available resources.

I visited a model boat-maker, Darwish Abdalla Saeed al-Zaabi, a retired sailor,[15] aged 70 years from Saham, who showed me how a *shāsha* is constructed. I had already collected information about this from the model boat-maker Abd Al-Amir in Bahrain a few years earlier.[16] The *shāsha* is made from the spines of date palm leaves. These are large leaves cut in a particular season. The palm stems (*jarīd* or, as they are called in Bahrain, *zōr*) are stripped and soaked in sea water from 4 to 7 days in order to allow them to become pliable.[17] 'This treatment', observed George Bertram (1948: 28), softens the palm fronds in a way that 'they may easily be pierced for sewing together and be curved into shape'. Taking them out of the water, the palm fronds are

13 Interviewed Abdalla Ahmed Saeed Al-Naqbi, Abdalla bin Fadil bin Abdalla Al-Shizawi, Ibrahim Muhammed Ali Al-Nawfali on 28 November 1996.

14 It all depends on the *shāsha*-maker's skill and material. Tom Vosmer told me (27 April 2000) that he and some colleagues videotaped the construction of a *shāsha* in 1992 and it took five days.

15 Interviewed on 29 November 1996.

16 Interviewed on 25 April 1991.

17 The Awazim of north-east Arabia buried the date-palm boughs in the sand for forty days before they are actually used (LeBaron Bowen, quoting Violet Dickson, 1952: 194). Bertram (1948: 28) notes that the *shāsha*-makers he visited at the Al-Batinah coast buried the palm fronds in damp sand by the sea for some 5 days. I think the number of days varied according to the type of boughs and how hot the temperature is before they are soaked.

trimmed with a curved knife and cut to some 10 feet long, ready for use. They need no drying. Some 40 fronds, if the canoe is designed for one person, or 50 if it is for two people, are placed neatly, one after the other. Holes, made by a sharp pointed file, are then bored in each frond: each hole lies horizontally some 8 to 10 inches from the other. When ready, the palm stems are collected in small bundles ready for sewing. The rope, made by the *shāsha* builder(s) from the beaten date palm stalk, is threaded from one hole to another, thus tightening the palm fronds. This bundle forms the keel of the *shāsha*. Then the sides are built up with 12 fronds sewn from the inside, and some twisting is done to the date-palm sticks, bending them upwards into a point at bow and stern. The hull is further strengthened on either side, including the bow and stern, by five pieces of wood from the *sidir* tree. It is lined internally by some 500 palm-stem butts (*karab*) so that the *shāsha* floats; the butts also ensure stability. The more stem butts that are used, the more balance the boat enjoys. A second layer of palm fronds, functioning as inside decking, is then laid on the stem butts. Sometimes the sides of the *shāsha* are raised by adding 15 fronds on each side to form the gunwale (illus. 39). A settee-shaped sail is hoisted on a mast made of Indian *baskīl* which consists of two small spars attached to the gunwales on either side of the boat amidships, and forming a triangle at the top where both ends are tied together. The paddles are made from pine (*snawbar*), but I noticed the blades nearly always vary in shape from one village to another in the Al-Batinah region: the circular and cricket-bat-shape blades are of common usage among the fishermen; other blades are angular like a boomerang, or are rectangular-shaped.[18] When completed, the *shāsha* is hauled down over rollers called *madrī* into the sea. The fisherman would row out to tend his nets and when the palm fronds became too waterlogged and heavy he would return to the shore, pull it on to the beach and leave it to dry (illus. 40). Several fishermen informed me that a *shāsha*-owner would have more than one canoe because as the craft is not waterproofed and absorbs too much water when at sea, he has therefore to beach it to get it dry. While drying one he uses the other at sea. Some fishermen owned two or three *shāsha*s for this reason. This information corresponds with what Bertram (1948: 28) in the 1940s, and Donaldson (1980: 483) in the 1970s have reported.

---

18 There is a variety of oars and paddles used by rowers throughout the dhow world: The general term for oar or paddle is CA *miqdāf* (pl *maqādīf*); GA *migdāf* (pl *magādīf*), Kt *mīdāf*; Dh *mīdāf* (pl *emyādīf* (from *mijdāf*; /j/ > /y/). Other spelling variables are *mijdāf*, *mijḏaf*, *mijḏāf*, *miqḏaf*, *miqḏāf*, *miġdaf*; the rectangular-shaped paddle is GA *migdāf*; the spear-shaped type is GA *ghādūf* < Aram (cf Syr *gādūpā*, 'oar'), see Glidden 1942: 72. Hawkins' (1977: 137) illustration of seven types of oars used from Iraq to Oman is quite informative.

39
A *shāsha* with raised sides at the gunwale, Umm Al Jaiz, near Saham, Oman

40
A *shāsha* laid on its side to dry, Saham, Oman

Almost all the *shāsha*s I saw had nylon cord instead of the date palm thread, and by replacing palm frond butts for polystyrene pieces, strength and longevity was added to the craft without interfering with its flexibility and manoeuvrability, as Donaldson (1980: 485) noted. He also remarked how Omani fishermen, finding the time right, adapted traditional patterns to innovations, making the craft cost-effective (ibid: 486). The only expense some Omani fishermen were willing to incur was to cut a rectangular hole in the *shāsha* to fit an outboard engine to the stern. Most of the Al-Batinah fishermen I spoke to had received grants from the Omani Ministry of Agriculture and Fisheries to buy outboard engines.

I was shown by Darwish a very small raft called a *zufāra* which was folded and laid on the side of a *shāsha*'s gunwale. This was the lifeboat in case the *shāsha* sank. I had never read or heard anything about this raft. He said that the *zufāra* consists of 20 to 25 palm stems all stitched together and tied to a piece of wood at either end. Its length is 3 to 5 feet and some 4 feet wide. Lying on his chest on the *zufāra* the man paddles his way to the shore with his feet.

The Bahraini firteh

In the fishing village of Malikiyah north of Bahrain, the *shāsha* is known as a *firteh* which is punted by a *khaṭra* made of bamboo. However, the Bahraini seamen of Muharraq and Manamah call the craft *wāriyya* as they do in Kuwait. I was told by Mohammed Abdallah Al Saqar (known as Bu Abdallah),[19] a model boat-maker in his late eighties, that the *firteh* is built out of a palm tree (called by the locals *marzabān*), from the best spines, which are strong and pliable. In his youth he remembers that practically all Bahraini fishing villages used the *firteh* for coastal fishing, and on festive occasions teenagers amused themselves by surfing in boat races using *firteh*s with sails: 'this was the only way that boys learnt to brave the sea by canoe races round the inner harbour', he added. When the boys became familiar with paddling their canoes, they would leave the harbour two or three miles out to where a large dhow was anchored, and then from there race back to the harbour. Typical of Malikiyah is what Mohammad Bashir Idham, a local fisherman,[20] called the *firteh chappār* (pl *chapāpīr*), used for net fishing. Both words are of Fārsī or Indian origin; in Urdu *chap'pu* means 'oar, paddle' (Qureshi nd: 249).

There are a few construction techniques different from those of a *shāsha*. I give here a brief description of making a *firteh* as explained to me by Hasan

19 Interviewed on 22 April 1991.

20 Interviewed on 28 April 1991.

Ali Al-Fardan Ibrahim bin Ali at Malikiyah.[21] The time for cutting the branches from the tall palm tree is during the winter months. The boughs (*saʿaf*) which are taken from the *marzabān* date palm tree are some 10 to 12 feet long and are shaved and put in the water for at least seven days. They are left for some time to dry thus becoming pliable for use. 24 palm fronds are shaved and placed on the floor in groups of twos or threes and nails of palm fibre called *shācheh* (pl *shjāyech*), are pierced through the frond spines, each nail placed at a distance of 5 inches from the other. The spines are sewn together with rope made locally from the *zaffān*, the date palm tree.[22] This is the first part in building the canoe, and forms the base which consists of some 20 to 25 stalks; several layers of bulbous ends are then placed onto this for buoyancy. The builder then takes another set of 24 spines pierced with palm-fibre nails and sewn together in the same fashion as before, and places them on the stem butts. The base is now firm. Now the sides of the canoe are built, following the same steps of piercing and threading; about 15 palm fronds are used for each side. When completed, they are both sewn onto the base, and both ends of the canoe, which form the bow and stern (*nashar*), are also sewn together. The gunwale, known locally as *dirʿān*, is the piece of timber going around the upper sheer strake of the boat securing the sides and protecting the oarsmen from any water coming through. The thwarts, made of local wood, are placed between either side of the gunwale and tied together to the spines. Sometimes ribs (*ʿiṭaf*) made of local wood are built into the *firteh chappār* to strengthen the sides of the hull. The circular-shaped paddles are worked against a thole pin called *ghass* or *ghiss*, next to the thwart. Sometimes, instead of paddles, one uses a *khaṭra*; a primitive sail is hoisted to two small spars lashed together at their heads and the other ends tied to either side of the boat amidships. The canoe can last up to three years and its flexibility enables it to cope well with heavy surf.

The Kuwaiti wāriyya

The palm tree-fibre boat of Failaka, an island east of Kuwait, is the *wāriyya* or *wariyya* (pl *wāriyyāt* or *wariyyāt*) which is ten feet long and used by fishermen. Iranian seamen I met in Doha, Qatar, use the same term and, according to them, *wāriyya*s can still be seen on the Iranian coast. Other names I heard for

21 Interviewed on 28 April 1991.

22 According to Shahina Ghazanfar, a botanist from the Ministry of Culture and Heritage (Muscat), in a personal communication with Tom Vosmer, no one has carried out any traditional taxonomic study on these varieties other than their recognition as different 'types' of trees, their dates perhaps differing in shape, size, or colour or taste (communication from T. Vosmer received 1 May 2000).

this beach boat were *wahriyya* and *warjiyya* in Failaka, and in Qatar my informants called it *hūriyya*. Dickson (1949: 480) speaks of *huwayriyya* and my Bahraini informant, a lifelong pearl-diver and a fisherman, Mohammed Yaqoob,[23] called it *hwāriyya*, a term which he recalled being used in his youth. That must have been a long time ago because at the time I interviewed him Mohammed was 112 years old, the oldest seaman I have ever come into contact with during my field trips to the Gulf. I visited Failaka in February 1985 and hardly any *wāriyya*s were left then on the island. Like the Omani *shāsha* and the Bahraini *firteh*, it is also made of date-palm spines. One technique similar to the *firteh* was the use of the nails of palm fibre pierced through the stalks and then tied together with string, while the Omani builders do not use nails but stitch the stalks together tightly. The bottom of the *wāriyya*, like the other beach canoes, is packed with *karab* (bulbous ends of palm stalks) to offer buoyancy so that the canoe lies flat like a raft. It carries one to two people with an oar fixed on either side of the thwart.

The Failaka name *warjiyya*[24] puzzled me. It sounds similar to the term *warjiwa* (if correctly transcribed phonetically) recorded by De Graeve (1981: 159); it is described as made of reed bundles and fitted out with wooden thwarts. No *karab* is mentioned, which suggests that the boat does not maintain the buoyancy required to keep it afloat. The name of the boat is contemporary but the make is ancient and probably refers to a Mesopotamian or early Persian usage. As a matter of fact we come across a similar Iraqi river craft on the Lower Tigris, described by Ritter and Moritz at the end of the nineteenth and beginning of the twentieth century (Ritter 1919: 143), made of reeds bound together and looking like a raft, poled, and occasionally with a sail: '[it is] only of any use for a fairly short journey', explains Moritz, 'as [it] soon absorb[s] the water and sink[s]' (Kindermann 1934: 59). Hornell (1942: 34) explains that this is what Bertram Thomas meant when he described this beach boat as being a 'frail wicker boat'. But Iraqis called this craft *shāsha*, we are told, not *warjiwa* or *warjiyya*, different names but very similar in design.[25] The Gulf *shāsha* is more robust and lasts up to three years. One detail I found interesting which no informant told me, is De Graeve's (1981: 159) comment on the oarsman sculling the reedboat by sitting at the prow of the

23 Interviewed on 24 April 1991.

24 Violet Dickson reported to have heard *warraga* (probably *warrāga*) (pl *wargiyeh*) which is used by Awazim fishermen in north-east Arabia (LeBaron Bowen 1952: 194).

25 LeBaron Bowen (1952: 196-7) comments that the shape of the Iraqi *shāsha* (and *huwayriyya*) seems to be similar to the *ṭarrāda* of the Marsh Arabs; the latter is a reed canoe covered with bitumen instead of the double bottom with bulbous ends in between, as you find in the Gulf beach canoes.

canoe and propelling it by oars, one placed on each side.[26] This method of sculling appears on two reliefs from the reign of Ashurbanipal (669-626 BC). A medieval *waljiyya* or *walajiyya* referred to (al-Muqaddasī 1906, III: 32), could be an ancestor of the present Failaki or Bahraini *wāriyya*, which is phonetically related to *warjiwa*;[27] the latter I believe has developed from the Iranain *varjī* (or *varjeh*), which Rowand (Lorimer 1986, I, iib: 2326) found at Zor some eighty years ago.

The zaᶜīma *coracle*

Made of wickerwork, the *zaᶜīma* was a rectangular coracle with rounded corners, 10 feet long and some 2 feet wide. None of these exist in the Gulf today. Bu Abdallah of Bahrain[28] informed me that these *zaᶜīma*s were essentially Iraqi craft though one or two were seen by him in Bahrain when he was small. They are made out of thin bundles of reed which are tied to one another. Marsh Arabs, wrote Young (1989: 58), skimmed about 'like mayflies' in these small reed canoes, coated outside with bitumen. The boat is similar in design to a *mashḥūf* (a slender, flat-bottomed longboat), Thesiger (1967: 128) wrote,[29] and for the locals it was the cheapest option. Frauke Heard-Bey, a Gulf historian,[30] told me that in the 1970s she saw a coracle made of reeds two feet high, in Quriyat, south of Muscat, but I could not find anyone who could give me information about it when I was there in April 1998.

The ramath

Regarding catamarans, the *ramath* (pl *anmāth*, *rimāth* or *rawāmith*) was the most popular among the Socotrans, on the west coast of India, and particularly around the island of Sri Lanka. They are still in the memory of many old Omanis in Muscat and in the Al-Batinah region, who recall the islanders of Socotra calling at their ports during the fishing season. Osgood (1854: 65) saw Muscati fishermen using catamarans but has no name for them; they were frail, 'constructed of two or three slender logs lashed together with a grass rope'. Unquestionably, these primitive craft are survivals from

26 Ritter's photo shows a frail *shāsha* with a rectangular sail, a man punting with a *khaṭra* and in front of him are two passengers sitting in the middle of the craft (1919: 143, Figure 42).

27 Voiced palato-alveolar fricative /j/; often an alveolar affricate with dialects of some Bahraini communities becomes a frictionless continuant /y/, see Holes 1987: 41.

28 Interviewed on 22 April 1991.

29 Gavin Young (1989: 26-7) writes about *mashḥūf*s that '[they] are carvel-built out of a mixture of Iraqi mulberry wood and wood imported from Malaysia and Indonesia . . .' Like their reed proto-Sumerian types, the *mashḥūf*s have a high curved prow and stern and their delicate wooden hull smeared with bitumen as their ancestors did. There are two bitumen Sumerian models of *mashḥūf*s from Ur in the British Museum in London.

30 Interviewed on 26 April 1998.

antiquity. We find two occurrences of this craft in a pre-Islamic poem by Abū Ṣakhr al-Hudhalī (mentioned at the beginning of this Chapter). The raft is portrayed as a romantic vessel by the poet, who longs to be on it with his beloved, on open sea –

> In my love for ʿUlayya, I wished that
> we were on board a raft [*ramath*] on the sea,
> without any wealth.[31]

And in a Ḥadīth (al-Zabīdī 1969, V: 265) it is narrated: A man came to the prophet and asked him, 'we embark on our *ramath*s and we have no water, do we make ablutions with sea-water?' The answer to which was that not only can you make ablutions with sea water before prayer but that you may eat of the fish therein! The background story may be peripheral, but what is important is the fact that the *ramath* by the early centuries of Islam must have been a common occurrence to find its way into the Ḥadīth, a religious literature, second in authority to the Qurʾān. The Spanish lexicographer Ibn Sīda (d 458/1066) listed this type of boat as being constructed of 'pieces of wood put together upon which one embarks on the sea' (1898–1903, X: 29); a general description, but historically its mention is important even though no details are given as to how many logs were bound together and what length they were to form a raft. The medieval sources are silent about this type until we come to the nineteenth century when it is recorded by western travellers, among them John Edye and Johann Ludwig Burckhardt. The latter (1822: 314) wrote that he sailed in Nubia on what he called a *rāmūs* which he described as 'a small raft of reeds'. In some other place however, he described it as a ferry boat formed of 4 trunks of date trees, 'tied loosely together, and is worked by a paddle about 4 feet in length . . .' (ibid 47). The Jesuit William Gifford Palgrave saw 1,862 catamarans (log rafts) off the Malabar coast in the Musandam Peninsula (1865, II: 314).

We have no information on how a *ramath* was built; I assume that the techniques were fairly universal in the maritime culture of the Indian Ocean, and both Edye's (1835: 4) description of a Sri Lankan catamaran off Cape Comorin, and Hornell's (1920: 153), of a boat catamaran off the Tinnevelly coast, would suffice to give us a general picture of this primitive craft. The raft is formed of 3 logs of timber,[32] some 20 to 25 feet in length and 2 to 3 feet

31 Translation by Montgomery 1997: 195.

32 John Edye (1835: 4) reports that the timber for the catamarans used in Sri Lanka, Madras and other parts of the south-west coast of India was from pine tree called by the natives *dúp* or *cherne-maram*.

in breadth, secured together by means of spreaders and cross-lashings; the central log is larger than the side ones. Hornell explains how these logs are held in position 'by a transverse two-horned block of wood at either end, whereto the logs are lashed securely by coir ropes passed through grooves cut in the sides of the logs'. It was navigated by one or two men and we are told that the catamaran was good for surfing on the beach. In the monsoons a light bamboo yard of 34 feet was placed, balanced with a small outrigger at the end of two poles, and using a mat or a triangular cotton-cloth sail. It was paddled by a double oar.

The word *ramath* is traced back to Demotic origin (the root being /r/, m/ and /s/) which refers to a papyrus *barque* or raft (Kindermann 1934: 33). The word also appears in Hieratic writing. It is a cognate term with Somali *ramsi*, *ramás*, *ramásh* and *ramísh*, 'a raft, fishing boat' and with Ethiopic, appearing in Kebra-Nagast (ibid 32), which shows evidence of this raft travelling from Ethiopia to Yemen, to Arabia on the Red Sea, and to Hadhramaut and the Dhofar region in Oman. It is possible that the Arabic *ramath* (*ramas* or *ramaṣ* in Socotri) comes from Ethiopic (Fraenkel 1962: 212), but the Arabic term could be as old as any Semitic form and therefore a diachronic reconstruction becomes more difficult. As the craft's design is primitive, locals would have learnt to make these rafts from time immemorial. Several Indian varieties of long-built catamarans can be found today on the west coast of India. As much as one would like to think that the idea of building a catamaran was borrowed by one community from another (LeBaron Bowen 1952: 193), it is more likely that coastal people applied similar techniques to build rafts, independent of one another.

On similar lines to the *ramath* there was in Bahrain the *rāddeh*, according to the 112-year-old Mohammed Yaqoob of Muharraq.[33] He described this as a raft which was used in Bahrain for fishing some hundred years ago and constructed of palm tree logs, between four and six tied together, the stronger and longer ones placed in the middle and the shorter ones on the side, to form a sturdy catamaran. It was punted in a standing position and was used for fishing on the coastline. The term may be linked with classical Arabic *rādda*, 'a piece of wood in the fore part of a cart' (Lane 1984, I: 1063–4) but there may be earlier links with Akkadian or Aramaic.

The qirba*: waterskin*

An earlier or perhaps concurrent method of sea transport was by means of an inflated skin, a waterskin *qirba* (pl *qirab*, *qirbāt*, *qirabāt*) used mainly by

33 Interviewed on 24 April 1991.

fishermen, at one time in Oman on the Arabian Sea, and in Bahrain and Iraq. When inflated, the skin was filled with water and bound together tightly; the fisherman lying forward with his chest on the waterskin paddled his way through the water with his feet.[34] It is a position clearly represented in antiquity on Assyrian bas-reliefs (Ritter 1919: 143): pictorial evidence of watertight animal skins employed by soldiers for swimming across rivers are rendered in palace reliefs from the reign of Ashurnasirpal II (c 883–859 BC) to Ashurbanipal (De Graeve 1981: 80–1). Numerous bas-reliefs show examples of skin-supported rafts, the type called by Iraqis *kelek* which are still used in some remote areas on the Tigris and the Euphrates rivers. The *Periplus* mentions 'rafts held up by inflated skins' on the Arabian Sea[35] and Pliny (6.176), also writing about the south Arabian coast, speaks of locals making rafts 'by spreading a plank over a pair of ox bladders'. In comparatively modern times, a fisherman sat on a single inflated goat or sheepskin, or a raft of two or more skins tied together by a piece of wood, fishing off the coast or chasing sharks or other big fish with nets, hooks and lines (Wellsted 1838, I: 79). When Bent (1900: 230) met the Janaba tribesmen of southern Oman he saw them swimming on inflated skins in pursuit of sharks. This ancient fishing technique was still being used until way into the 1950s, on the Dhofar coast opposite Kuria Muria islands in Oman, or so Basheer Saeed Rabee from Marbat informed me.[36] The Janaba fishermen, I heard from locals of the fishing village Al-Ashkharah,[37] used to catch sharks for the fins and tails which they sold to passing vessels on their way to Muscat; these parts of the shark were then shipped onward to other destinations in the Far East, particularly Japan. Several western writers gave accounts of these sheepskin floats, which were prevalent in south Oman and they were surprised to see how safe they were on heavy surf. Haines (1847: 141) stated that in his own experience, approaching the coast by a sewn boat, strong and flexible though it may be, is more hazardous than on an inflated skin pushed to the shore with a surf.

In conclusion, *shāsha*s are still actually being used on the same shore where they must have been invented during early prehistoric times. It would be interesting to find what connection they might have with the ancient-style reed-boats of the Tigris and Euphrates of some 3,000 years ago. The *shāsha*s are light and they are handled by fishermen who depend upon them to move

34 This information is based on the photograph of a fisherman on a waterskin taken by Ritter (1919: 136) on his trip to the Euphrates in 1917.

35 The quote is from Schoff's translation (1912: 32 [27]); Casson translates: 'rafts of a local type made of leathern bags' (1989: 67 [27]).

36 Interviewed on 16 November 1996.

37 Interviewed Hamad bin Jumaa al-Jafri, Hamad Salim Mohammed al-Mardi and Hamid bin Jaaruf al-Balushi on 15 April 1998.

from place to place. As with the early skiffs, they are made of reeds for lightness, and are coated with pitch for waterproofing. But they are not the only primitive craft to have survived: dug-out canoes, like the *hūri* and the *balam*, are also fascinating relics of the past. The Indian *hūrī*s I saw in Sidab and Qantab near Mutrah were actually hollowed out by fire or stone tools, cleanly cut and as cleverly constructed as a manufactured boat. Here we are at the beginning of the twenty-first century with the stitched beach boat and the dug-out canoe still in use, while at the same time other shores of the Gulf are seeing vessels built of planks and ribs.

7
BUILDING THE TRADITIONAL WOODEN CRAFT

وسار بي والليل ظلمة
ورموني بغبة زرقة

I travelled so far until the night was dark
Sailing on this deep blue sea[1]
(Mohammed Ali Hammadi al-Shihhi from Khasab)

The construction of wooden dhows is still a living tradition in the Gulf. It is one of the most evocative images of the past but is now having to survive against the onslaught of modern technology, turning many of the old craft into museum objects. The isolation of dhow-builders was something that struck me during my research. Gone are the days when the master-builder went around in the market, meeting his fellow craftsman – the blacksmith, ropemaker, flax spinner, weaver and sailmaker – to discuss with him exactly what he wanted. The carpenter in the shipbuilder's yard is practically the only craftsman that survives and holds together the art of building a dhow. It is this craftsmanship that I will discuss here; we will look at the traditional methods of construction, the tools, and the stages in the building of a dhow, in this instance, the *būm*.

Shell construction method

The stages of development which the dhow has undergone relate to particular changes in the shipwright's art and to the shape and purpose of the vessel. Thus, in the past century and beyond, the large vessels, the *baghla*, *ghanja*, *kūtiyya* that traded to foreign ports, had a high square stern and often a poop. The double-ended *būm* was designed, though it was smaller, to carry the same weight as the large vessels and, as *nākhōda*s reported to me, to sail even faster. I asked the Kuwaiti builders why a *būm* has a sharp stern. They seemed to think that it made it safer in a seaway and more manoeuvrable than the unwieldy stern of the *baghla* (the dhow that was replaced by the *būm* at the beginning of the twentieth century). This is possibly true;[2] the fishing *badan*,

1 'Wa-sāra bī wa-l-layl ẓulma/wa-ramūnī bi-ghabbat zarqa' – sung on a journey at night (interviewed on 26 November 1996).

2 There is that optimistic thinking that a *nākhōda* always hopes to sail in more or less good winds. In Chapter 4 we saw what financial effects a storm can have on a shipowner who

baqqāra and *battīl* were built to break the surf, convenient for beaching and for use under oars.[3] Following the discovery of oil the traditional wooden dhow was mechanized, necessitating some changes to allow the installation of inboard engines. Fibreglass motor boats have replaced the dhow in almost all coastal areas of the Arabian Gulf and Oman, some keeping the same design of the traditional fishing *sanbūq* or *shūʿī*.

One important development often noted about Gulf craft, and which presumably took place after the arrival of the Portuguese in 1498, is the transition in the construction of ships from planks hewn and fastened together by coconut-fibre cord and treenails, to the introduction of iron-nailed framing in the hulls. The early Arab and Indian ships were probably double-ended, designed as such to mount a steering oar close to the sternpost. The double-ended hull (Ar *haykal*) in Alan Villiers' (1952: 70) judgement, was of old favoured by Arabs and Iranians because it provided greater safety. A good example of transition from a double-ended to a square-sterned type is the *sanbūq*, at one time sewn, and remnants of which I saw in Taqa near Salalah on the Dhofari coast of the Arabian Sea. In the memories of the seamen I spoke to, the *sanbūq* of the Gulf was always square-sterned. On closer inspection I could see how the design evolved from its early ancestry to having the rudder fully exposed with a scutcheon-shaped transom, features of which were current in the days of the sixteenth-century Portuguese *caravel*. Some *sanbūq*, *shūʿī* and *jahāzī* have their athwartship timbers and the overhang of the stern, painted. The lofty poops, broadened by quarter galleries, are characteristics of the fifteenth- and sixteenth-century Portuguese and Dutch vessels which found their way to the beautifully carved sterns of the Arab *baghla*, *ghanja*, Indian *kotia*, the Perso-Arab *sanbūq* and the Arab *shūʿī*. Space and decoration, therefore, are the features of square-sterned dhows but they are technically less hydrodynamic: 'the waves are heavy and break unequally' explained Yacoub Al-Hijji, a boat researcher,[4] on my visit to Kuwait. He told me that Kuwaiti experience has shown that double-ended vessels prove to be more seaworthy;[5] waves break evenly against the stern.

The Portuguese influence is clearly shown in shipbuilding techniques, which we can trace in the Gulf nautical vocabulary; Johnstone and Muir (1964: 299–322) have already pointed this out in the Kuwaiti marine

invests his capital on the ship and cargo. Some shipowners in Kuwait and Bahrain, I am told, were never able to recover financially from the loss of a large dhow.

3 Tom Vosmer in a personal communication (3 September 1999) informed me that the raised stern of these craft was related to their being beached stern-first.

4 Interviewed on 5 May 1998.

5 One may draw parallels with north European boat design between 900 and 1450, see Crumlin-Pedersen 1972: 182-92.

repertoire. The list shows that many terms are of Portuguese origin and that some were in use at the time of the explorations (Leitão and Lopes 1963), though understandably there is also evidence of Fārsī and Urdu usages.

I met two builders in the Gulf who could work from plans and drawings but generally the construction work is carried out without such aids and all measurements for the variations are memorized by the boat-builders. When discussing the building of a dhow with his customers, the master-builder will squat and draw the ship on the sand or sketch it with a piece of chalk on a plank, detailing some parts. It should be said that the Arab dhow-builder is a master craftsman and would not be too happy if the customer pinned him down to providing exact dimensions. Once, during my stay in Sur in December 1996, I managed to follow a conversation between a builder and a few customers who came around to the boatyard to place an order for a *shūʿi*. After greeting each other and the usual kissing on foreheads and noses they moved around the yard talking in terms of how large and how slender they wanted the dhow to be, then roughly the completion date and finally, the price was agreed and was sealed by a handshake. It was extraordinary, how short a time was taken in ordering a vessel. Basically, there is nothing to discuss, the craftsmanship is in the hands of the artist. He will provide the best for the price you offer. It is his accuracy of eye and experience which determine the measurements of the vessel. Hull-shape templates are, nonetheless, applied, to shape the planking, though it should be noted that this practice did not exist with sewn boats, as discussed in Chapters 5 and 6.

Almost all the dhows I have seen built in the Gulf follow the shell construction method whereby the frames (the ribs of the ship running from the keel to the side rail) are inserted after the planks on the outside have been fitted in. The initial building stage in the west is the opposite and consists of a rib-skeleton to which the planks are subsequently fixed. However, I have watched *hūrī*s in al-Butteen boatyard at Abu Dhabi where the builders set up the frames first, followed by the planking. Here, *hūrī*s are being built as a class of boat for racing; the same method was applied at Ma'alla in Aden for the big *sanbūq*s (Hawkins 1977: 44).[6] Historically, nautical information extracted from Sumerian, Akkadian and Assyrian sources seems to point out that craft used on the Tigris and Euphrates during the first two thousand years BC were built keel first followed by close-set frames,[7] though a re-study

6 The rib-skeleton method is according to Hawkins (1977: 44), applied in southern India for the construction of the Tuticorin *thoni*.

7 The nautical data are found in Salonen 1938: 3-23; 1939: 1-199; 1942: 1-118.

of construction methods in the light of underwater archaeology shows that some of the data presented by Salonen are by no means conclusive (Casson 1967: 286). I found that in Iraq ships are of carvel build, the technique of which closely follows that of Europe. When the keel, the stem and the sternposts are laid, the frames (ribs) are then fitted in position and to these the planks are nailed. This Iraqi technique is not necessarily an indication that there is a continuity in the tradition of how ships were built from ancient times in an unbroken line. Many cultures have adopted frame-first construction, after a shell-built tradition of many centuries. Not much is known about early techniques until after the arrival of the Portuguese in the Gulf and India. It is difficult to establish whether inserted framing was replaced by pre-erected frames, nor is it possible to find out how one method evolved into the other, particularly as the construction of keel first, then stem and sternposts, is a common process with both methods.[8] In the past, no manuals were written to describe how a dhow was built. The attempt made recently by a few Arab researchers to describe the building of such dhows is indeed commendable.[9] But the fundamental question as to why Gulf builders apply the shell-first construction is still puzzling. It is of course impossible to build a sewn hull by any method other than shell-first. I thought that an answer to this intriguing question might be found in the smaller dhows like the *badan*, *battīl* and *zārūka*. On a trip in November 1996 to Kumzar, a fishing village in the rugged and remote Musandam Peninsula, Zaid Ahmed Abdallah Al-Kumzari,[10] a dhow-builder, showed me some features of the *battīl* which have disappeared from more recently-developed types. I was familiar with much of his explanation on sewn boats but one detail he pointed out raised some hopes in my long search for the link between antiquity and recent times. Wooden boats, like the *badan*, *battīl* and *zārūka*, were completely sewn in the past; today, the only parts to be stitched are the stem and the sternpost timbers (with date-palm fibre), onto the end of the planks, and this contsitutes the frame of the hull. The planks are fastened to the frames (ribs) with iron nails. Sewing, however, is still used to secure the athwartship

8 Underwater archaeology in the Mediterranean shows plentiful evidence of frames put into place after the hull shell; good examples are the Punic Ship, Yassi Ada and Serçe Limani wrecks, see Bass 1972: 50-65, Katzev 1972: 50–1, Van Doorninck 1972: 137-9, Greenhill 1995: 50 and Farrar 1997: 212-3.

9 In particular, ʿAbdallāh (1987) for Qatar, Shihāb (1987) for Yemen and the Red Sea, al-Ḥijjī (1988) for Kuwait, al-Shamlān (1990) for Bahrain; also, the dictionary of nautical terms compiled by the late al-Rūmī (1996) is an extremely useful tool for the study of shipbuilding and Arab seafaring.

10 Interviewed on 25 November 1996.

timber (or the beams) to the sides of the hull. These beams in fact lock the sides together, a technique that was apparently found in the ancient Mediterranean and medieval northern Europe (Hanseatic cogs, for example).[11] 'The projecting beams are there to hold the planking in a secure position', explained Zaid Ahmed, 'in doing so, they help to hold the shape of the hull'. The builder then fits the frames and fastens them to the planking. Indeed, the process of building a boat in this fashion explains the shell construction method and why Gulf Arabs, for generations, have adopted it.

Size and tonnage

The building season starts some time in October and ends in early June, often earlier if the weather is too hot. A dhow can take anything from 3 months – a *shūʿī* for instance – to 8 or 9 months. Of course, it depends how many carpenters are hired to do the job. For example, one 30-year-old shipwright, Naseem Mubarak Al-Araimi from Sur[12] informed me that a small *shūʿī* takes three months to build with at least 4 to 5 carpenters involved. Smaller boats such as a 40-foot racing *jālbūt* in al-Butteen boatyard in Abu Dhabi would take six weeks to construct, involving 4 workers.

Dhows come in different sizes depending on their type and function. Precise information on length of dhows and cargo weight was hard to obtain. It is true that Gulf Arabs and Iranians do not keep registers, or if they do, I have never seen any. I discussed the matter of weight capacity with two Suri *nākhōda*s, Shaykh Nasser Hamad Khilfan al-Bilal al Makheini and Shaykh Ali bin Musallam bin Jumaa al-Alawi,[13] and confirmed what other *nākhōda*s had informed me: large dhows such as the *ghanja*, *baghla* and *būm* could carry a cargo from 100 to 400 tons, *sanbūq*s varied from 70 to 400 tons, and a *badan*, from 30 to 70 tons. The older generation did not speak of tons but of the number of sacks a dhow was capable of carrying. One term used in Khor Fakkan, Ajman, and Umm al Quwain was *jūniyye* (*yūnya* in Sur) for 'a sack of rice' or sometimes another food product. The following information was given to me by Ahmed Salih Husain al-Hamash (known to the locals as Bu Hamash),[14] a captain from Khor Fakkan, and Saeed Mohammed Rashid al-Fanna al-Araimi, an experienced *nākhōda* from Sur,[15] who dealt with trade and customs for some fifty years: the largest craft such as the *kūtiyya*, *baghla*

11 I am told by Tom Vosmer in a personal communication (3 September 1999), that this is a practice which still prevails with small types of craft in south and south-east Asia.

12 Interviewed on 3 December 1996.

13 Interviewed on 11 April 1998.

14 Interviewed on 17 April 1996.

15 Interviewed on 12 April 1998.

and the *būm* could carry between 4,000 and 5,000 sacks,[16] a *sanbūq* about 3,000 sacks, a *ʿuwaysī* some 1,000 sacks, a small *shūʿī* from 100 to 300 sacks and a small *badan*, 50 to 100 sacks. Saeed Mohammed roughly estimated that 10 sacks weighed a ton; thus, 4,000 sacks would be about 400 tons. In Kuwait, early this century, bales of dates were used to figure out the cargo capacity: *baghla*s had an average carrying capacity of 2,000[17] and *shūʿī*s, 1,200; coasters would carry fewer, some 700 bales (Lorimer 1986, II c: 1053). A dhow-builder could tell the capacity of the ship if he were given the length of the keel; for example, a 66-foot keel on a *būm* would be about 300 tons or 3,000 bales of dates. On the basis of how many bags of rice, or bales of dates a dhow could carry, taxes were levied at the customs accordingly.

Most builders hardly ever give exact measurements of a dhow. They speak in terms of length, that is from bow to stern, in the Gulf, while in south Oman and the Dhofar region on the Arabian Sea coast, the calculation is done on the length of the *hīrāb* (*bīṣ* or *bīs* in the Gulf), 'keel'. You often get the measurement in *dhirāʿ* ([pl *adhruʿ*] = 1.64 feet or approximately 18 inches), being a forearm's length (or a cubit); for example a *sanbūq* has a keel of approximately 25 *dhirāʿ* (about 41 feet), a *badan* from 15 to 25 *dhirāʿ* (25-41 feet) and a *hūrī* from 6 to 8 *dhirāʿ* (10-13 feet).

The unit of measurement for the cargo ships in the main ports of the Gulf and Oman is the ton (s *ṭunn*, pl *aṭnān*). Customs officers talk about cargo capacity in register tons (*ṭunn musajjal*) but rarely about tons deadweight of a dhow. I could not find a way to determine either the depth of hold of a cargo ship or its draught at sea. The LBD (Length, Beam, Draught) formula produced by Prins (1965: 88), largely depends on the ship type and gives an approximate tonnage figure. For a 50-ton *jahāzī* the tonnage is calculated by applying:

$$\frac{\text{Length x Beam x Draught (in feet)}}{130} = \text{tons deadweight}$$

The dhows are usually measured in cubic capacity. In measuring the length it is not taken on the Load Water Line as it would be when measuring

16 I think Hess's figure of 50,000 sacks of rice, quoted by Kindermann (1934: 13), on board a *būm* he saw early the twentieth century is an exaggeration. It should read 5,000. Again, in connection with a *shūʿī* Hess claimed that it could transport roughly 30,000 sacks (ibid, 52); this could not be right, I am told by my older informants. One other measure mentioned is *irdabb* (pl *arādib*), a dry measure, but this, I was told, is Egyptian.

17 Villiers (1948: 410) sailed on a *būm* carrying 2,000 date packages (estimated 150 tons), with a crew of 28. The vessel's cargo was full of salt and rice and it carried some 120 to 180 passengers.

displacement tonnage (ibid). The length is taken on deck, from the forward deck at the stem under the bowsprit, to the after side of the sternpost; the beam is measured to the outside of the hull-planking (at maximum point) and the draught of its hold, below the main deck. The hull measurement of a 48-ton *jahāzī* is: length, 60 feet x beam, 15 feet x draught, 7 feet, divided by 130. If we take a 216-ton *būm* with an LBD measurement of length 97 feet, beam 29 feet and draught 10 feet, the tons deadweight is calculated by dividing the product of these three data by 130.[18] I am told by the shipwright Yousef Al Majid of Doha, Qatar,[19] that with trading vessels between 100 to 300 tons, the master-builder has to consider the economics. If the trading dhow is smaller than 100 tons, it is unlikely to be efficient and seaworthy on ocean crossings because it would be unable to carry a lot of weight and consequently would be expensive to run. On the other hand, to build a dhow larger than 100 tons is costly;[20] in addition, the shipowner has other annual expenses to worry about, namely, the cost incurred of annual maintenance.

Tools

My first impression on walking through the doorway of the shipyard[21] was the smell of timber, mainly teak and the powerful odour of shark oil that filled the air. All sizes of wood lay on the floor while the sawdust and chips of wood blended into the sand (illus. 41). Untidy piles of adzed branches of trees, *jangalī* 'jungle wood',[22] lay about here and there while stacks of timber for all parts of the dhow are generally ordered for easy access. I was welcomed in all the shipyards I visited with true Arab hospitality, the builders were open-minded enough to share the secrets of their trade. Enthusiastic though I was to start collecting information, it was considered polite on my part to sit down on the mat with my legs folded for long periods while sipping bitter

18 Villiers (1962: 114) measured a 115-ton *būm* as follows: Load Water Line length, 85 feet; Light Waterline length, 76 feet; length of keel, 63 feet; length of sternpost to bow, 104 feet; extreme beam, 29 feet 3 inches; depth of hold 9 feet 6 inches.

19 Interviewed on 19 April 1992.

20 Discussing building costs with Tom Vosmer (28 March 1998), he told me that they increase roughly by the cube of the length, ie a 40-foot boat costs about eight times as much as a 20-foot ($40 \div 20 = 2$, $2^3 = 8$).

21 I did not hear any Gulf Arab referring to a specific word for shipbuilding yard; the commonest was *wirsha* (pl *wirash*) from English 'workshop'; but in the Emirates I heard *mūshara* or *muwarsha*, the first being from *washar* (*yashir*) 'to saw (wood)' (al-Zabīdī 1974, XIV: 362; De Landberg 1920–42, III: 2923), the second term is a hybrid structure of Ar *mūshara* and Eng 'workshop'. The Yemenite verb *washar* (*yūshir*) 'to build a ship', as noted by Serjeant (1974: 87), does not occur in the Dhofari repertoire.

22 A few 'jungle wood' types are: *Artocarpus lakoocha* 'jackfruit', *Acacia arabica* 'babul' and *Thespia populnea* 'portia'.

41
All sizes of wood are found in the dhow-building yard, Sur, Oman

coffee followed by several cups of *shāy* (tea) from a kettle boiling on a fire which blazed with scraps of wood (*qishbār*) collected from the yard. I had to do all the explanation as to who I was and why I was studying boats. The introductions served to bring us to a mutual level of understanding before I started my interviews. The trade of carpentry is an inherited one passed on from father to son. In Sur, boat-building is a family affair and while teenagers go to school in the morning they are in the yard shortly after *ʿaṣr* (afternoon prayers) with their father, learning the family trade. Indians and sometimes Pakistanis had been hired as carpenters in all the shipyards I visited in the Gulf. They are the finest carpenters I have ever seen, and, like their masters, work solely by eye and experience. Their work is supervised by a highly experienced master craftsman whom they address as *ustād* or *ustādh* (pl *istādiyya* or *istādhiyya*). The dhow-builder in the Gulf is called the *gallāf* or *jallāf* (pl *galālīf* or *jalālīf*),[23] and is assisted by the *ẓarrāb* (pl *ẓarrābīn*), a carpenter who fastens planks with nails, the *imzawrī* who carries the timber

23 The skilled artisan is CA *qallāf* and *qilāfa* is the abstract noun for the profession of shipbuilding. CA *qalf* is the practice of 'securing the ship's timbers with palm fibres' (al-Zabīdī 1987, XXIV: 283). Another CA usage is *ṣāniʿ al-sufun* (pl *ṣunnāʿ l-sufun*). A place where dhow-builders meet in Kuwait is the 'Dīwāniyya l-Galālīf' (Dhow-builders' Centre), established in Kuwait in 1982. It is open to all builders and members of their families. I have conducted some of my interviews with dhow-builders and seamen there during my second visit to Kuwait in May 1998.

from the yard to the ship, and the *iwlēid* (CA *walad*), the boy who collects the scraps of wood to use on the fire for cooking.

The tools are rudimentary. On some of my early visits to a boatyard in Kuwait in December 1984 and February 1985 I observed logs being cut into planks by a *migsām umm idēn* (pl *magāsim umm idēn*), pit saw; this would take several days of concentrated skill, sometimes in intense heat. Pit saws were in use in Sur until recently. Where nails are fastened to the planks, the carpenter bores holes using an electric drill. Some shipwrights like Abdalla Naseeb Al-Araimi, an experienced master-builder for thirty years in Sur,[24] uses a *migdāḥ* (pl *magādiḥ*) or *majdāḥ* (pl *majādiḥ*), a bow drill, muscle-powered, to bore holes for the iron fastenings.[25] When showing how the bow drill worked he said: 'an electric drill, though efficient and quicker, may burn the wood, and worse, damage it; the *migdāḥ*, truly, is slower but cleaner and safer'. The *migdāḥ* consists of a piece of round wood, cylinder-shaped, with a metal drill fixed to one end, and a bow. The string of the bow (*gōz* or *jōz*) is looped around a groove carved around the middle of the wood. The carpenter moves the bow backwards and forwards, operating it like a violin, while pressing the point of the drill to bore a hole (illus. 42). With an adze (s *juddūm*, *judūm* or *gudūm*, pl *jadāyim* or *gadāyim*), a thin arching blade set at right angles to the handle, a carpenter fairs off the planks with gentle strokes (illus. 43). In addition to these tools the carpenters use a hammer (s *maṭraga*, pl *maṭārig*),[26] chisel (s *mingar*, pl *manāgir*),[27] hand saw (s *minshār umm idēn*, pl *manāshīr umm idēn*),[28] plane (*randa*),[29] vise (s *milzama*, pl *malāzim*),[30] auger (*ghawār* or *kōbār*) and pincers (*shabāṣa*). Sawing manually is still practised; in Sur, I observed carpenters adzing to shape, every piece of 'jungle wood' with great accuracy. Except for the introduction of electric saws, not much has changed in traditional Arab

24 Interviewed on 3 December 1996.

25 There are three types of bow drills: (a) *migdāḥ tifshīt* with two points at the tip of the drill, (b) *migdāḥ taysīr* for wider gaps, (c) *migdāḥ būrīma* for narrow gaps.

26 Three types of *maṭraga*: (a) *maṭraga umm nīr*, ordinary hammer, (b) *maṭraga umm shaghwa*, claw, (c) *maṭraga khashbiyya*, wooden hammer; the latter is used in Bahrain. I also heard the Indian carpenters in the Amiriyyah boatyard in Doha, Qatar using the word *hamar* (of Hindi or English origin?) for an ordinary hammer.

27 Also *mafrāṣ* in Kuwait, *izmīl* in Qatar; two other types of *mingar* are: *mingar wilāyti*, a chisel with changing blades from a quarter of an inch to four inches and *mingar kalfāt*, a caulking iron.

28 Other hand saws are: (a) ميشارة قبّا or منشار قبّا or منشارجبّا a large saw, (b) ميشارةتصريح or منشار تشريح a medium saw, (c) ميشارة العودة, a small saw, (d) ميشارة ناعمة or منشار تنعيم and زبن a very small saw for carving wood, see ʿAbdallāh 1987, III: 165 and al-Shamlān 1990: 36.

29 Other names are: *dayl al-fār* (in Sur), *kishtir* [?] (in Qatar) and *ṭarḥa* (a long plane).

30 Also known by the older seamen as سكنجة، هواسة or سكني , see al-Shamlān (1990: 38).

42
The carpenter using the *migdāḥ* (bow drill) to bore holes

43
Fairing off the plank with a *juddūm* (adze)

tools; the axe, adze, saw, chisel and auger are recorded as tools which were used for building Punic ships though Farrar (1997: 212–3) thinks that the Punic builders must have also had a plane to trim rough edges. The Gulf Arabs rarely use metrication. They measure in feet (s *qadam*, pl *aqdām*) and inches (s *būṣa*, pl *būṣāt*) but they also calculate sizes by *shibir* (pl *ashbār*), span of the hand, which is 9 inches, and by *dhirā*ᶜ (lit 'a forearm'). I learnt from the Kuwaiti dhow-builders that nails to fasten the planks are manufactured locally by ironsmiths in Bahrain and Kuwait, as are hinges for doors and gudgeons and pintles for rudders. Some Indian carpenters told me, however, that iron nails from India are preferred because they are considered harder. The nails have names and are used for different purposes; of course, they come in different lengths (illus. 44): *chāwiya*[31] 16 inches or longer, are used for the keel; *mismār* (pl *masāmīr*) *jasad* 12 inches, for decking and planking; *mismār maghlaṭānī* 10 inches, for planking in general;[32] *mismār bū shibir* 9 inches (a span); *mismār bū fitir* 7 inches (small span); *mismār ṣaff kibīr* 5 inches; *lingūtī* (< [?] Port *linguete*),[33] a rivet 2 to 3 inches long, for joining knees and beams; *mismār satḥa* 3 inches, for decking only, and *mismār saḥāra* 2 inches, a small-headed nail.[34] I could not count the number of holes they bore in one large dhow; I am told that 800 to 1000 is quite possible. After the holes are driven into the planks, the workers chisel out with an auger, a shallow hole for the nail head so that it can be countersunk (illus. 45). The long thin nails are driven (bored) right through the planks and the frames (or ribs). I asked Yousef Al Majid[35] why Gulf Arabs use iron nails rather than the galvanized type which last longer. 'Iron is firmer and more durable. We carefully wrap our iron nails in oiled fibre before they are bored', said he, 'thus sealing them off against rust' (illus. 46). It may seal them to some extent. Yet I saw thirty-year-old dhows with rusty nails, in boatyards all along the Gulf coast. Howarth (1977: 79), an experienced boat-builder, is right to say that caulking on iron nails soon wears off and would allow the vessel to be badly damaged. Rusty heads are, as Howarth put it, 'a blemish on the beautiful surface of the teak'. Severin and Awad (1985: 201), having experienced how rusty nails in warm saline conditions eat away the surrounding timber, argue that the only way to salvage the dhow is to replace the iron nails or abandon it. Like several other Gulf builders, Yousef Al Majid sees no danger with caulked iron nails: 'if dhows have a regular maintenance at least every eight months they should

31 *Chāwiya* (pl *chāwiyāt*); cf Leb جويط or برنيه (al-Rūmī 1996: 80).
32 Al-Shamlān 1990: 35.
33 Da Silva nd: 976 and Johnstone and Muir 1964: 319; see also al-Ḥijjī 1988: 387.
34 See Johnstone and Muir 1964: 320 and ᶜAbdallāh 1987, III: 163.
35 Interviewed on 19 April 1992.

enjoy a longer life', explained the master-builder. I learnt only recently that galvanized nails are much more expensive than iron nails. In any case, clenching would damage the galvanizing.

44
Various sizes of nails from 2 to 16 inches in length (photo courtesy of Rainer Hartel)

45
With the *ghawār* (auger) the carpenter chisels out a shallow hole for the nail head to countersink

46
Wrapping nails in oiled fibre

Construction of the *būm*

I have wandered around in shipyards all along the Gulf coast observing closely how dhows are built. Arab ship-masters use the rule of thumb methods of tradition, often giving no explanation as to why things are done one way and not another, whereas European builders follow plans and drawings scrupulously. This does not suggest in any way an inferiority of technique on the part of Gulf Arabs, for indeed many of their dhows are sturdy, seaworthy and handsome craft. Kuwait was famed for dhow-building, and first-class vessels were built there over many years.[36] I watched a few dhows under construction during my field trips and was able to collect information on building a *būm* (the keel's length was 90 feet, the prow 28 feet and the stern 30 feet long) during my first field trip in 1985, from two Kuwaiti master-builders, Hasan Abd al-Rasool and Khalil bin Rashid and their partner builders.[37] Subsequently I went back and forth to other shipwrights

36 CDRAD-IOR R/15/1/504, 1927, p 13.

37 Interviewed on 12, 21, 26 December 1984 and 14, 21 and 28 February 1985. On parts of dhow I have consulted al-Dujaylī's two articles 'Asmāʾ mā fī l-safīna' and 'Adawāt al-safīna' (1912c and 1912d) both cited frequently by Johnstone and Muir (1964); I have cited the latter in this chapter. I have also consulted al-Ḥijjī's (1988) *Ṣināʿat al-sufun al-shirāʿiyya fi l-Kuwayt* (1988), an informative work on the construction of a *būm*, the one of its kind; Grosset-Grange's *Glossaire nautique arabe ancien et moderne de l'océan indien* (1993), a

to clarify some technical data I had recorded in my field notes. However, my interest lay primarily in the language of the parts of a dhow. Much of what I was told applied to other types of dhow, with a few exceptions, namely: the trading vessel *battīl* in Doha (Qatar), trading or fishing *sanbūq* in Dubai, and fishing *shūʿī* in Ajman and Sur. Some terminology and techniques varied, not unexpectedly, though in general it must be said, they were common to all types, depending of course on the size and shape of the hull.[38]

The keel, stem and sternposts

Most of the dhows I saw under construction were built under cover of a sack-rag or palm tree roofing, supported by wooden poles or strong bamboos. The tent-like roofing is high, providing, on very hot days, a cool area for the builders and carpenters as well as for visitors who come to look around. The yards were filled with piles of massive seasoned logs.

At the beginning of the construction of a dhow the master-builder orders one of the boys to clear the area. A new tent is set up, but only when an old one needs replacing. The keel (*bīṣ* or *bīs*)[39] is laid first. The wood, of the jungle (Ar *jangalī* < Hin) type,[40] is normally kept under sea water to protect it from splitting as a result of the intense heat that hits Kuwait during the summer months from June to September. There would be several long pieces of wood lying in water and the builder examines the wood carefully to make sure it is strong and straight enough.[41] The wood for the keel having been chosen, it is carried and laid on building blocks, called *ṭuʿūm* (s *ṭaʿm*).[42] The horizontal level of the wood is checked with a spirit level. After the wood is squared off, the master-builder draws a middle line on the wood using a string and chalk; into each end of the keel a nail is lightly hammered, each positioned carefully opposite the other in a straight line (illus. 47). This done,

comprehensive dictionary with valuable notes, though not always reliable on phonetic representation; and finally, al-Rūmī's *Muʿjam al-muṣṭalaḥāt al-baḥriyya fī l-Kuwayt* (1996), is, indeed, an excellent dictionary of parts of a dhow with an attempt to include alternative terms used in Lebanon, Egypt and Tunisia. In all instances where technical terms quoted from Arabic sources had no vocalization I have maintained the Arabic script.

38 The reader is referred to a table of parts of a *jālbūt* in al-Shamlān 1975-8, II: 569, of the parts of a *ghanja* in Hawkins 1977: 87 and *battīl* in ʿAbdallāh 1987, III: 175–209.

39 Possibly of Hindi origin; SA and Dh *hīrāb*; see also Johnstone and Muir 1964: 303, al-Ḥijjī 1988: 377; cf Egy and Tun مرينة ; Leb بريم (al-Rūmī 1996: 32).

40 The *Terminalia alata*, *Terminalia coriacea* 'Indian laurel', of brown colour, with a height of 93 feet, is the ideal wood for the keel, see al-Ḥijjī 1988: 53; also Hawkins 1977: 40, 99.

41 For the *battīl* the keel consists of two parts scarfed together; the *bīṣ* in this case is the forward part, larger than the *kwēsiyya*, the latter part (Johnstone and Muir 1964: 303).

42 Cf Egy درا فيل ; Leb فرشات ، فرشة ; Tun كرسي (al-Rūmī 1996: 65).

the builder rubs the string with chalk and marks the line. Then, a carpenter carves a narrow groove along this line in case the drawing fades away. It looked fairly simple to me. Only when the work progressed could I see the importance of this middle line – the balance of the vessel.

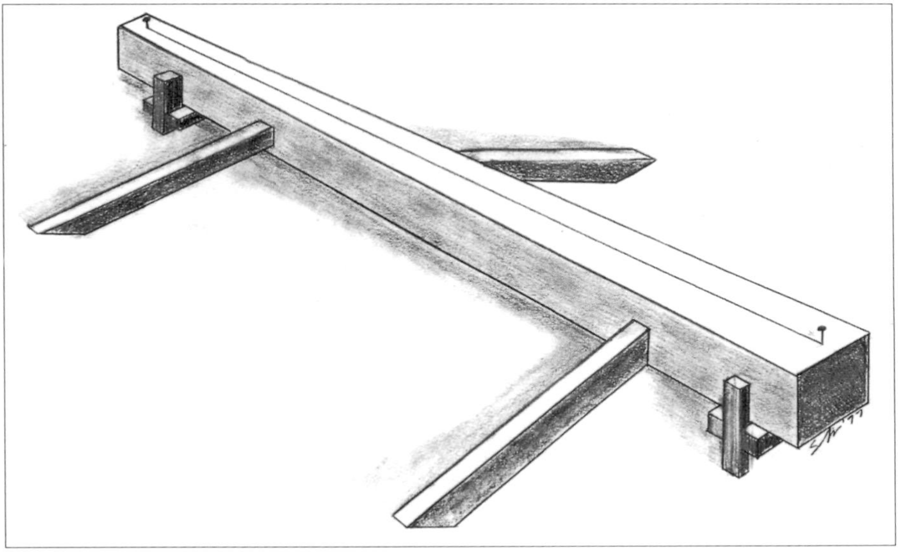

47

A middle line on the squared-off wood is drawn and two nails are positioned at either end of the keel

Many old superstitions existed in the past around the early stages of building the dhow. One story I have heard relates how the dhow-builder takes every precaution to protect the new keel from the evil eye once it is laid on building blocks. A night watchman is hired to guard the keel because it was firmly believed that if a barren wife leaps over it, before the planking is high enough to prevent her, something terrible will happen to the ship; it would not be fit to face tempestuous weather and would subsequently sink. If, however, the barren wife manages to cross over the wood keel she will give birth to a male child. This traditional belief like many others preserved in the memories of the older seamen, has become a thing of the past.

Setting up the stem and sternposts comes next (illus. 48). The wood is usually of teak (*sāj or sāy* < Hin *sagawan*).[43] The *būm*'s stempost, called *mēl*

43 *Tectona grandis* 'teak', a golden colour, is strong and durable. It has an oily membrane called *dasam* (in Kuwait), which makes its timber water resistant. The tree reaches a height of 133 feet.

48
The early stages of construction – setting up the stem and the sternposts (photo courtesy of Rainer Hartel)

is-sidr,[44] is a long piece of wood which will be positioned at an angle as we shall see. I asked several master-builders to what purpose was this projection of the wood; none could say why they did it. The stempost is squared off. On the side of the post touching the keel, two parallel lines, some four inches from the middle line, are drawn half-way up. Each line is rabbeted, making a groove (2 inches wide and 2 inches deep), called *wādira* (pl *wādirāt*),[45] and designed to receive the sides of the garboard strakes, as we shall see later in this Chapter. The master-builder then, saws this side of the timber post at an angle of 48 degrees (or 8 *khann*s, as I will explain below) and sets it up so it leans forward on the keel and is one foot in from it. In order to temporarily hold the stempost, two large poles standing on the ground are fastened to it and a large nail is driven into the keel. I then watched the master-builder closely as he calculated how far the stempost should lean forward. He took a *handāza* (< Per *āndāz*),[46] which is a quadrant inscribed in degrees with a plumb line (*bild*)[47] attached; there are 15 *khann*s (pl *akhnān*), each divided into 6 degrees, totalling 90 degrees. Hasan Abd al-Rasool then placed the quadrant

44 GA *mēl* (pl *amyāl*); SA and Ir *mīl* (Johnstone and Muir 1964: 321); see also al-Ḥijjī 1988: 388; cf Tun قوس (al-Rūmī 1996: 92). The forward end of the vessel is generally called in the Gulf *mugaddam* or *mujaddam*.

45 See al-Ḥijjī 1988: 389.

46 Steingass 1977: 108.

47 A cord having a lead (shaped like a 'top') weight attached to one end, used to determine the true vertical or perpendicular line.

beside the stempost while the carpenters moved the wood slowly forward and backward until the required angle was reached, 8 *khanns* or close (illus. 49). If an imaginary perpendicular line is drawn from the joint points of the keel and the stempost from point (a) to a point (b), the angle from points (c) to (d) would measure 8 *khanns* and the angle from points (e) to (f) would be 7 *khanns* (illus. 50). The plumb line determines whether both the stempost and the keel are lined up perpendicularly. This done, the builder sets to work chiselling-out a *guful* ('tongue') from the stem in order for it to fit into the keel. This is another job that demands a fair amount of patience and accuracy. With a *galam* (a compass), a line is drawn on the wood of the stempost from the lower end, ie from points (a) to (b). Opening the *galam* almost 2 inches wide, the master-builder draws a straight line from points (c) to (d) and then from points (d) to (a) (illus. 51). The same lines are drawn on the other side of the wood. The carpenter will also chisel out a 2 inch groove in the keel for the stempost to fit in position. The plumb line is applied to check that the middle position is maintained. The stempost is tenoned into the keel and the joint is fixed with a rivet. To set up the *mēl it-tifr* (sternpost),[48] the same procedure is applied; the angle, however, will be 7 *khanns*. If an engine is to be installed inside the ship, a curved *karwa* is constructed at the stern, to which a shaft and propeller is later fitted.

49

The stempost leans forward on the keel when the building of the dhow is completed

48 The term *tifr* (or *tufar*, see al-Rifāʿī 1985: 66) is perhaps an English borrowing, *taffereel* ('panel', diminutive of *tafel*, 'table'; originally *taffeleel*), 'the upper part of the flat portion of a ship's stern above the transom, usually ornamented with carvings etc.' (OED 1982, II: 3220). Kemp (1992: 854) notes that the term *taffrail* meaning 'the after rail at the stern of a ship' did formerly refer to the curved wooden top of the East Indiaman. It does seem that the Arabic *tifr* was borrowed from India at the time when nineteenth century Gulf ship owners or timber merchants frequented Beypore shipyards where *baghla*s and *ghanja*s were being constructed before they were introduced to the Arabian/Persian Gulf.

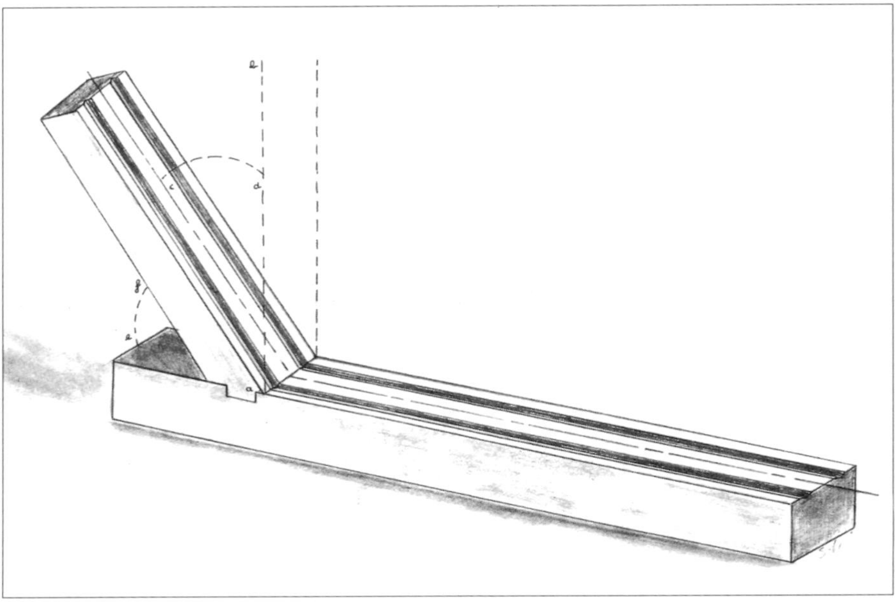

50
Measuring the *khanns* (degrees) from the joint points of the keel and the stempost

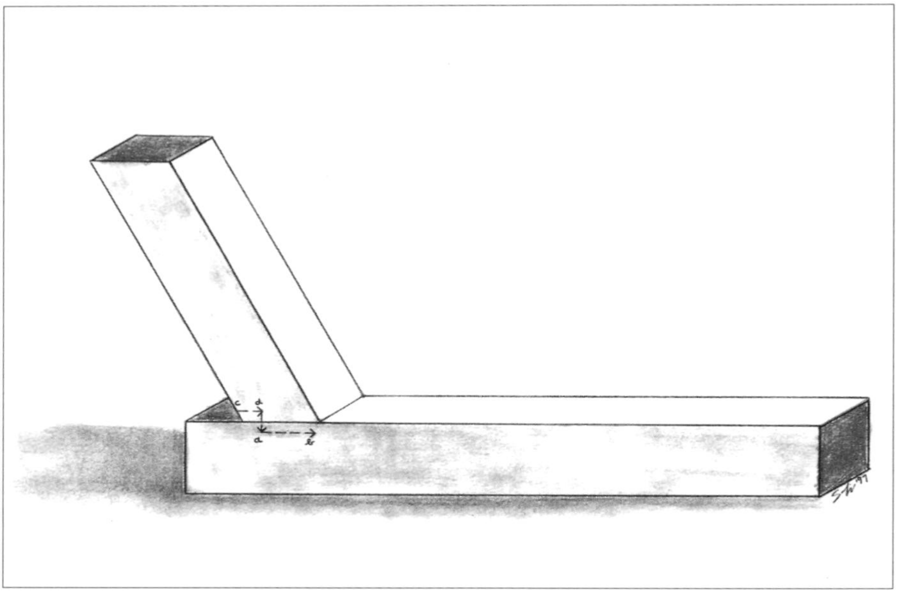

51
Fitting the stempost in the keel at an angle

I asked the master-builder, Yousef Al Majid of Doha (Qatar), how builders would know that the posts were in perfect line with the keel. He replied that traditionally the shipwright would pin a string on top of the middle of the stemhead and run it along to the other end pinned also on the middle of the sternpost. Attached to the middle of the string would be a plumb line which should fall right on a middle point of the keel. At this stage, some adjustments would be necessary until all woods are in line.

Fitting in the garboard strakes

The hull is constructed from teak wood. Seasoned teak ordinarily came from Malabar and has always proved to be the ideal marine timber because it does not split, crack or shrink in seawater. Several people informed me that teak wood is highly resistant to decay, an important factor because the Gulf waters are very salty, and salt, as well as sea worm, has always been thought to destroy wood. Recent findings, however, have shown that salt is a good wood preservative. Salt water is much better than fresh water for preventing rot. The salt carriers of North America, for example, were renowned for their longevity.[49] As we shall see below, the dhow's hull was treated with lime below the waterline and the planking was caulked with coir treated with fish oil.

Before planking starts, grooves are chiselled out of the keel 2 inches deep and 2 inches wide, set parallel with the grooves made in the stem and sternposts. One technical difference I noticed from the European and Mediterranean methods is that the first garboard strake, what the Gulf Arabs call the *mālich* (pl *mawālich*),[50] is not nailed from the outside into a keelson but rather is rabbeted into the keel, the stem and the sternpost. I was told that preferably the *mālich* should be one piece of plank, 2 to 3 inches thick, with no faults.[51] The planks are from *manṭīj* (< Hin)[52] and *sāj*. Each plank is a complete longitudinal run from stem to stern. The carpenter cuts the

49 Private communication from Tom Vosmer, 27 April 2000.

50 CA general term for plank is *lawḥ* (pl *alwāḥ*) (Lane 1984, II: 2679–80); the GA *mālich* is often called *mālich al-awwal* (the first strake), see also Johnstone and Muir 1964: 320, al-Ḥijjī 1988: 387 and Grosset-Grange 1993: 47; cf Egy لوح الملف; Leb لوح النار (al-Rūmī 1996: 86).

51 The *shūʿī*s I saw being constructed in Sur had about three strakes, each one being stapled to the other temporarily. Apparently, this is a technique I was told in Kuwait that goes back to antiquity and I noticed in Sohar the same technique being applied to planks fixed to the gunwales of a *hūrī* in order to increase its freeboard.

52 *Lagerstroemia lanceolata* 'benteak'. In Kuwait I was informed that for the third part (from below) of the dhow, *manṭīj* planks are used while for the rest of the craft (above the waterline) *sāj* wood is preferred, the reason being the *sāj*, unlike the *manṭīj*, is heat resistant and copes well with dryness, see al-Ḥijjī 1988: 52.

ends of the garboard strake at an angle of 8 *khanns* (48 degrees) and 7 *khanns* (42 degrees) respectively, to match the inclination of both erected posts. The edges of three *shaghghārs* (pl *shaghāghīr*) crooks or battens, one metre long, are now nailed temporarily on to the sides of the keel, one placed in the middle, and the other two, one third of the keel length in, from each end. Other crooks called *ṭārī* (pl *ṭawārī*),[53] some half a metre long, are also clamped to the garboard strakes and to the keel, on each side. The crooks are temporary, to hold the planks in position until they are permanently fastened. They are only taken down when the construction of the planks and ribs is completed. Measuring the ends of the garboard strake, cutting and setting it to fit the grooves was by no means an easy task. I watched three workmen holding the *shaghghārs* while bending the garboard strake into position in the grooves with the master-builder guiding them to tilt the strake at an angle of 7 *khanns* (42 degrees). The bottom end of the plank is wrapped up in a cloth dipped in *dāmir* (gum) (< Mal)[54] to protect the wood from sea worms. Next, the Arab dhowbuilder carries on planking the dhow. On top of the first garboard strake comes the *khadd* (pl *khudūd*),[55] consisting of two pieces of timber and tilted further out to the *mālich*, at about 8 *khanns* (48 degrees). The third planking is referred to as the *thālith mālich* which is fitted even further out to the *khadd*, measuring 9 *khanns* (54 degrees) (illus. 52). None of these three are easy to fit, they need a twist and much tapping and hammering is required to get them right on the butts. The dhow's seaworthiness depends on the correct positioning of the planks. Once the three plankings are completed on side (b), seven other planks are fitted in on each side of the keel (illus. 53). The planks will not lie together in a free state; the builder, therefore, puts in a short piece of framing to hold them together and each side is bent into position with a *shaghghār*. The initial planking done, four more strakes are laid reaching up to the waterline; none of these has any name. I remember for the first time seeing a half-built dhow in Kuwait in February 1985, I thought the whole thing was going to collapse until I was reassured by the builder and assistants that this would not happen. Hasan Abd al-Rasool jokingly told me: 'we have been building dhows this way for centuries; I don't see why it should now spring apart and collapse'. Yes, of course! This was a technique that dates back to the times when dhows were sewn together. What we have here is the clinker-building technique in which the builders of sewn craft fastened each plank as they laid it: it is indeed remarkable, as Howarth (1977:

53 See also al-Ḥijjī 1988: 383; cf Leb عيرة (al-Rūmī 1996: 64).

54 A resin derived from various evergreen trees, *Agathis*, of the pine family; the Arab *dāmir* is extracted from East Indian trees, *Hopea shorea*. Cf Egy قلفونية (al-Rūmī 1996: 97).

55 See also Johnstone and Muir 1964: 307 and al-Ḥijjī 1988: 379.

65) pointed out, that Gulf builders today, still follow the same technique with carvel planks 'which are not fastened to each other at all'.

52
The first strakes following the keel (shell-construction method) in Sur, Oman

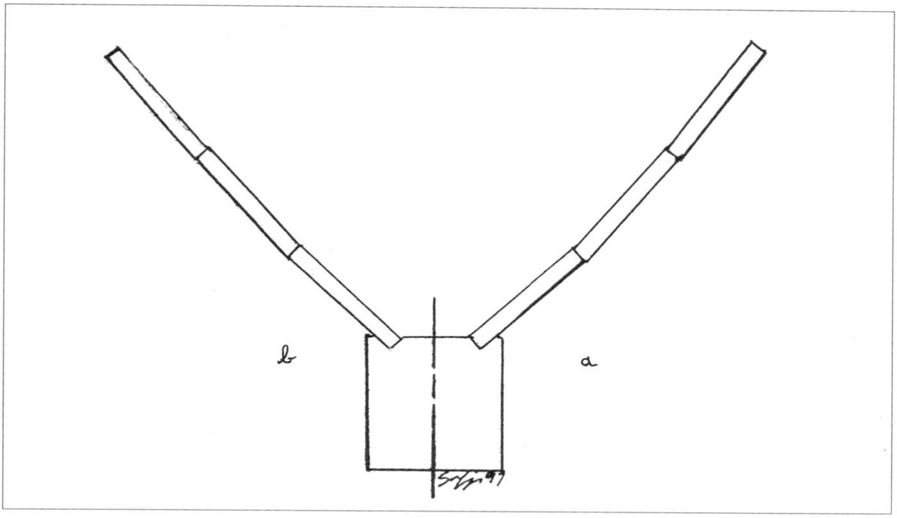

53
Fitting in the garboard strakes

The templates

So far, we have the shell of the *būm*; now for the work inside. First the *ʿaqrab*,[56] a piece of wood some 2 feet long which fastens the stem and sternposts with the joints between the fourth and sixth planking (illus. 54). A long piece of timber called *chaftōh* (keelson) is bolted so as to clamp down the inner edges of the *mālich*, thus preventing any water from entering. The keelson is extended to include two pieces of timber on top of the *ʿaqrab*, forcing the garboard strakes firmly into the grooves. Once more a piece of cloth dipped in *dāmir* is fitted on to each side of the keelson blocking any existing gaps, a job called *kalfāṭ* or *kilfāt* (< [?] Port *calafeto* or *calafate*),[57] ie caulking, which we will see later, on completion of the dhow. The middle line which was drawn on the keel at the beginning of the construction of the dhow is now marked on the keelson with chalk. When the seven planks are laid, gaps appear at the rear of the hull; these are filled by a number of timbers, named *jazrāt* (s *jazra*) (stealers) which are fastened to the planks.

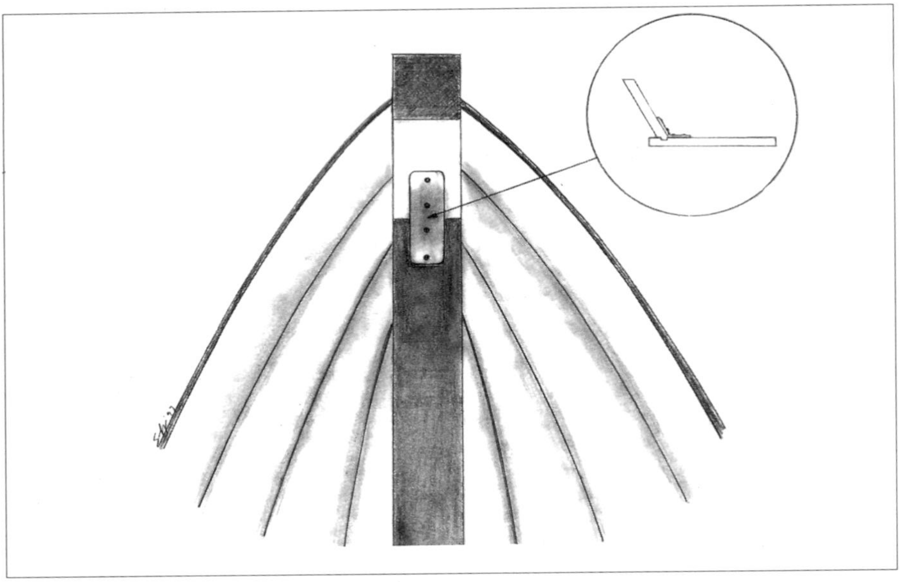

54

Fastening the *ʿaqrab* to the stempost with the joints between the plankings

56 See also al-Ḥijjī 1988: 384; cf Egy and Leb ملقط (al-Rūmī 1996: 67).

57 Note also Arabic *qalfat*, *ghalfat*; an old term, possibly of Indo-European origin (note Ur *kalpattī*), reached Greek via the early Semitic languages, borrowed by the Arabs through Greek, hence the addition of /t/. CA *qallafa* (Form II) 'to caulk' and *qalafa* (Form I) 'to bark (a tree)' (Wehr 1966: 787). See Da Silva nd: 278, Johnstone and Muir 1964: 319, al-Ḥijjī 1988: 386 and Grosset-Grange 1993: 53.

The proportions of the dhow was another intriguing subject. How would an Arab builder calculate the dimensions of a vessel? The figures I was given were all calculated approximately. The builder divides the keel into three equal parts measuring the distance by a piece of string and marking an 'x' with chalk at each dividing point. Simply by the accuracy of his eye the master calculates the width of the dhow in ratio to its length and breadth. For example, for a *būm* with an overall length of 42 feet, width 17 feet and depth 7 feet (from the sheerline to the keel), a builder calculates the dimensions by measuring its breadth (2.5) in proportion to the length (6) and depth (1).[58] I guess it is by sheer instinct that an Arab builder gives his dhow a relatively accurate cross-section. Undoubtedly this is very crucial because, after all, the boat's stability depends on it. It is interesting to note that I found no permanent ballast on the dhows I examined; the *būm* in particular, when it has discharged its cargo, needs some additional weight to give it stability. 'As we lay the strakes', Hasan Abd al-Rasool told me, 'we make sure that the dhow is stable solely by the eye; we adjust planks as the work progresses'. It is difficult to explain it, but there we are, the skill is handed down from father to son. Each dhow is the builder's creation, formed in his own mind and it is the hands of craftsmen that make it.

The shape of the planks is maintained by erecting temporary templates (s *furma*, pl *furmāt* < Port *forma*)[59] against the outside of the hull. Once in position, the templates dictate the shape of the hull. 'Each master owns his own *furma*s', Hasan Abd al-Rasool explained, 'they are not borrowed or sold; in fact they never leave the shipyard'. Of course, templates vary from one ship to another. Production of these templates demands both care and skill

58 The measurements have been recorded by al-Ḥijjī (1988: 97); Howarth (1977: 65-6) gives the following dimensions of *shūʿī*s which he jotted down from a local *gallāf* in Ras al Khaimah:

Length overall	beam	ratio/length/beam
52'	15½'	3.35/1
52'	11'	4.73/1
41'	11'	3.73/1
32'	9'	3.55/1
23'	10'	2.30/1

The variation of ratio, however, could not be determined whether it were planned or purely by chance, as Howarth remarked, for boat-builders would politely avoid giving you such information. On this matter Tom Vosmer wrote to me (27 April 2000): 'A rough rule of thumb is that as length increases, beam or width becomes proportionally less; for example, a small boat will have a LOA (length overall) to beam ratio of 3.1 (approx) while larger vessels can commonly be 6.1. Basically, it comes down to a compromise between stability, speed and capacity'.

59 Da Silva nd: 767, also borrowed in Urdu and Turkish (Johnstone and Muir 1964: 316).

on the part of the carpenters. Seven temporary templates are fixed in position by clamps and rivets (*chāwiya* and *lingūṭī*). The master-builder determines the location of each template,[60] the first being one third from the fore keel, a position known as the *furma d-digil* (the place where the main mast is laid).[61] The two sides of the template are fixed to a wooden horizontal, placed on the keel, and attached to the middle of it by means of a plumb line, the master then calculates the middle point corresponding with that of the keelson. The other template of the *būm* is located on the second third of the keel; this template is known as the *furma kabirt* (< Port *coberta*)[62] and is wider than the first; the extra width being necessary to provide stability in the middle of the ship because of the weight of the merchandise carried. Also because if the ship uses sails, the proportions of the sail area and hull volume must be fairly equally distributed. The third template, *furma l-waṣṭ*, comes higher (by 5 inches) I am told, than the first two (illus. 55). Each dhow is different, so some adjustment is needed until the builder is satisfied with the proportion of the templates laid in position (illus. 56). Having laid down the seven templates required, they are then removed and the carpenter makes copies, each (copy) rib being called *shilmān* (pl *shalāmīn*).[63] The ribs are of the *fanaṣ* (< Hin) type of wood.[64] Nails are then driven through the planks, countersunk and clenched over on the inside of the ribs. All nails are coiled with a wick soaked in *dāmir* or fish oil to prevent water seeping through. With the smaller vessels like the *sanbūq* and *shūʿī*, I noticed that almost all the ribs are crooked branches (ie natural bends of 'jungle wood'), which the workers gather from the back of the yard; they take them onboard and then, after hewing off the outside with an adze, they start to match them to fit the inside shape of the hull

60 For a 40 foot *jālbūt* that I saw being built in al-Butteen, Abu Dhabi in April 1997, there were 8 templates, the middle ones 5 feet apart and those nearer to the fore and aft keel some 3 feet apart. Sultan Al Zaabi (interviewed on 12 April 1997) called these templates with different names: the three in the middle of the boat are known as *rāmī*, all of the same size, the one at the front is called *al-ʿālī*, the template close to the aft keel is the *rigʿa* and the two before it are the *hībeh*.

61 CA *daql*, *daqal* (pl *adqāl*), coll *daqala* 'mast' (Lane 1984, I: 898); *diql*, *diqil* (Tibbetts 1981: 52). pl *daqālāt* (Grosset-Grange 1993: 105); other terms, *id-digil il-ʿōd* (Tun صاري ترانكيت), 'mainmast', *id-digil il-ghulamī* (Tun قلمي مسطر), 'mizen-mast' (Johnstone and Muir 1964: 309, al-Ḥijjī 1988: 380 and al-Rūmī 1996: 46).

62 Da Silva nd: 374 and Johnstone and Muir 1964: 318; see also al-Ḥijjī 1988: 385.

63 Unrecorded elsewhere except the Gulf; of Indian influence, it may be related to Hin (-Skt) *śal*(*āka*), 'small stick of wood, brace, rib' (Glidden 1942: 71); CA *ḍalʿ* (pl *ḍulūʿ*); cf Egy عيدان ; Leb عيدان , عودان (s عود); Tun قربوص , ضلوع (al-Rūmī 1996: 59).

64 *A. Hirsuta*, *A. Integrifolia* 'jackwood', of brown colour, is stiff, strong, and resists heat and dryness. It is often used for the square base of the mast, see al-Ḥijjī 1988: 54; Hawkins 1977: 58.

(illus. 57). This might take a number of days. The master-builder rigorously inspects the shape of each rib and monitors closely where each is positioned in the hull before the workers finally fasten them to the planks. Between one *shilmān* and another, a *ʿuṭfa* (pl *ʿuṭaf*),[65] a naturally grown floor rib almost v-shaped, is fitted on top of the keelson with a huge clench (*chāwiya*) driven right through the keel (illus. 58). All dhows would have these v-shaped floor timbers scarfed to futtocks, to form alternate ribs of the hull (illus. 59). 'Once the planking of the hull is fastened to the frames [ribs]', remarked Abdalla Naseeb Al-Araimi, a dhow-builder in Sur,[66] 'you cannot make any changes'. He also told me that the master-builder has to be absolutely sure that the templates are measured correctly before any copies are made because, he continued, 'any mistake can lead to errors difficult to correct later on during the construction of the vessel, and, needless to say, [would be] costly'.

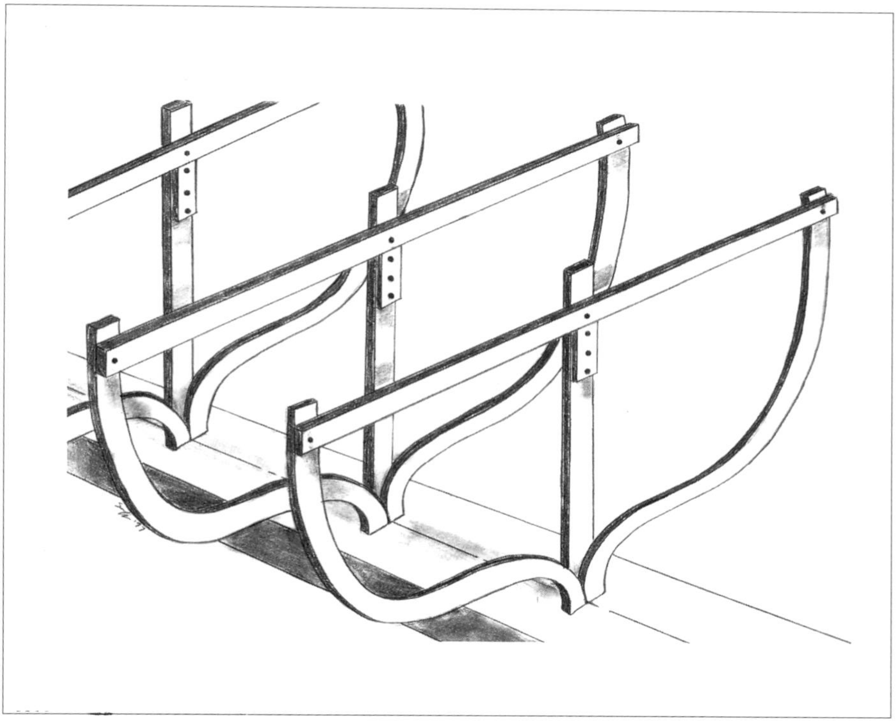

55
The middle template, *furma l-wasṭ*

65 See also Johnstone and Muir 1964: 315 and al-Ḥijjī 1988: 383; Grosset-Grange (1993: 149) has s *ʿaṭfa*, pl *ʿuṭuf*.

66 Interviewed on 3 December 1996.

56
The carpenter holds the *shaghghār* and, with the help of another carpenter, bends the strakes into position and adjusts them accordingly in proportion to the templates

57
Layout of the *furmas* (templates) giving shape to the hull of a *shūʿī*, Umm al Quwain, United Arab Emirates

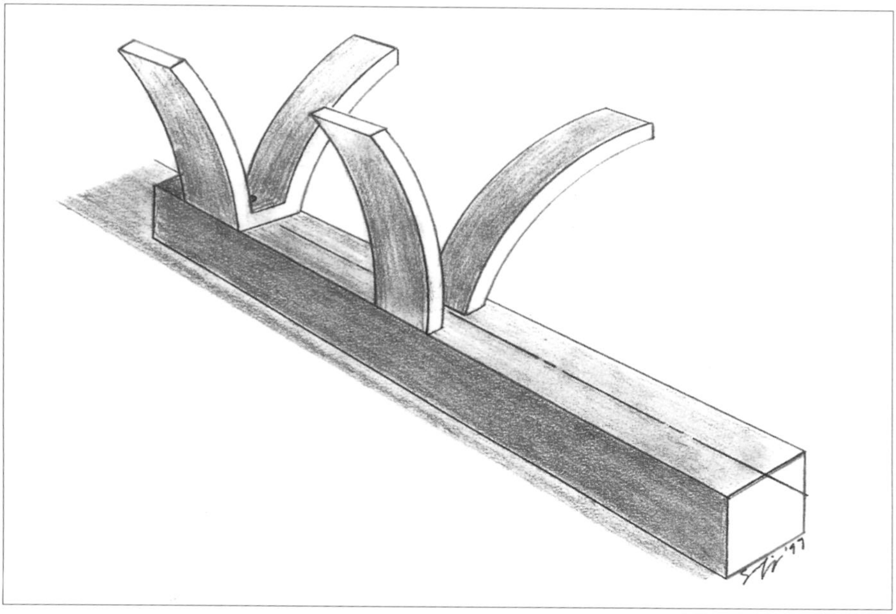

58
The ribs fitted to the keel alternate between the *shilmān* and *ʿuṭfa* (v-shape)

59
Crooked branches of *jangalī* wood are carefully chosen and positioned inside the hull (photo courtesy of Rainer Hartel)

Other planking

The skeleton of the dhow is now completed. On the outside the workers fit in one more plank, called *kamar* or *kamir* (< Per and/or Ur),[67] which is the waterline wale. More pieces of timber (*ṭawārī*) are temporarily nailed to the planks to secure their positions and for shaping the hull. The work of planking continues in sequence; the ordinary hull planks some 2 inches thick are narrowed at the bow and stern. Onto the *kamar*, five wales (s *manẓara*, pl *manāẓir*)[68] are bolted to the sides; they are positioned below the gunwale and are often known in the West as rubbing strakes. An extra strake, the *gēṭān* (only found on *būm*s, *baghla*s and *ghanja*s),[69] is added on top of the *manẓara*. At the final stage, about six upper strakes, each called *tirrīch* (pl *tirrīchāt*),[70] are bolted to the ribs; they serve to protect the merchandise and sailors from falling off the deck. The Indian carpenters now fasten a number of stringers to the frames; these are designed to strengthen the frames by holding them firm in the fore-and-aft line. They also act to add longitudinal strength and reduce hogging. First, the carpenters start with the lowest stringer, the *naʿāsh*,[71] next to the keelson, to prevent water from entering the bottom. The *naʿal* (pl *nuʿūl*)[72] is the next, which is almost 6 inches in width, followed by eight more stringers, called *ḥzāmāt* (s *ḥzām*),[73] 'belts', laid across the ribs, two feet apart (illus. 60). The number of *ḥzām*s I observed varied between three and eight depending on the size of the craft; for example, a *shūʿī* I observed in Sur, took six. Practically all the inner hull planking was put on at the same time as that on the outer hull.

67 Johnstone and Muir 1964: 319. Per *kamar*, 'the middle of anything; the waist' (Steingass 1977: 1048-9) and Ur *kamar*, 'waist loin' (Qureshi nd: 496). According to Grosset-Grange (1993: 48) the *kamar* on some dhows is found lower than the 'waist', while with others it is placed higher. There is no indication as to which dhows he was referring; see also al-Ḥijjī 1988: 386.

68 This strake is much lighter than the one you find in the West (Grosset-Grange 1993: 48), which perhaps explains why the Gulf Arabs called it *manẓara* (< *naẓara*, 'to gaze, glance'), purely for decorative purposes; see also Johnstone and Muir 1964: 321 and al-Ḥijjī 1988: 388.

69 See also Johnstone and Muir 1964: 318 and al-Ḥijjī 1988: 385; *gītān* and *qiṭān* (Grosset-Grange 1993: 47); cf Egy حزام الوقاية ; **Leb** الخيزرانة (al-Rūmī 1996: 79).

70 See also Johnstone and Muir 1964: 305, al-Ḥijjī 1988: 378 and Grosset-Grange 1993: 47; cf Egy سور (al-Rūmī 1996: 32).

71 Cf Egy فرش ; Leb فرشة (al-Rūmī 1996: 93).

72 Johnstone and Muir (1964: 321) have pl *niʿūl*; see also al-Ḥijjī 1988: 388 and Grosset-Grange 1993: 100; cf Tun رباط (al-Rūmī 1996: 94).

73 See also Johnstone and Muir 1964: 306, al-Ḥijjī 1988: 378 and Grosset-Grange 1993: 100; cf Egy رباط , مرصادة , حزام داخلي ; Leb سكوجات , سكوجة (al-Rūmī 1996: 38).

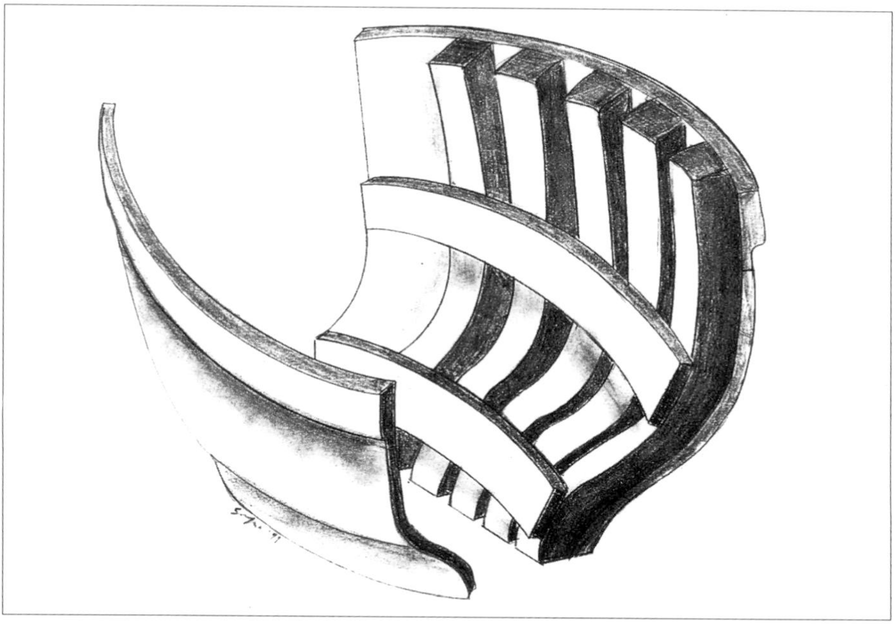

60
The *ḥzāmāt* (belts) laid across the ribs

Decking the beams

Fitting in the *fils* (mast-block) involves more work inside.[74] The *fils* holds the main mast (*id-digil il-ʿōd*) in place[75] and it is not clenched to the keelson as you would find with a western mast-block. The *fils* is positioned firmly by two fore and aft carlings (*mashāy*).[76] On the upper deck, a pair of stout stanchions (*gāyim*),[77] about six feet long, are set along the side, next to the *furma kabirt* (illus. 61). I was told that the posts act as a crutch appendage when the mast is unshipped. In other dhows the athwartship spars are secured in postion at the top of the posts. Before fitting in the deck

74 Grosset-Grange (1993: 105) gives *fals*; see also Johnstone and Muir 1964: 317 and al-Ḥijjī 1988: 384; cf Egy قاعدة الصاري; Tun دوّا , دوي (al-Rūmī 1996: 72).

75 All ocean-going Gulf dhows categorized as *saffār* (see Chapter 3) carried the main and mizen masts: the *būm*'s main mast was a stout and heavy spar, stepped amidships with a great rake forward and the mizen mast (*ghulamī*) was a small spar with a less forward rake; cf Tun main mast صاري ترانكيت and mizen mast صاري مسطرة (al-Rūmī 1996: 46).

76 See also Johnstone and Muir 1964: 320 and al-Ḥijjī 1988: 387; cf Leb حاجب الكوبرتا (al-Rūmī 1996: 89).

77 Grosset-Grange (1993: 47) lists CA *qāʾim*, which none of my informants used; see also Johnstone and Muir 1964: 317 and al-Ḥijjī 1988: 385; cf Tun قايمة (al-Rūmī 1996: 74).

61

The stout stanchion (s *gāyim*) is set on either side of the front of the upper deck

beams, a shelving called *salbīs* and made of *fīnī* (< Hin)[78] or *jangalī* wood, is fitted in, running the whole length of the *būm*. This is the deck shelf on which the deck beams rest, as we shall see. Below this shelf, the *durmēt* (< Port *dormente*),[79] an extra stringer not as thick as the *salbīs* and shorter in length, is fastened to the frames. At this stage the ship is ready to be decked with beams, *ṣuwār* (a collective usage for *ṣwāra*, one beam),[80] which are strengthened by a curved *karwa* (< Port *curva*),[81] knee. The transverse

78 *Palauium ellipticum*, pali wood, is also used for stringers, and other internal planks that strengthen the hull's ribs; see al-Ḥijjī 1988: 55.

79 Da Silva nd: 568; translated by Johnstone and Muir (1964: 309) as 'the sleeping shelf'; see also al-Ḥijjī 1988: 380 and Grosset-Grange (1993: 100) gives *darmīd*.

80 See also Lorimer 1986, I, iib: 2332; other variations, s *swāra*, pl *swārāt* and coll *ṣuwar*; see Johnstone and Muir 1964: 312; Grosset-Grange (1993: 45) has pl *ṣuwārī*; cf Egy بنك ; Leb مرصادة (al-Rūmī 1996: 63). There are three *ṣuwār*s: (a) *ṣuwār al-mugaddama*, 'the foredeck crossbar', (b) *ṣuwār id-digil*, 'mast crossbar', (c) *ṣuwār it-tifir*, 'the aftdeck crossbar'.

81 Da Silva nd: 462; also borrowed into Urdu from Portuguese (Johnstone and Muir 1964: 318).

frames (ie the beams) are laid on the deck shelf; there are four main deck beams, two of which, laid 2 feet apart from each other, are found in the first third of the hull close to the *furma d-digil*, and the other two, thicker, are located on the last third near the *furma kabirt* (illus. 62). Other deck beams, one (marked a) is placed six feet from the bow, and a few thinner ones are placed at the rear, two feet apart from each other. In the middle part of the ship (marked b), between the *digil* (pl *adgāl*) and the *kabirt*, two carlings running fore and aft are laid at an angle of 12 degrees (marked d and e) with the wider sides (marked f and g) facing the stern (marked c) (illus. 63); smaller deck beams are fitted on either side. When the workers have finished laying the deck beams, a waterway, named *ʿanch*,[82] is fitted on the outboard edge of them and fastened to the frames. At the bottom of the *ʿanch* a few scuppers, *marāzīm* (s *marzām*),[83] are chiselled out of the wood to let water out.

62
Skeleton of the hull before decking

82 See also Johnstone and Muir 1964: 316 and al-Ḥijjī 1988: 384.
83 Cf Egy بنته ; Leb مكسوس , بونيه (al-Rūmī 1996: 87).

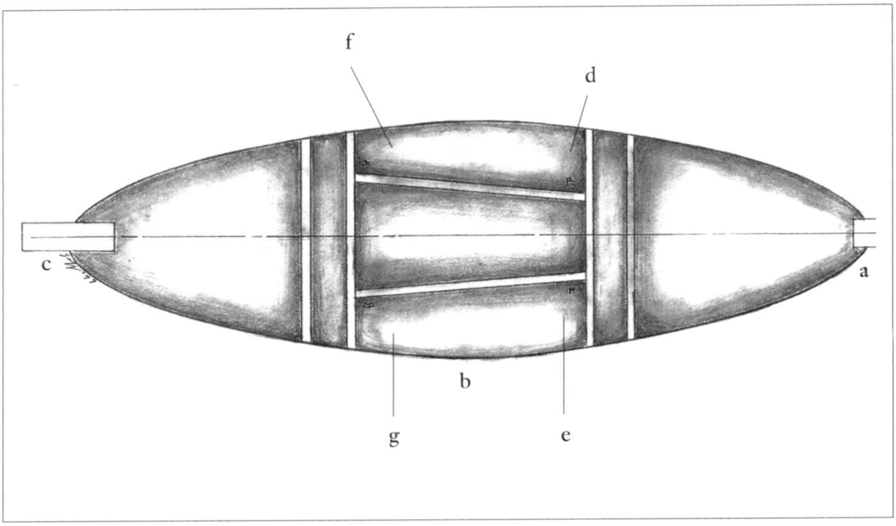

63
The *kabirt* (carlings) laid in the middle part of the dhow

Horizontal platforms made of teak are now fastened to the beams, and form the main deck of the ship (illus. 64). Some gaps are left for later work. It needs mentioning that only large dhows are fully decked, the small fishing vessels, the *sanbūq* and the *shūʿī*, are only decked at the forecastle and the poop. Fitting the *ʿubaydār* (or *ʿobīdār*)[84] is the next job: it is the knight, a heavy angled post anchored to an athwartship beam, used in order to multiply the power exerted on a halyard tye for raising sail. Set at an angle of 12 *khann*s (72 degrees), the stout timber is fixed between the *ṣwāra kabirt* and the one in front of it. Four apertures (s *fakhdh*, pl *afkhādh*) are made in a block called a *gāfiyya*,[85] to fit in four iron pulleys (s *bakra*, pl *bakrāt*),[86] operated by one sheave pin (s *ṣanfir*, pl *ṣanāfir*).[87] The apertures of the pulleys are for the ropes of the mast. Another job was to fit four pieces of timber (crescent-shaped) on

84 Grosset-Grange (1993: 105) has *ʿubīdār*; see also Johnstone and Muir 1964: 315 and al-Ḥijjī 1988: 383.

85 SA s *qūfiyya*, pl *qawāfi*, *qafāfi* (Johnstone and Muir 1964: 317); see also al-Ḥijjī 1988: 385 and Grosset-Grange 1993: 126.

86 See also Johnstone and Muir 1964: 302 and Grosset-Grange 1993: 126.

87 Cf Egy دبوس ; Tun كوريل (al-Rūmī 1996: 62).

64
The main *ṣuwār* (deck beams) are laid on the beam-shelf (photo courtesy of Rainer Hartel)

either side of the foredeck, each piece being called *zand* (pl *zunūd* or *zinūd*),[88] and to which the anchor cable is made fast.

The work on the deck progresses slowly and each part is checked by the master-builder who painstakingly chooses the wood most fitted for the work assigned to the day. The poopdeck *nīm* (< [Per])[89] or half deck is next. This is where the skipper (*nākhōda*), and the helmsman (*sukkūnī* or *sukkōnī*), live. The space the *nīm* occupies is approximately a third of the lower poopdeck, from the *gāyim* to the *khiyyīsa* (see below). The work on the poopdeck also includes the *ghulamī* (mizen),[90] the steering wheel (*charkh* < Per),[91] and a cabin for women passengers named *dabūsa* (< Per or Ur).[92] Two large

88 Johnstone and Muir (1964: 311) state that it is made of iron; see also al-Ḥijjī 1988: 381.

89 See also Johnstone and Muir 1964: 321 and al-Ḥijjī 1988: 388.

90 Ur *kilmī*, *kalmī*; SA *galmi*, *galami* (Johnstone and Muir 1964: 317); Grosset-Grange (1993: 105) gives two other Arabic variations *qalamī*, *qalāmī*. I was told from various sources that on Gulf dhows you would generally not find more than two masts, the smaller dhows had only one mast.

91 Also known as *dūlāb*; cf Egy طارة الدومان (al-Rūmī 1996: 34).

92 Per *dabūsa*, 'cuddy' (Steingass 1977: 503 and Johnstone and Muir 1964: 308); see also al-Ḥijjī 1988: 379 and Grosset-Grange 1993: 77.

aftermost stanchions (s *khīsa*, pl *khiyyīsa* or *khiyāsa*)[93] are erected at the stern: the poles are positioned on the *salbīs* and *durmēt*, leaning at the top on the inside (illus. 65). Their function is also to support the aft *tiʿrāḍa*[94] (a stout beam), on which the main yard called *firman* or *firmal* (< Per *farman*)[95] is lowered. Once the *nīm* is completed the carpenters start working on the sides of the poopdeck: first they fit in the railings from the *gāyim* to the *khiyyīsa*, called the *ribūsh*, *ribsh*[96] or even *rēl* (< Ur or Hin or Eng)[97] on each side of the *nīm*. The second job is setting up the *ʿēbāt*, wooden uprights alternating with iron ones, and on top of these uprights comes the handrail, *fālkī*.[98] A small *ẓulla*,[99] awning (canvas or reed canopy), for protection from the sun, is spread over a ridge rope above the poopdeck and secured to stanchions fixed on either side (illus. 66). Then, a wooden bench is constructed 2 feet high, and placed under the canvas canopy above the poopdeck; the bench is called *kātlī* (< Port *cátel* or *cátele*),[100] and the *nākhōda*, or sometimes the senior crew members, sleep on it. Behind the *nīm*, the stern comes round in a curve called *ʿanāfa*[101] (only found on *būm*s): rails are set up to secure the curved head, the latter being the highest structure of the ship, ie the *kashtīl it-tifr* (the after-castle) (illus. 67).[102] On some dhows, like the *sanbūq* or the *jālbūt*, the *kashtīl* serves as the place where the *nākhōda* sleeps. On the foredeck (*kashtīl is-sidr*), the grapnels (s *anyar* or *anjar*, pl *anāyir* or *anājir*)[103] and the ropes are stored.

93 See also Johnstone and Muir 1964: 308 and al-Ḥijjī 1988: 379.

94 See also Johnstone and Muir 1964: 305 and al-Ḥijjī 1988: 378.

95 Pl *farāmin* or *farāmil*; see also Johnstone and Muir 1964: 316 and Grosset-Grange 1993: 42; others noted Kt *fármen*, Ir *farmal*, Had *tarmāl*, *tirmāl*, *turmāl*, Yem *farramān*, Meh *formēl*, Tig *tormēn* < Hin *paravān* < Skt *pramāna* > NP *farman*, *farvand* (Glidden 1942: 71).

96 *Ribūsh* also includes, according to Johnstone and Muir (1964: 310), 'the carvings at the stern'. The railings surrounding the poop are also known as *mashiār* (Grosset-Grange 1993: 47).

97 I heard this word more often than *ribūsh*; see Johnstone and Muir 1964: 310 and al-Ḥijjī 1988: 381.

98 See also al-Ḥijjī 1988: 384.

99 Also SA *ẓalla* (Johnstone and Muir 1964: 315); some informants said *ʿarsha*; also recorded by Lorimer (1986, I, iib: 2330).

100 Da Silva nd: 325 and Johnstone and Muir 1964: 318; see also al-Ḥijjī 1988: 385.

101 Grosset-Grange (1993: 78) gives *ʿannāfa*; see also Johnstone and Muir 1964: 316 and al-Ḥijjī 1988: 384; cf Leb قادومة ; Tun شلبورة (al-Rūmī 1996: 67).

102 *Kashtīl* < Port *castelo* (Da Silva nd: 322 and Johnstone and Muir 1964: 318); see also al-Ḥijjī 1988: 386. I heard *saṭaḥ guddām* or *juddām* in the northern Gulf; also recorded by Grosset-Grange (1993: 125). For smaller dhows like the *battīl* or *zārūka* in the Musandam Peninsula the locals refer to the foredeck as *fanna*, see also al-Rūmī 1996: 82.

103 Other types are *sinn*, a killick good for anchoring on coral; the grapnel was apparently introduced by the Greeks (hence < Gr *āgkura*) and *bawra*, fisherman's anchor (< Eng *bower anchor*), see Johnstone and Muir 1964: 301 and for more details LeBaron Bowen 1957: 288-93. Other information on the use of stone anchors in south-east Oman, see my forthcoming book *People of the Dhow*.

65
Horizontal platforms made of teak are fastened to the beams forming the main deck

66
The *nīm* (half deck). The work on the poopdeck also includes the *ghulamī* (mizen) and the *charkh* (steering wheel). Two large aftermost stanchions, *khīsa*, are erected on the stern

Both decks are constructed in the same manner as the main deck. I observed in some of the larger ships, such as the *ghanja*, *baghla* and *kūtiyya*, that the forecastle was used to wash table utensils, dishes and receptacles, a convenient location because it had several drainholes to let water out. In fact the whole area gets splashed with sea water as the bow cuts through the waves. Scuppers are normally found on decks but one main drainhole (*magarr*)[104] is found at the bottom of the keel.[105]

Work on deck

About two to three feet from the curved head of the bow, a cat beam, named *chalb* or *chalba*,[106] projects on either side to form the catheads (*ʿabīd*). The *chalb* is a common feature that you find on every dhow, big or small.[107] Usually the anchor ropes are tied around the catheads. The last piece that the workers make is the *ṭabla* (pl *ṭablāt*) (< Port *tábua*),[108] an area which is forward to the cat beam: triangular-shaped, it is located between the *sāṭūr* or *ṣāṭūr* (stemhead)[109] and two pieces of timber on either side known as the cheek, *wisāda* (pl *wasāyid*).[110] The next job is to do with the *sāṭūr*, the part projecting above the forecastle deck, the shape of which, it has been said, is like a butcher's cleaver (illus. 68). I was under the impression that the *sāṭūr* was typical of the Kuwaiti *būm* because of its unique shape, yet several Bahraini and Qatari builders I spoke to were also referring to *sāṭūr*s when they were talking about *sanbūq*s and *bānūsh*es.[111] They look almost similar but I found the Kuwaiti

104 Grosset-Grange (1993: 109) lists *maghar* and *magharr*; Johnstone and Muir (1964: 320) have *sachācha*, 'a bung to fit the drainhole in the hull'; see also al-Ḥijjī 1988: 387; cf Egy سدادة ; Leb أنبار (al-Rūmī 1996: 90).

105 In a course of correspondence (4 October 1999), Tom Vosmer told me that he saw scuppers on *battīl*s and *zārūka*s in Musandam, plugged with a piece of wooden dowel (tapered).

106 See also Johnstone and Muir 1964: 319, al-Ḥijjī 1988: 386 and Grosset-Grange 1993: 60.

107 With smaller boats like the fishing *battīl*s and *zārūka*s in the Musandam Peninsula, Tom Vosmer informed me (3 September 1999), that the *chalba* (as known by the Shihhīs and Kumzaris), was too weak for either the anchor or for dragging on the boats. In fact the through-beams were used to drag the boat, and a beam aft of the foredeck was used to secure the anchor.

108 Da Silva nd: 142-3; recorded by al-Ḥijjī 1988: 383 and Grosset-Grange 1993: 124; also called *ṭabla t-tifr* (Johnstone and Muir 1964: 314).

109 Various terms used for different types of dhow: *rās is-sidr* or *gubēt* for the *baghla*, *ghanja* and *balam*; *qādūm* or *yadūm* or *tāj* for the carving on the stemhead of the *ghanja* or *kūtiyya*; see Johnstone and Muir 1964: 304-5, 317 and Grosset-Grange 1993: 81.

110 Recorded as s *wasād*, pl *wusūd* (Grosset-Grange 1993: 60); see also Johnstone and Muir 1964: 322 and al-Ḥijjī 1988: 389.

111 One can find sketches of stemheads of some dhows in the Japanese work of Kamioka and Yajima 1979: 58.

67

The railings (*rēl*) are fitted with *ᶜēbāt*, wooden uprights alternating with iron ones and the *fālkī*, the handrail. A *ṣīrī*, the wooden ladder on the right leads the crew from the main deck to the poopdeck and a *ẓulla*, awning (canvas or reed canopy) is built to protect the *nākhōda* (the captain) and his assistant from the sun

sāṭūr much stouter and longer. As we pointed out earlier, in the initial stage of constructing the *būm*, the master-builder sets up the stempost in position with the keel leaving a gap of one foot from the end: the gap is where an outer stem, the *barmēl*[112] (also found on *sanbūq*s or *shūᶜī*s), referred to in the West as the false stem, is secured to the existing stempost. The *barmēl* (pl *barāmil*) functions as a fender against the crushing waves. At the bottom curve of the stem where it joins with the keel, a wooden beakhead, *daᶜūma*[113] is fixed. To complete the work in this area, the stempost and the *barmēl* are tightened with cramp-irons, *būlūlē*, which protect the wood from splitting; they are also used to connect the *barmēl* to the stem, rather than through-bolting fore and aft (illus. 69). One other job related to the sternpost is the *sukkān* or *sikkān*[114]

112 The term is perhaps a hybrid of Persian *bar*, 'on, over' and *mēl* 'stem or sternpost' (Johnstone and Muir 1964: 301); see also al-Ḥijjī 1988: 377; cf Egy فيدوة (al-Rūmī 1996: 29).

113 Known as *būmiyya*, 'supporting knee to shore stem and sternposts, connecting these with keel' (Prins 1965: 281); see also Johnstone and Muir 1964: 309 and Grosset-Grange 1993: 49; cf Egy حجر بدن; Leb روسطانية; Tun رِجِل (al-Rūmī 1996: 42).

114 CA *sukkān*, well known term in early Islam (Lane 1984, I: 1394), Ir *sikkān*; Meh *sekkōn*; Tig *sukan*; Som *šukan* < Ak *sikkānu* via Syr *sawkāna* (Glidden 1942: 71); see also Johnstone and Muir 1964: 312, al-Ḥijjī 1988: 382 and Grosset-Grange 1993: 90–1; cf Egy and Leb دفة ; Tun دفة , دمان (al-Rūmī 1996: 54).

68

The *ṭabla* located on either side of the cat beam forming the cheek, *wisāda* and finally the stemhead, *sāṭūr* projecting above the forecastle deck

(rudder), which is hung by several pintles (s *narr*, pl *nurūr*) and gudgeons (s *māda*, pl *mādāt*),[115] allowing lateral movement from side to side as required. A piece of wooden bar *kāna* (tiller)[116] fits into the head of the rudder by which the latter is moved by yoke lines attached to the ends of the yoke and operated by the helmsman.

The construction of the *būm* is now almost finished. If you look at it from a distance you see a shell with ribs jutting out. These are the *shilmāns* (ribs) which now need to be sawed and trimmed to the level of the *tirrīch* planking. The *zabdara*,[117] gunwale, is fastened atop the upper sheer strake to bind in the

115 Both terms *narr* and *māda* are used to represent in the language of the dhow, 'male' or 'female' respectively. Specifically used in Kuwait (Johnstone and Muir 1964: 320-1); note Ur *nar*; GA *māda* < Per (ibid); in other Gulf states you often hear s *dhakr*, pl *dhukūr* (ie male) for pintle and s *nathiyya*, pl *nathiyyāt* (ie female) for gudgeon; also s *unth* or *uns*, pl *anās* (ie male) (Grosset-Grange 1993: 84); cf Egy صباع (pintle),سكرجة(gudgeon); Leb زبار pl زبارات; Tun دكرا (pintle), لتنا (pintle or gudgeon) (al-Rūmī 1996: 93).

116 From Hin *kāna* 'ear, helm of boat' (Glidden 1942: 72) or Port *cana* (Da Silva nd: 292); recorded *kana* or *kanā* (Grosset-Grange 1993: 91); SA *kāna ḥagg as-sukkān* (Johnstone and Muir 1964: 318); Egy يد ; Tun ملوينة , منويلة (al-Rūmī 1996: 80).

117 Other variations known *zbadara*, *zibadra* or *zabdāra*, see Johnstone and Muir 1964: 311 and Grosset-Grange 1993: 100 < Port *cevadeira* (Da Silva nd: 342 meaning 'the whiskers or spreaders of the bowsprit shrouds', see Johnstone and Muir 1964: 311); Ur *sabdarā*, 'bowsprit' > **sbadara* > Kt *zbadara* (ibid, 311); see also al-Ḥijjī 1988: 381 and Grosset-Grange 1993: 100; cf Egy حافة ; Egy and Leb باطوس ; Tun بروّة (al-Rūmī 1996: 51).

69
The stempost and the *barmēl* (false stem) are tightened with *būlūlē* (cramp irons) (photo courtesy of Rainer Hartel)

top work; it prevents the inflow of sea water when the vessel heels over. The gunwale in a v-shape at the fore and aftercastle is called *sdīrī*, though I also heard *jilinga*.[118] Finally comes the caulking (*kalfat* or *kilfāt*), the operation of driving a cotton rope impregnated with fish (shark) liver oil or coconut oil into the seams of a dhow's sides in order to render them impervious to water. With smaller vessels such as the racing *hūrī*s I saw in al-Butteen in Abu Dhabi, there is a different technique to block gaps between the planks, which the boat-builder Mhammed Khamis Bu Haroon[119] referred to as *rass* or *tanzīl al-alwāḥ* (ie securing the planks together). For this, a *kawra* (or *milzāma*), which is a pointed piece of wood three inches long looking like a chisel, is placed between the planks and, starting from the bottom, ie the garboard strake, the carpenter hammers each plank down in position fitting them together tightly (illus. 70). If any gaps show, they are blocked by a *shkhāsa* (stealer). It is at this stage that the carpenters fasten the ribs and planks together.

The outside of the *būm* is coated with hot pitch or some other composition to prevent fouling. Shark's oil is applied to the topsides and the interior, thus

118 See also Johnstone and Muir 1964: 305, al-Ḥijjī 1988: 378 and Grosset-Grange 1993: 149; cf Leb حشوة (al-Rūmī 1996: 36).
119 Interviewed on 12 April 1997.

70
The carpenter is applying a *kawra* to tighten the strake down in position

preventing the timbers from splitting and warping. The oil gives warmth to the wood and adds richness to the mahogany colour of the dhow. The *sāṭūr*'s head is painted white and black and the tiller is also painted using the colours in reverse, black and white. Other accessories to the *būm* are: the *ṣīrī*, a wooden ladder fixed to the right side of the upper deck; the *dirīsha* (pl *darāyish*) (< Per *darīcha*, 'window'),[120] a stern port for loading poles; *jālī* (< [?] Ur 'lattice, grating'),[121] a hatch leading to the *khinn* (< Per),[122] the hold; *sarēdān*,[123] a moveable wooden box, open at the front, with an iron sheet lining the inside for cooking with charcoal or wood, and usually located at the front of the dhow (illus. 71); *zūlī* (or *zōli*),[124] a semi-circular box with a hole at the bottom

120 Steingass 1977: 577; see also Johnstone and Muir 1964: 309 and al-Ḥijjī 1988: 380; other variations are s *daraja*, *darija*, pl *darāʾig*; on the *baghla* it is known as s *shabbāk*, *shubbāk*, pl *shabābīk* (Grosset-Grange 1993: 137).

121 Qureshi nd: 233 and Johnstone and Muir 1964: 305; see also al-Ḥijjī 1988: 378 and Grosset-Grange 1993: 119.

122 Steingass 1977: 475 and Johnstone and Muir 1964: 307; given as *khann*, *kann* (Grosset-Grange 1993: 51); see also al-Ḥijjī 1988: 379.

123 Ad *ṣurīdān* (Johnstone and Muir 1964: 312).

124 SA *zūli* (Johnstone and Muir 1964: 311); see also al-Ḥijjī 1988: 381 and Grosset-Grange 1993: 62.

71

Sarēdān, a moveable wooden box, opens from the front with an iron sheet covering the inside for cooking with charcoal or wood, located at the front of the dhow

used as a men's latrine and found attached outboard at the stern (I noticed that some dhows fix it at the bow);[125] *finṭās* or *khazzān il-moy*, a caulked water cistern tank located on the main deck near the poopdeck; and finally on the side of the poopdeck the *katāt* or *kitāt*,[126] davits projecting over the *chanta* (gunwale) to which the small lifeboat, *māshuwwa* (in the case of the *būm*), is hung. Once all the accessories are fitted in, the carpenters set out to smooth the outer planks, fairing them off by cutting rough edges with an adze, an operation often referred to as *tadrīkh* (or *tashdīb* in the Emirates). Finally, a motor engine is installed and a propeller (*barwāna*) is fixed to the *karwa* unit just above the end of the keel at the stern. A flower decorated with white and sky-blue petals in a circular pattern, is painted on a wooden frame in the middle of the railings of the poopdeck (illus. 72).

Preservation of the dhow

On completion of our *būm*, the workers cover below its waterline with a coating made of boiling oil and animal fat mixed with burned lime (*chunam*),

125 It is possible, Tom Vosmer wrote to me (10 October 1999), that the position is related to the usual wind direction relative to the boat, ie downwind, the *zūlī* would be fixed in the bow.

126 See also Johnstone and Muir 1964: 318 and al-Ḥijjī 1988: 386.

72
The flower pattern painted in the middle of the railings of the poopdeck

to deter barnacles and other growth from attacking the bottom. The anti-fouling paint permeates through the teak and strengthens it. The teredo (Lat *teredo* [*navalis*] < Gr *terēdōn*), commonly known as ship worm, has notoriously damaged thousands of wooden ships. The Greek Theophrastus, as early as the third century BC, wrote about this sea creature that 'has a large head and teeth'. Some worms are as long as three feet, and nearly an inch in diameter. 'The harm done by the *terēdōn*', warned the Greek botanist, 'cannot be undone'.[127] The Sumerians smeared wooden hulls with bitumen which they extracted from the (present day) town of Hit in Iraq.[128] It is well-documented in medieval times that fish oil, particularly from the whale, was used to protect a ship's hull from the sea. We find mention of third/ninth century fishermen from Sīrāf cutting whale blubber, extracting the oil from it and mixing it with other substances and rubbing it into the joints of ships' planking (Reinaud 1845, I: 146). At Al-Radah in the Al-Batinah region I was told that fishermen were still applying shark liver-oil which they called *ṣall*

127 Theophrastus 1916, Book V, Chapter IV: 4–6.

128 Two kinds of bitumen were used for caulking ships in Mesopotamia: one was a hard impure substance mixed with loam, chopped straw, filler and fibrous materials, the other was a soft but pure asphalt used mainly to refine or coat the hull from the inside. The name of the town Hit derives from *ittu*, the Akkadian term for bitumen (De Graeve 1981: 105).

(some of my sources said *dehen*).[129] The seamen placed the shark's liver in a *barmīl* (cauldron) and boiled it for an hour or so. They then let it cool off until it became thick like paste and ready to use. Not only does the fish oil protect the wood against the *teredo* but it strengthens the boat against dryness caused by the sun. The smell of the fish oil was terrible almost to the point of fainting.

The bottoms of *baghla*s, not too long ago, were coppered, but often you would have found some of them sheathed with thin planking, having a mixture of *dāmir* (resin), lime and coconut oil, or smeared with this mixture from the bottom up to the waterline. This process was renewed periodically otherwise the sea-water worm crept in causing rapid and extreme damage. Large vessels in the Gulf are not soaked and scoured with oil just once but after each inspection (every eight months). This process is called careening. You see a dhow laid up on the beach in summer, since this is the season for cleaning hulls and refitting. However, in December 1996 I saw a number of Omanis cleaning and treating the interior timber of large *shūʿī*s in Mutrah and Sur. The vessel in Sur was put aground with the help of the tide. The preparation of *shūna*[130] (a mixture of *wadach* or *shaḥam*, 'fat' and *nūra*, 'lime') takes place alongside the dhow. When the mutton fat has boiled in an iron pot the dhow-man mixes it in a *mankaba* (pl *manākib*),[131] wooden container, with lime which makes it into a thick paste. Then, after scraping off the weed and barnacles, the mixture is plastered by hand over the underwater part of the hull accompanied by chanting. Apparently, the *chunam* (fat and lime) coating dries after a few weeks; Severin and Awad (1985: 202) tell us it hardens, then cracks with the movement of the dhow on the sea. Severin's experience on the *Sohar*, a replica of a medieval Arab stitched trading vessel built in 1980,[132] has proved that when the anti-fouling flakes off, the dhow is exposed to the attack of ship worm which

129 Interview with Hamad Saeed Al Breiki on 29 November 1996.

130 It is possible that Arabic *shūna* was borrowed from Fārsī (through Hindi) *chūnāh*, 'quick lime' (Steingass 1977: 403), also Urdu *chooʼnā* 'lime' (Qureshi nd: 261). In Tunisia the process of careening is called *tashḥīm*, see al-Rūmī 1996: 98-9.

131 In Kuwait *manchaba* (pl *manāchib*), the wooden container imported from Malabar is used by divers to store rice and preferred to metal as a better resistant to heat, see al-Rūmī 1996: 115.

132 The length of the hull was 80 feet, a beam of 20 feet and 4 inches, and the length of the waterline was 63 feet. The sewn dhow sailed from Muscat, Oman to Canton, China in excellent condition, Tim Severin being the captain of the Omani and Western crew. The voyage was funded by His Majesty Sultan Qaboos and sponsored by the Ministry of National Heritage and Culture of Oman, whose minister, His Highness Sayyid Faisal Al Said gave his fullest support (Severin 1982: 10-1, 235-9).

bore cylindrical holes in the planks to the point of disintegration. Some planks (test pieces) of the *Sohar* voyage, unprotected by the traditional anti-fouling, were attacked by worms and consequently 'snapped with one's bare hands like wafers', Severin reports (1982: 127-8, 132). Anti-fouling is done far more frequently in the Gulf and Oman than anywhere else, presumably the salty water corrodes far quicker, though it must be said that the danger of teredo is the more important factor. Removing the boat from the water for several days also kills the teredo.[133]

The launch ceremony

I understand from my informants that, in the old days, much labour was involved in sliding a large dhow into the sea and many men would flock to the scene to help. In towns, a lot of the folklore practices had disappeared much earlier than in fishing villages. Some fishermen in Raysut[134] recalled, before Sultan Qaboos came into power in 1970, how the master-builder would inform the village *imām* of the launching of the *sanbūq*. The news then spread to all the villagers through market stalls, shop owners, police and of course the mosque. Everyone was invited and hundreds of men would flock to the beach for the launch ceremony and for the big meal consisting of sheep's meat and rice. The women would follow in groups, ullulating. Several men grabbed the necks of sheep to be sacrificed for the happy occasion, and after slaughtering the animals the blood was sprinkled on the outside and inside of the boat, while the women continued ullulating in jubilation. About one hundred men would lift the large *sanbūq* and carry it to the sea, followed by the beating of the drums and the singing of young men. The *sanbūq* moved gracefully out to sea, while the crew hauling the mainsheet to set sail, chanted: *yā allāh*, *yā allāh al-muʿīn*, 'O God, O God help us (on our way)'. Although these folklore rituals sound in the distant past, the slaughtering of goats and sprinkling of blood on the *battīl* and *zārūka* is still being practised in Khasab and Kumzar in the Musandam Peninsula. There was other sea lore: sailors sung prayers to keep the dhow on course, or to avert shipwreck. During the construction of the dhow and after the vessel was completed workers would sacrifice animals and wash the timbers to prevent them from getting rot.

Almost every boatyard I visited in the Gulf stood right at the water's edge. A new *būm* was hauled down to the sea over 'built-up skids and log rollers placed under the bilges' with a wire tackle attached to a *dawwār* (capstan)

133 Information given to me by Tom Vosmer (30 March 1998).

134 Interviews conducted with Sabi Khamis, Musallam Saeed Ahmad, Muhad Ali Amer, Mubashir Khamis Ragab, Hafiz Awad and Raghab Khamis on 19 November 1996.

providing the motive power.[135] The people helping to launch the vessel are divided into two groups: the one consisting of sailors on board the ship, turn the wire of the capstan round, while the other group, workers who the *nākhōda* hires for the occasion, rotate the capstan's wire on the shore; chanting (called *dawwārī*) or improvised singing (*ḥinda*, *ḥanda*) accompanies the work (al-Rifāʿī 1985: 132). After many hours of work the dhow was slowly hauled to the sea. It sounded very simple to me but when one of my sources described to me the launching of a large *sanbūq* some 20 years ago in Abu Dhabi,[136] I realized how much more complicated it was. The day the master builder wanted to launch the boat, many men from nearby locations came out to help. When the dhow was ready to be launched, the path leading to the sea was cleared; this was done by a bulldozer. Log rollers rubbed with grease were laid on the path for the dhow to slide on. Meanwhile, truckloads of old tyres were placed on the left side of the dhow (ie the *burd*) facing the sea, and placed on top of them, a large plank smeared with *wadach* (fat).[137] There was a lot of shouting and arguing before the master-builder finally gave the order for the men to fit a huge rope around the keel of the dhow and then to attach the end of the rope to the bulldozer. They also attached a rope to the stemhead and another to the sternpost and pulled sideways while some other workers knocked away the props[138] which held the dhow upright during its construction. They pulled the dhow until it subsided on to its left side where the tyres were placed. The next thing was to place planks under the keel. The bulldozer then pulled the dhow slowly on the rollers into the sea.[139] It was odd to see the dhow sliding on its side into the sea. But there it was on the sea gradually becoming upright again; having reached a certain level of water the bulldozer could not proceed any further and in order for the dhow to reach the deep sea it was pushed by the bulldozer with tyres attached to its shovel. It gently pushed the boat until it found deep water and glided proudly out on the green-blue sea, followed by a lot of singing and dancing, beating of drums and clapping of hands from the watchers on shore. In the days of the sail, when the dhow was afloat the masts were manhandled to the water and stepped by the sailors after which they set up the rigging required for sailing.

---

135 See Hawkins 1977: 100, and also 46: steps of launching a *būm* are shown in an illustration though there is no mention of wire tackling on board the ship.

136 Interviewed Yusuf bin Naser Al Zaabi on 12 April 1997.

137 Al-Rūmī 1996: 105. Ar *wadk* > GA *wadsh* (/k/>/sh/ known as the *kāf mukashkasha*, a common phonological feature in Gulf Arabic).

138 In Kuwait a prop is called *mindī*, pl *manādī*.

139 Cf al-Rifāʿī 1985: 132-3.

Conclusion

The shell-built method of construction, ie laying the planks first, tightly butted together, then adding the frames later, is a tradition that goes back to the times of antiquity. The builder knew from experience how to shape the strakes which determined the final design of the dhow. The long tradition of dhow-building in the Gulf and Oman is today being threatened by the fibreglass dhow industry, very active in Ajman. Yet, the traditional boat continues; it does not owe anything to industralization. It is the product of pure craftsmanship which is in the hands of individual artists, who work solely by eye. The master shipwright pictures the plan of the dhow in his mind and modifications are made without compromising its seaworthiness.

8
Dhow Types: An Overview

يا الله بصباح الخير
يا الله بصباح الخير
أول صلاتي على النبي
رزقك على الله يطير

O Allāh, may this morning be fine
O Allāh, may this morning be good
I pray: May Allāh bless the prophet,
May Allāh grant you a swift voyage.[1]

(Khamis Abdallah Khamis al-Shayhi)[2]

Technological transformation

Like many visitors to the Gulf I fell into the trap of romanticizing the apparently age-old and picturesque dhows as 'fossilized remnants' (Prados 1997: 185) of antiquity. A year into my field trips, I became aware that this was not completely true, and there is undoubtedly a continuum with the past which is evident today. Ships of course evolve in response to technological developments, and modifications are made according to market needs as well as economic pressures. Shipping is not static, it is dynamic and dhows are constructed for a number of needs. It is with the development of maritime trade that the design alters or modifies. These changes can be seen in the hull shape and construction of double-ended craft, which continued concurrently with square-sterned vessels. Inboard and outboard engines replaced the sails and the traditional anti-fouling application continued as underbody paint. Commercial anti-fouling was applied at Ghubbat Ali in Musandam over the traditional coating but was not very successful; it flaked off.[3]

It has often been claimed that the double-ended design is a relic of the past. This belief is based on a number of illustrations from medieval sources representing Islamic double-ended vessels of the Arabian/Persian Gulf and Indian Ocean (Nicolle 1989: 168-97). The double-ended *būm* and *samʿa* of Kuwait and the Emirates respectively, are, however, totally modern inventions of the late nineteenth and early twentieth centuries, which are often mistaken

1 'Yallāh b-ṣabāḥ al-khayr/yallāh b-ṣabāḥ al-khayr/awwal ṣalāt-ī ʿalā n-nabī/rizqak ʿalā allāh yaṭīr' – sung by fishermen in Qalhat before sailing.

2 Interviewed on 29 March 1998.

3 Information given by Tom Vosmer in a personal communication (21 April 2000).

for vessels of the past. The Yemeni *sanbūq* is perhaps an interesting example, as it was originally a double-ended craft which, with European contact, evolved into the classic transom-sterned vessel of the sixteenth century. Today it has become again in Yemen the archetypal double-ended craft.

It is generally believed that the *baghla*, *ghanja*, *kūtiyya* and *battīl* vessels of Arab and Indian design, have a Portuguese and later a Dutch influence, with their high poops and transom-stern belonging to early carvel construction. The use of nails for construction is understood to be of European or Chinese influence. R. B. Serjeant (1974: 132) and other scholars believe that the twentieth-century dhow has not changed much since the sixteenth and seventeenth centuries. It is interesting how some old technologies have persevered in certain remote areas of Oman, as Pâris' nineteenth-century illustrations of a *badan* show (1841, Plates 7 and 9). There you can find a steering oar on each side of the craft, a technology of the eleventh century that pre-dates the use of the rudder. But with these lateral oars, I was informed by Suri *nākhōda*s, it was impossible to tack, to sail against the wind, or for that matter to sail when the sea was rough. A tiller, operated by a seaman on deck, was attached to the rudder which was fixed at the dhow's stern, and moved just below the surface of the water.

Builders modified designs. The *abūbūz* was created by mating the *sanbūq* with a European type of sailer. Deep-draft dhows cannot anchor wherever there is low tide or shoals that dry at low water and therefore *jālbūt*s with shallow-drafts were designed to navigate in these waters. Shipbuilders made some adjustments to the *baghla* and *ghanja* to enable them to carry bulk cargos of mangrove poles from East Africa to Sur and Kuwait. The *sanbūq* in the Arabian/Persian Gulf has fore and aft planking bulwarks built above the deck to prevent the waves coming over the gunwale. This of course protects the vessel's cargo from spray.

Dhows have always had to adapt to the changing winds and ocean currents, according to the season. The sail was the principal motive force until the introduction of the diesel engine which transformed navigational techniques as dhows became less dependent on seasonal voyages controlled by the monsoon. With oil profits in the early 1970s, shipowners found diesel-engined dhows more profitable for running their trade with India and East Africa. Prados' (1997) empirical study of dhow activity in the Yemen, from October 1993 to May 1994, shows what impact market forces, technological developments and cultural contacts can have on the way dhows are designed. Competition in trade is what keeps traditional shipping active; the shipbuilder, shipowner or captain, navigator and merchant, are part of the development and change over the centuries. As the profits from competition with high-capacity freights started to decrease and the buying of building materials from India in particular, became increasingly costly, shipwrights began to look for newer methods of cutting costs in construction materials and time (Hornell 1942: 23–4). Hence the double-ended Kuwaiti *būm* had virtually replaced the *baghla* within a space of 35 years (1892 to 1927).[4] On a smaller scale the Yemeni double-ended *sanbūq* has gone through changes and adaptations for economic and practical reasons. Also, like the Omani dhow-builders, Yemeni builders saw the advantage of building square-sterned *hūrī*s with an outboard engine, in that the number of fish they can carry makes them more economical to run (Prados 1997: 193).

Like Prados, in my field trips to the Gulf and Oman I have noticed, though not an architect myself, some examples of technological transformation. I spent long hours with shipwrights observing the building of the dhow in Kuwait, and in all the shipyards I visited in the Gulf and Oman I was under the impression (and the local shipwrights always claimed) that construction practices remained traditionally unchanged. The assertion is that the shell-first method was always practised in the Arabian/Persian Gulf and Oman. However, in Abu Dhabi, dhow-builders were not applying the shell-first method to construct their racing *hūrī*s; instead, after laying the keel, stem and stern and the garboard strakes, they were installing seven permanent ribs. Having done this they would then decide the lay of the rest of the planking. The method was similarly observed by Prados in Yemen who noted that builders there 'plank and frame the vessel concurrently' (ibid, 195). He believed that such methodology was an 'intermediary evolutionary step' between shell-first and frame-first construction. Admittedly, whichever methods are being applied, master-builders are individual architects who build their dhows according to what they think fits the needs of the buyer. There are no plans or drawings which would enable a dhow design to be replicated – each vessel is unique. It is solely by the accuracy of the eye that the dhow is built, yet it is strong enough to stand up to the roughest weather.

Except for racing dhows, sails have been replaced by inboard and outboard engines. All over the Gulf, dug-out *hūrī* construction is being changed to plank-built, with a transom-stern to fit an engine. These are the fishing *hūrī*s: they are bigger than the dug-out boats and the space allows for a good sized catch. Foreign fishing trawlers made of fibreglass (the so-called *ṭarrād* or *ṭarrāda*), mostly imported from Japan (at least the ones I saw), may eventually bring the existence of the wooden dhows to an end. In the Gulf and Oman, builders are changing their methods; but even though the traditional wooden vessels are now being replaced by fibreglass dhows in places such as Ajman, they retain the same design and they keep their

4 CDRAD – IOR, 15/1/504 (1927), fol 13.

ancestral name. The builders, who are in their twenties, build mainly *shūʿī*s; they are economical, easy to build and maintain and of course, are lighter to use out at sea. Gone are the handsome wooden *sanbūq* and *shūʿī* of the Gulf; they are following in the wake of the Kuwaiti *būm*, the Omani *badan* and the *baqqāra*, on the long voyage to extinction.

Transition of designs

It is true to say that there is to some degree an unchanging tradition in shipbuilding in the Arabian Gulf and Oman. The sewing of boats until fairly recently shows a continuity in traditional shipbuilding based on the availability of material, ie wood and coir. With larger seagoing vessels, wood was imported mainly from south-west India. No wood suitable for shipbuilding was available on the whole of the Arabian coast, the Iranian coast of the Gulf nor the African Red Sea shore. Only for primitive boats, such as the *sanbūq ẓufārī*, could builders find local wood readily available from the *wādī*s and hills of the Dhofar region of Oman, as we pointed out in Chapter 5. The materials for larger vessels and perhaps sometimes the techniques of shipbuilding, have been imported into these areas from India since the third millennium BC. There is evidence to suggest that similar boats have sailed in the Gulf and Indian Ocean for centuries. Undoubtedly there exists a long maritime tradition in the Indian Ocean civilization and, like many seafaring communities, they tend to be conservative and stick to tried and tested building techniques and to make use of local materials. Changes occur as a result of local requirements and from influence by foreign designs.

How much influence the Greek ships had on Arab craft in early times, is a question that is hard to answer unless tangible evidence such as a shipwreck, is available. Boats and building techniques have continued to change and this is quite apparent from our surveys on dhows (Chapters 4 to 7); a number of examples of dhows that were in common use in the past two hundred years have disappeared, and we have seen the introduction of newer designs. It is interesting to note that out of a list of 36 ship types mentioned by al-Muqaddasī in the fourth/tenth century (1906, III: 32; Agius 1997: 303–29), only four remain in the modern daily repertoire: *markab*, *qārib*, *safīna*, and *zawraq*. The names prevail but we have no information about their hull design and function. We have little information from medieval accounts as to the weight that large vessels could carry. However, with the discovery of stone anchors in Qalhat harbour in April 1998 (Vosmer *et al.* 1998; Vosmer 1999: 301–2; Agius 1999: 187–194), and all over the Western Indian Ocean, it is possible to go some way in determining vessel weights, though this remains hypothesis until a shipwreck is found in the Gulf or Oman.

In terms of economics, a dhow never grows old because parts of it are gradually replaced over the years; a new dhow is bought because the owner has lost the old one in rough seas. Many were the owners who purchased trading and fishing vessels, and today, few would order any dhows (the *shūʿī* being the most popular). The fibreglass dhows are becoming increasingly available in the Emirates and it is the prevalence of racing dhows in the shipyards of the Gulf and Oman which are taking the lead in the twenty-first century.

Classificatory problems

All dhows look similar to western observers because their rig does not vary much. Variations depend on the size and the hull design. The hull could be a recent or traditional design according to local specifications and shipbuilding techniques. Arab dhows are recognized as belonging to one region or another, so to a boat researcher, a *kūtiyya* is clearly an Indian design, which has remained unaffected and essentially the same for many years; but for the Suris the craft is called *ghanja*, as the name became identified with the area, irrespective of its ethnic origin. The maritime literature is sometimes not clear on the use of terms. When Villiers (1940: 396) was writing about his Red Sea voyage he kept using *sanbūq* for *zārūq*, interchangeably, because of the similarities that exist in the bent stemposts of both craft. While both Hornell (1942: 23, 25) and Villiers (1940: 396) correctly identified the craft as a double-ender, there were other subtle differences which Hawkins (1977: 79) noted, in that the *zārūq* had a lower stempost and sternpost. We find interesting observations made by boat researchers in the maritime treatises but these are sometimes not backed up by information from local seamen as to names and features of different dhows.

Arabs classify craft on the basis of their hull shape and functionality. Craft types and labels vary from region to region and identical terms may apply to different vessels while others may apply to structurally similar craft. In Bahrain, a *bānush* represents a *jālbūt* or a *shūʿī*. There may be peculiarities or inconsistencies that the Western boat researcher finds, which the Arab shipwright or the coastal community brushes aside as unimportant. Some boat-builders I spoke to knew the ships by shape; the seamen and fishermen rarely bothered about shapes and when they called them by name, they often used the incorrect names. Confusion of terms and designs is frustrating for the researcher. One is struck by the similarity of dhows in their overall design, while the dhow types such as the Emirati *ʿāmla*, the Omani *shāḥūf*, and the Musandam and Iranian *zārūka* look the same in many respects, differences are found in a few features of design and size, hence it is understandable that locals confuse the names. The same confusion surrounds the names *baqqāra* and *shāḥūf*; both are structurally similar dhows but with disparate regional names. Our survey indicates that from Majis, north-east of Sohar, a *baqqāra* was called a *shāḥūf*, and from beyond the border of Oman into the Emirates it is no longer a *shāḥūf* but a *baqqāra*. What is also confusing is that in Liwa, north of Majis, the fishermen called a *baqqāra*, *ʿāmla*, again because of similar design features and characteristics of these craft. The locals did not argue with the present researcher, as far as they were concerned the terms were 'hiya hiya' (one and the same), the regional name for them is a pragmatic matter. A long-stemmed *zaʿīma* in Aden is functionally called a *sanbūq* by fishermen involved in net fishing even though structurally these dhows are dissimilar. In the eyes of the local fishermen it is the fishing location which classifies a boat: the *sanbūq* was traditionally the fishing dhow and therefore a *zaʿīma* is a *sanbūq*, type and design are irrelevant.

A taxonomic classification

For the Arabs, dhows are differentiated either by their sterns or their bows, or a combination of both. The *baghla*, *sanbūq* and *shūʿī* are distinguished by their sharp bow, while the stern of the *baghla* and *sanbūq* is almost a replica of the square-transom stern of the European galleon. The *jālbūt*, on the other hand, is different; the bow with its upright stem is unique among the rest of the dhows. Prins (1972-4: 164–5) correctly identified three general distinctive categories: a) the broad-beamed double-ended vessels such as the *būm* and the early *dangī*, b) the slim rakish double-ended craft such as the *zārūka*, *battīl* and *badan*, and c) the transom craft, long- or short-keeled, examples of which are the *sanbūq*, *jālbūt*, *shūʿī*, *ghanja* and *baghla*. Each of these has been structurally influenced by distinct local features, some going back to antiquity, and their names, though only a few have been identified as genuinely Arabic, are borrowed from languages within the Semitic family or from Fārsī or Hindi.

There are several questions as to how dhows are distinguished, who or what determines their categories and why one term can represent different dhows, or several terms can be used for one identical dhow. A taxonomic classification, as we illustrated in Chapters 4, 5 and 6, is an attempt to categorize dhows according to hull design. Admittedly this is not an ideal way to look at types of dhow. On the other hand, distinction of dhows according to their function cannot be determined by the terminology the seamen use because one dhow can function as a cargo vessel while the other could be for fishing. The dhows can look similar but may have separate functions. A small *sanbūq* could have only operated as a fishing craft but a larger vessel could be used for fishing, pearling or trading. Some larger vessels, such as the *būm*, *baghla* and *ghanja*, could typologically be identified as cargo carriers, which were occasionally used for pearling or fishing. The very small types of craft such as the *māshuwwa* or the dug-out *hūrī*, were usually found in the fisheries, but also functioned as passenger boats, to ferry people among the numerous creeks.

Our survey has shown how difficult and often complex it is to suggest an overall classification, with rules that can be applied all over the Indian Ocean world. If the informant wishes to use a more inclusive term like *khashaba*, a term common in most parts of the Gulf and Oman to signify 'launch', or to use terms of purpose such as the Kuwaiti *saffār* for ocean-going vessel, the Emirati *sammāk* for a fishing dhow, *mehmel*, which seamen use when they are talking about a cargo dhow, or *ʿabra* to refer to a ferry boat, the boat researcher would still not know what type of ship it was. The distinction between ship types, functioning as cargo, pearling and fishing vessels, is only expressed in general terms but the names of individual types do not figure in this general terminology. Dhows of similar design could be cargo or fishing vessels though some exceptions do occur. One category which a boat researcher comes across is the universal term *lanch* used by Arab and non-Arab seamen for all transom-stern vessels fitted with an inboard engine. In some instances in lieu of *lanch*, the names *sanbūq* or *shūʿī* were used. The other problem is the size of the dhow. When we speak of a Kuwaiti *būm*, a Suri *ghanja*, a Bahraini *bānūsh*, an Emirati *kalba* or an Omani *badan*, are we referring to a large, medium or small vessel; a *ghanja* is a large vessel, but what size is large? My informants gave rough tonnage figures of weight capacity and by that, one is expected to draw a picture of the size of the vessel; for example, a 300-ton *būm* as opposed to a 450-ton *ghanja*. As so many dhows do look alike, sometimes locals identify them by their approximate shape rather than their size.

Because names given to dhows are not representative of shape or design, it is only after a dhow is marked by some name that it becomes identified by its own characteristics. The shipbuilder's perception of a dhow may differ from one region to another; the case of the *baghla*, as it is called in Kuwait, and the *ghanja* in Sur for the same type, is a good example. Hawkins' (1977: 24) view is that there never was a dhow type called *ghanja* as such. About the name *ghanja*, Suris adapted the nomenclature from the Indian *ganjo* and *gunjo*, names given to ships generally, and not to a specific type. In fact the type the Suris were dealing with was the Indian *buggalow*, which Kuwaitis called *baghla*. A *hūrī* in Masirah represents what the rest of the Gulf calls a *sanbūq*. There are no answers to such wrong coinages. Locals may designate different names to those which the boat researcher identifies as the same type. The discrepancies are many whether they are to do with name coinage, hull design or function. Our study has conveniently applied a taxonomic classification where it has been possible to draw inter-relationships or proportionate significance of facts or information, as considered from a particular point of view.

Unanswered questions

There are still questions unanswered as to how one recognizes differences in hull design, why names of types change drastically from one region to another, who determines what type a certain vessel is, and so on. These and other questions of classificaton and designation methods are crucial to the study of boat typology. Who gave the name to a ship type? The shipwright, owner or captain, or the coastal community? Is the name borrowed or locally created? What about transitional names? One name can give way to an older name. The Bahraini *bānūsh* replaced the Gulf name *shūʿī*. Prados (1997: 192) believes that the term *sanbūq* in the Yemen has 'quietly displaced common usage of the term *zārūq*'.

The name *sanbūq* is an old term, the origins of which could be the *shabūq* as recorded by al-Muqaddasī (1906, III: 32) in the fourth/tenth century; the craft was an Indian Ocean vessel, found from the Red Sea to the Seas of China. In different languages (see Chapter 5), cognates of this term point to a universal name. Moreover, the *sanbūq* was a versatile ship which plied the Indian Ocean as a cargo vessel, fishing and pearling boat, and many a time as a coastal ferry boat.

Another question needs to be addressed: How many of the dhows built in India can be credited as being Perso-Arab in design and name? Hornell (1946: 219) observed that the sailing craft of the Indian west coast for about 100 miles south of Bombay, show a strong influence from Arab designs. The *sanbūq* was often built at Beypore, south of Calicut on the north of the river Chaliyar (Wiebeck 1987: 96). Immigrants from the Yemen, Hadhramaut, Oman and the Iranian littoral of the Gulf, settled at one time on the west coast of India, and whether they brought new technical ideas for building ships and introduced new (Arabic or Fārsī) names for ships, or whether Indian names prevailed in spite of the migratory movements into the area, it is difficult to say. One good example is the Hadrami sayyid family, Al-Jifrī, who settled in Kerala in the late eighteenth century. Their descendants were timber merchants and shipbuilders, whose workshops were located in Beypore, south of Calicut. For generations, Arab shipowners from the Gulf came to them for their dhows to be built (Dale 1997: 181–2). As much as they applied their Hadhramaut shipbuilding techniques from the early years of their settlement in India, it is assumed that they also borrowed Indian technical ideas which they then introduced to the Gulf when trade links between India and East Africa became increasingly strong in the nineteenth century. The fact needs to be stressed that up to the present day Indian carpenters in the Gulf and Oman are considered the best skilled workers for the construction of dhows.

Could names of types signify an animate or inanimate object? Folk beliefs among the seamen on the origins of names of dhow types are plenty. For example, the *baqqāra* is related to the shape of a cow, a *badan* is understood to represent the figure of a human body, while the *battīl*'s hull shape is that of a pregnant woman. The name *shūʿī* is believed to come from a type of tree called *shūʿ*. The names *būm* and *ghurāb* seem out of place, but for the common seamen and fishermen the fact that the names stand for an owl and a raven respectively seems perfectly natural. There may be some precedent for this because medieval names of ship types such as *ṭayra* meaning bird, or *ḥamāma* for pigeon, were used in the fourth/tenth century (al-Muqaddasī 1906, III: 32). Whether they represented birds as such is not known. However, the metaphorical imagery of likening a ship to a bird is found among medieval writers, such as the historian Abū Shāma, who tells us that the *ghurāb*s are war galleys, called as such because 'they spread their wings like those of a dove' (wa-tansharu min ḍulūʿi-hā ajniḥat al-ḥamām) (1872–98, IV: 210). Another comparison, the ship/camel, either metaphorically or literally, is a classical theme in pre-Islamic poetry. The camel in the desert is superimposed on the image of the vessel in the ocean. The portrayal of such an identification is lively, as in the poem of the panegyrist Zuhayr b Abī Sulmā (dc 6/627), comparing riders guiding their camels into the desert with sailors sailing their ships on the open sea:

yaghshā l-ḥudātu bi-him waʿtha l-kathībi ka-mā
yughshī l-safāʾina mawja l-lujjati l-ʿaraku

(The guides direct them to the fine-sand of the dune just as
the sailors direct their ships to the waves of the sea)[5]

Ships with sails were compared to camels carrying howdahs (or litters) in the verses of Bishr b Abī Khāzim al-Asadī (d c 535 AD):

fa-ka-anna ẓuʿna-humu ghadāta taḥammalū
sufunun takaffaʾu fī khalījin mughrabi

5 Translation from Montgomery 1997: 186.

(Their camel-borne litters, on the morning they departed, resembled
ships tossed about on a watercourse with humped waves)[6]

One cannot help noticing the *sāṭūr* (bow) of a *sanbūq* or *būm* which protrudes like a long camel's neck. The comparing of ships to animals is an interesting study which could yield some important results from a literary, linguistic and cultural perspective.

More puzzling is the gender of the names of ship types. There are no definitive answers to such mysteries, though I heard one explanation by Sabil Abbas[7] at the Deira boatyard in Dubai. He told me that the *sāṭūr* makes the difference; if it is thick, the name is feminine such as the *samʿa*, *baghla*, and *ghanja*, while if it is longer and thinner and looks fiercer, the name is masculine, for example the *būm*, *sanbūq*, *shūʿī* etc. I discussed this with other seamen but received a mixed response. It is an interesting idea which demonstrates the workings of folk belief and how people relate names of material culture to nature. Folk belief can be seen here as the imaginative expression of the attitudes and cultural values of a people.

The holistic approach to the lingusitic inquiry

The inquiry to examine linguistically the nomenclature of ship types and terminology of ships' parts is virtually new territory. My attempt to limit my study to the Arabian Gulf and Oman was fundamental and the holistic approach in this book should present a framework for further linguistic and historical studies in the area. Before embarking on a more ambitious study on the language of the dhow across the Indian Ocean, future studies should incorporate the Iranian coast of the Gulf, the south-west Arabian coast and the African Red Sea coast.

Our study has shown the limitations of the technical sources and the historical written sources, hence the importance of local specialist knowledge. A combination of documentary evidence as well as fieldwork is essential in such research. It is important to note that technical Western sources are of great use for the boat researcher but she/he must be aware that many of the writers in this field are non-Arabists, only a few spoke some Arabic, and they were certainly not historical linguisticians.

My research set out to establish that one cannot examine material–cultural terms as separate entities in dictionaries. They are to be taken in the context of the culture of the community, its customs, ideas and attitudes, which are transmitted from one generation to another. Language is the chief agent

6 Translation from Montgomery, ibid.
7 Interviewed on 15 April 1996.

of culture transmission. In studying the nomenclature of ship types and technical terms for the parts of a ship, one has to take account of the fact that the names and uses for things, peculiar to one community, may be adopted by other communities through culture contact. Although the dhow, as an object of the material culture, is a thing of aesthetic value in itself, by looking at the language pertaining to the dhow we can find out so much more about the interaction of the Gulf communities with India, Southern Arabia, and East Africa.

One has to be aware that an inquiry into the material–cultural terms, in our case the names of ship types and terminology of ships' parts, is seriously hindered by the lack of proper tools. The researcher will discover sooner or later as I argued in an earlier work (Agius 1984: 59–87, 313–28), that Arabic lexica are biased against any material–cultural terminology, let alone nautical terms. The lexica consider that technical terminology with dialectal affiliation is improper and does not deserve a place in the dictionary, written as it is in the language of the Qurʾān. Basically these dictionaries are only practical for philologists who, arguing about roots of words, are only concerned about the correct form of the classical language. Our interest is not merely in what the form may mean but in how the word was used in the context given for the speaker or writer of the time. Basically there are no Arabic dictionaries on historical principles, they are descriptive. Nor do we have good dictionaries of Arabic dialects, certainly not for the area I have studied. With this deficiency in linguistic research, one resorts to literary works and documents as well as oral history. One seeks to see, in the entirety of the words investigated, the intellectual process of the speakers who use them, and to understand them against the whole background of the language they pertain to, not only in their actual use, but also in their literary and social value and in their innumerable relations with other words. These were the principles by which I conducted my inquiry, the results of which have shown the value of combining, by a holistic approach, the linguistic, documentary and fieldwork sources into one overall picture of the dhows in the Arabian Gulf and Oman.

A diachronic investigation into the nomenclature can only be done if more archival material comes to light; unless this is so, several names will remain in doubt. One important thing which has emerged in our study is the Fārsī element in the nomenclature of parts of a ship, which points to an early Persian dominance in boat-building, from antiquity to modern times. This, together with other evidence of the presence of Shīʿite Arabs of Iranian ethnic origin and of their culture, as portrayed in the floral patterns on dhows and the doors of houses, adds to our understanding of maritime ethnography in the Arabian Gulf and Oman.

Appendix

The following figures, although not to scale, represent the different sections of the *būm* with a glossary of technical terms for the parts of the vessel[1] as discussed in Chapter 7.

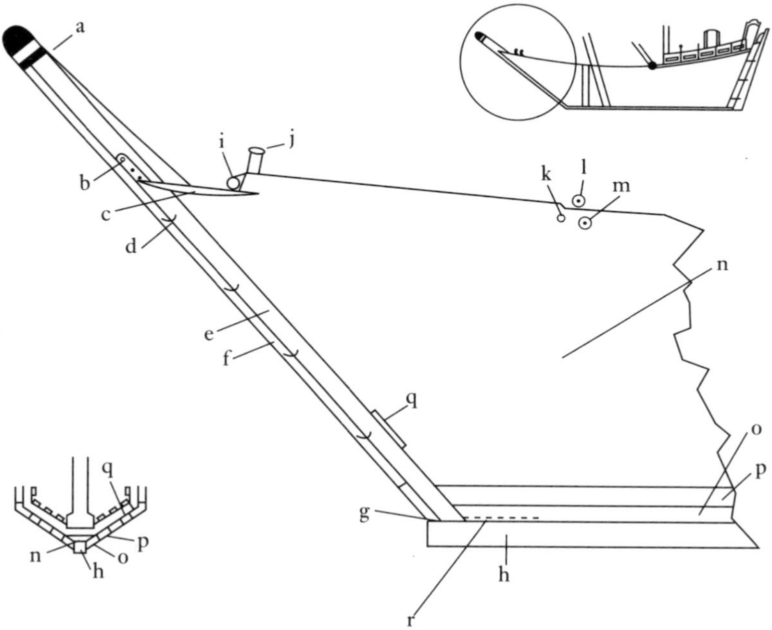

Figure 1
The front side

(a) *sāṭūr* or *ṣāṭūr* (also *sidr* or *sidir*) bow fender, (b) *fakhkha* or *fakhkh* cramp, (c) *wisāda* (pl *wasāyid*) cheek timber, (d) *būlūle* or *bilūla* crampoon, (e) *meyl is-sidr* stempost, (f) *barmēl* outer stem, (g) *daʿūma* cutwater, (h) *bīṣ* or *bīs* keel, (i) *chalb* or *chalba* cat beam, (j) *rummāna* bollard, (k) *marzām* (pl *marāzīm*) or *mirzāb* (pl *marāzib*) scupper, (l) *ḥmār al-baḥr* or *ḥmār baḥḥār* moveable spar, (m) *ḥāshya* fixed spar, (n) *burd* (< Port *bordo*) the side or board of the ship, (o) *mālich* (pl *mawālich*) garboard strake, (p) *khadd* (pl *khudūd*) bottom (second) plank, (q) *ʿaqrab* crosshead, (r) *chafīōh* keelson.

1 Cf Johnstone and Muir 1964: 299–332; al-Ḥijjī 1988: 73–146; Groset-Grange 1993: xi–xx; al-Rūmī 1996.

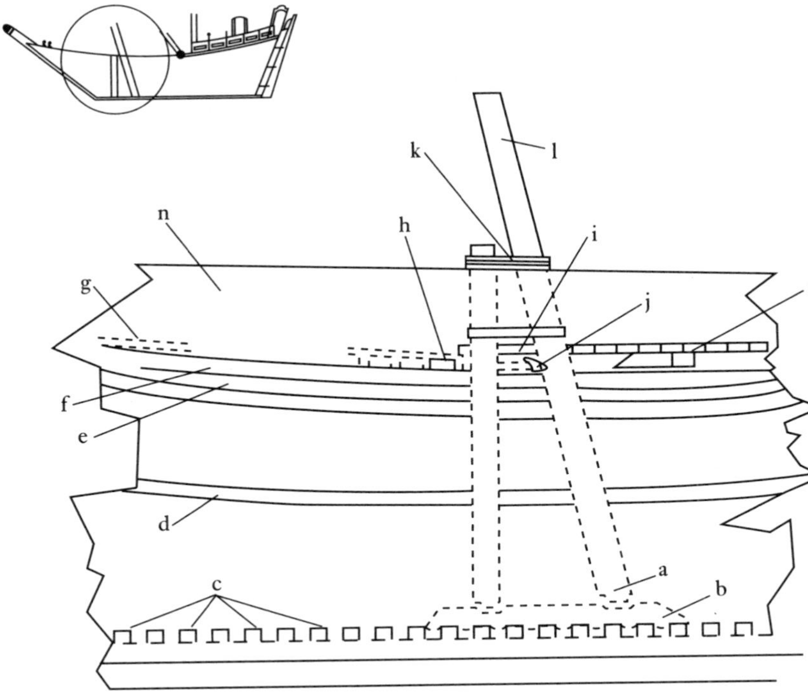

FIGURE 2
The front middle side

(a) *sikk* mast step, (b) *fils* mast block, (c) *ʿuṭfa* (pl *ʿuṭaf*) or *ʿiṭfa* (pl *ʿiṭaf*) floorboard rib, (d) *kamar* waterline wale, (e) *manẓara* (pl *manāẓir*) bulwark, (f) *gēṭān* wale, (g) *tirrīch* sheer-strake, (h) *zand* (pl *zinūd*) tie-beam, (i) *ṣuwār id-digil* mast cross-bar, (j) *gudri* padding, (k) *zīār* rope lashing, (l) *digil* or *dagal* (pl *adgāl*) mast, (m) *jālī* (pl *jawālī*) hatch, (n) *darrāba* (pl *darārīb*) moveable weatherboard.

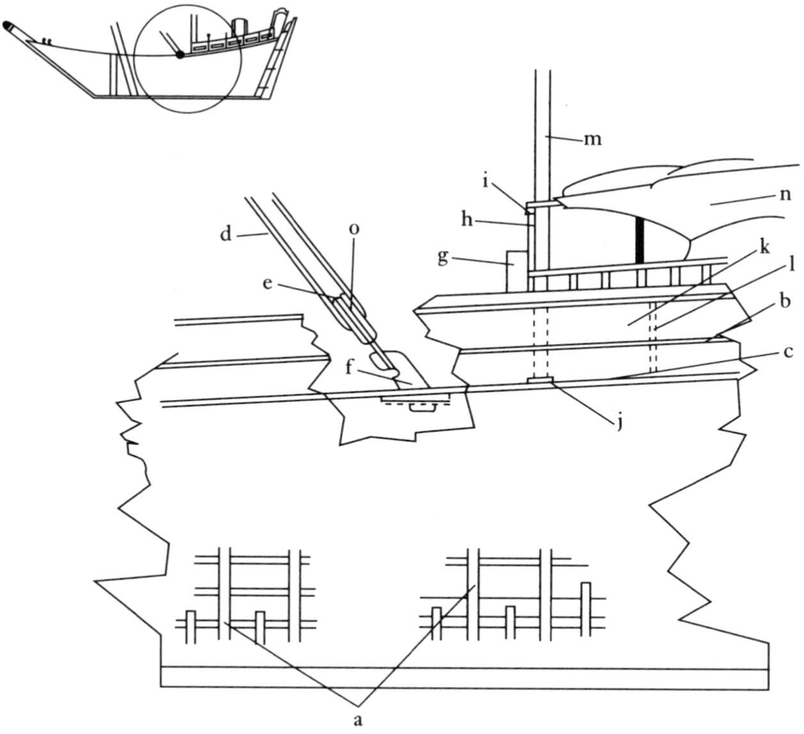

FIGURE 3
The rear middle side

(a) *shilmān* (pl *shalāmīn*) rib (frame), (b) *zabdara* gunwale, (c) *saṭaḥ* deck, (d) *bāssa* or *makhāṭif* main tackle, (e) *jāmaʿa* or *yāmiʿa* ramhead, (f) *ʿubaydār* or *ʿobīdār* knight, (g) *gāyim* bitt for the lower rigging, (h) *khīsa* or *khīyāsa* large aftermost stanchion, (i) *gafla* cross beam that rests on the aft stanchions, (j) *fatan* centre-line plank, (k) *fanna* open poopdeck, (l) *falkī* bulk-head, (m) *digil* or *dagal* (pl *adgāl*) mast, (n) *ẓulla* awning, (o) *gāfiyya* block.

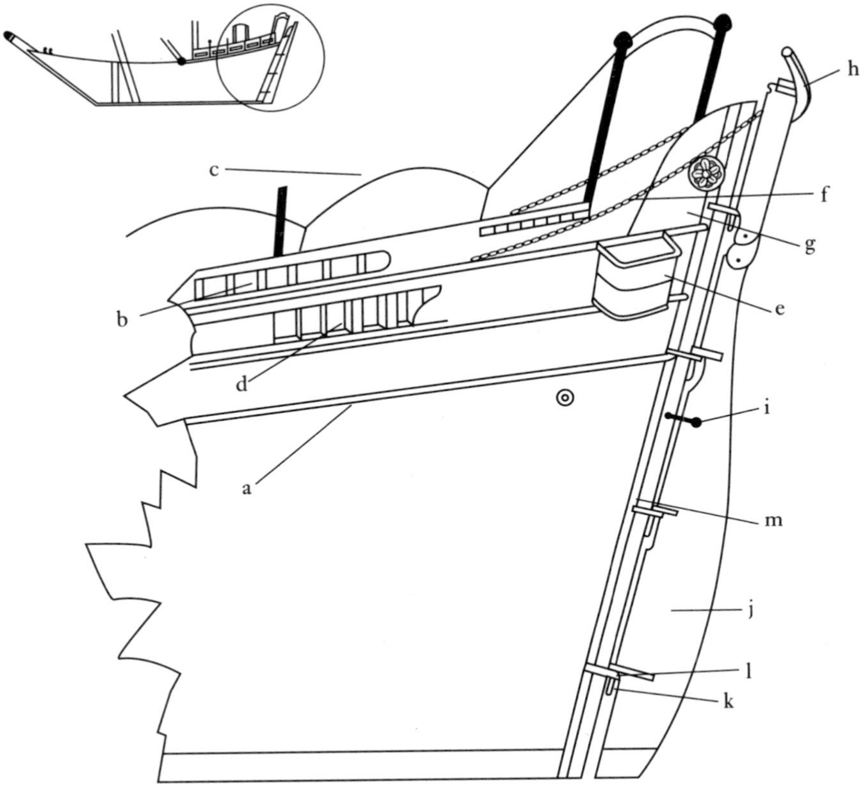

FIGURE 4
The stern side

(a) *ānsāb* rubbing strake, (b) *ribūsh* or *rēl* or *mshāya* poop rail, (c) *ẓulla* awning, (d) *dīrīsha* (pl *darāyish*) or *darīcha* (pl *darāyich*) port-hole, (e) *zūlī* or *zōlī* male's toilet box, (f) *sangal* or *ṣangal* (< [?] Hin) chain pull, (g) *ʿanāfa* or *ʿannāfa* curved stern head, (h) *kāna* tiller, (i) *salāma* safety-rope, (j) *sukkān* or *sikkān* rudder, (k) *narr* (pl *nurūr*) or *dhakar* (pl *dhikūr*) pintle, (l) *māda* (pl *mādāt*) or *nathiyya* (pl *nathiyyāt*) gudgeon, (m) *mēl it-tifr* sternpost.

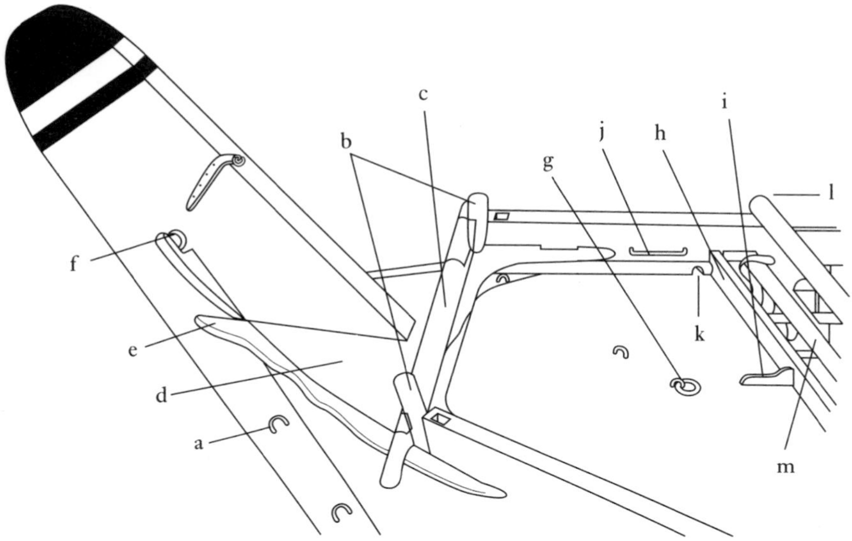

FIGURE 5
The foredeck

(a) *būlūle* or *bilūla* crampoon, (b) *rummāna* bollard, (c) *chalb* or *chalba* cat-beam, (d) *kashtīl is-sidr* forecastle, (e) *wisāda* cheek timber, (f) *fakhkh* or *fakhkha* cramp, (g) *ḥalga* ring, (h) *ḥajir* brakewater, (i) *mākrī* (pl *mawākrī*) stop-cleat, (j) *zand* (pl *zinūd*) stout iron rail, (k) *marzām* (pl *marāzīm*) or *mirzāb* (pl *marāzīb*) scupper, (l) *ḥmār al-baḥr* or *ḥmār baḥḥār* moveable spar, (m) *ḥāshiya* fixed spar.

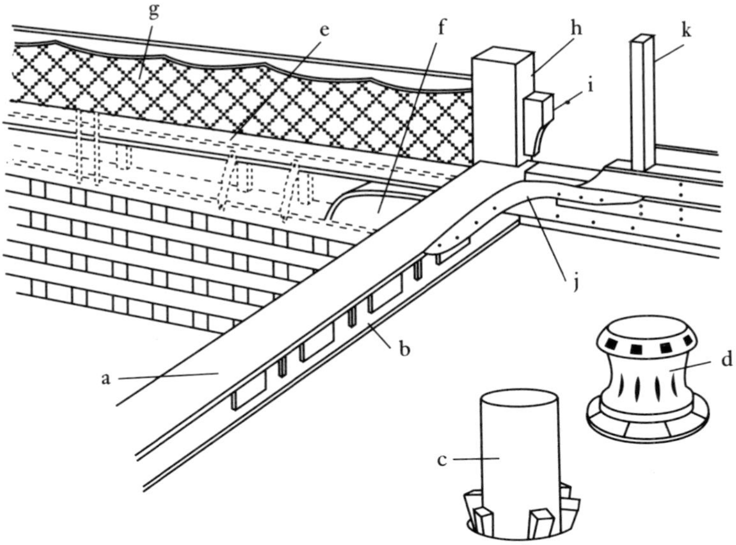

FIGURE 6
The middle part of the deck

(a) *fālkī* or *jāmlaw* (< [?] Hin) hand-rail, (b) *ʿēbāt* support rail, (c) *ghulamī* (< [?] Hin or Ur *kilmī* or *kalmī*) mizen mast, (d) *dawwār* capstan, (e) *darrāba* weatherboard, (f) *ḥiyāb* or *ḥayāb* small bulwark, (g) *talbīs* or *tilbās* plaited tress, (h) *gāyim* stout stanchion, (i) *mākrī* (pl *mawākrī*) stop-cleat, (j) *karwa* (< Ur or Port *curva*) or *milzāma* knee, (k) *ḥīsa* crossbar-stanchion.

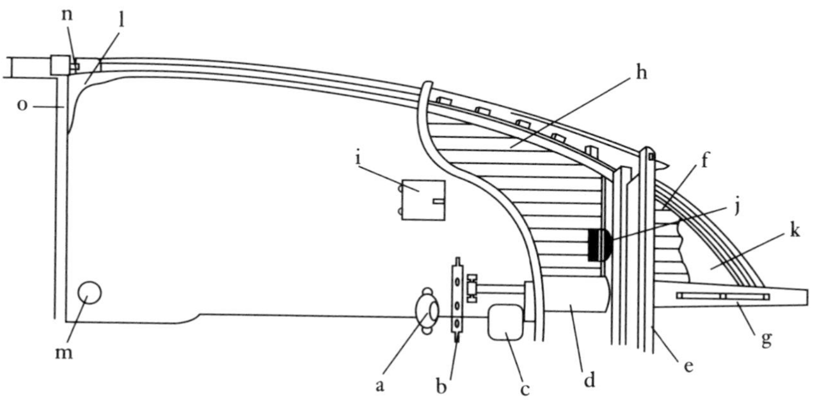

FIGURE 7
The stern deck

(a) *dēra* compass, (b) *charkh* or *dūlāb* (< Per *dūlab* 'waterwheel') steering wheel, (c) *kursī* box or bench, (d) *ṣandūg as-sankal* chain-box or cover, (e) *gafla* cross-beam, (f) *kashtīl it-tifr* stern-castle, (g) *ʿanāfa* or *ʿannāfa* curved stern head, (h) *nīm* poopdeck, (i) *kamira* (Port *câmara*) hatchway, (j) *kātlī* bench, (k) *ṭabla* aft platform, (l) *karwa* or *milzāma* knee, (m) *ghulamī* mizen mast, (n) *mākrī* (pl *mawākrī*) stop-cleat, (o) *fālkī* or *jāmlaw* hand-rail.

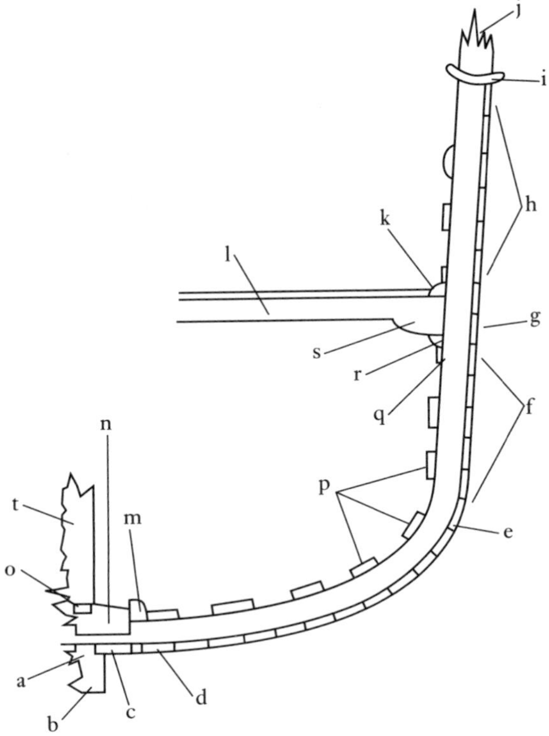

FIGURE 8
Vertical section of the hull

(a) *chaftōh* keelson, (b) *bīṣ* or *bīs* keel, (c) *mālich* (pl *mawālich*) garboard strake, (d) *khadd* (pl *khudūd*) bottom (second) plank, (e) *kamar* waterline wale, (f) *manẓara* (pl *manāẓir*) bulwark, (g) *gēṭān* wale, (h) *tirrīch* sheer-strake, (i) *zabdara* gunwale, (j) *darrāba* (pl *darārīb*) moveable weatherboard, (k) *ʿanch* waterway, (l) *ṣwāra* beam, (m) *naʿal* (pl *nuʿūl*) stringer, (n) *naʿāsh* (lowest) stringer, (o) *fils* mast block, (p) *ḥzām* (pl *ḥzāmāt*) belt, (q) *durmēt* counter-clamp, (r) *salbīs* clamp, (s) *karwa* or *milzāma* knee, (t) *id-digil il-ʿōd* main mast.

Glossary

ʿabbāra (pl ʿabbārāt) – south-eastern Omani ferry boat

ʿabīd – the cathead (a beam projecting over the dhow's bow to which the anchor is secured)

ʿabra (pl ʿabrāt) – a generic term for a ferry boat

ʿabrī or ʿabriyya – a Dhofari small sailing stitched boat; a Suri deep-sea cargo ship

ʿabriyya – see *ʿabrī*

ʿabriyya sanbūq – the Mahri and Suri double-ended *sanbūq*, long and wide with a long prow

abūbūz – a fishing boat with similar features to a *sanbūq* except for the rounded stern

alāt as-safīna – ship's instruments

ʿanāfa or ʿannāfa – the curved stern head

ʿanch – a waterway (piece of wood fitted on the outboard edge of the deck beams and designed to channel water out)

anjar (pl anājir) – see *anyar*

ʿannāfa – see *ʿanāfa*

ānsāb – the rubbing strake (a fender to protect the side of the dhow when coming close to another vessel or mooring)

anyar (pl anāyir) – a grapnel

ʿaqrab – crosshead (an internal knee – piece of wood – which fastens the stem and sternposts)

ʿarāgiyya – a large Iraqi cargo river boat

arīr – *Delonix elata*, grows to a height of about 16 feet in the Dhofar region; the fibrous centre of the trunk is used to make ropes and nets, while the timber is used to make ribs for small boats

ʿarīsh – an open hut made of palm-tree branches

ʿarsha (also ẓulla) – the awning (canvas or reed canopy)

athab – *Ficus salicifolia*, grows to a height up to 20 feet, found in Arabia and Oman; timber is used for ribs on small boats in Dhofar

bachchāra (pl bachāchīr) – see *baqqāra*

badan (pl badana or bdāna) – Omani coastal trading vessel; also fishing boat, double-ended and double-keeled with a long slim hull having a sharp needle-nose stem and high unswept sternpost, one mast

badan safar – seagoing trading *badan*

badan ṣayyād – fishing *badan*

baggāra (pl bagāgīr) – see *baqqāra*

baghla or bghala (pl bghāla) – ocean-going Kuwaiti vessel with a low bow and a high unswept quarterdeck, characterized by the square, galleon-type stern with rear windows and quarter galleries, rigged with two or three masts

bahwī – a medium size Musandam *battīl*; has features of the eighteenth- and nineteenth-century *battīl*

bajra – a nineteenth-century Iranian pleasure boat with a high stern and flattish rounded bottom

bākhira (pl bawākhir) – a steamship

bakkīs – cowrie shells

bakra (pl bakrāt) – iron pulley

balam or belem (pl ablām or blām) – Malabarian dug-out canoe, round bottomed; the Iraqi type is flat-bottomed, carvel-built with high sides, with its prow and stern carved and decorated. It is punted or sailed

balam ʿashārī – Iraqi passenger or light cargo boat

balam fūdrī – Kuwaiti sharp double-ended vessel

balam naṣārī – Iraqi freighter, fishing or pearling vessel

ballām – an Iraqi term for rower

bandar (pl banādir) – harbour; commercial centre

bānūsh (pl bawānīsh) – a generic term for a Bahraini square-sterned vessel with features of a *sanbūq* and *shūʿī*

baqqāra (pl baqāqīr) or bachchāra (pl bachāchīr) or baggāra (pl bagāgīr) – double-ended fishing boat, transport and pearling vessel, some hybrid features of the *badan* but with a sharp-pointed bow

barmēl or barmīl (pl barāmil) – the false stempost (a protective outer stem); cauldron

barmīl – see *barmēl*

barriyya – whitebait

barwāna – the propeller

bāssa (pl basīs) – the main tackle

batel – see *batella*

batelha or batel – medieval Portuguese small boat (sixteenth and seventeenth centuries)

batella or batel – north-western Indian cargo vessel of the mid-nineteenth century with a square flat stern and a long stemhead

batellus or batus or battus – a Latin term for boat

baṭīra or batīra – high sided double-ended vessel with a swept back stemhead from the northern Gulf, one mast

battīl (pl batātīl) – coastal trading and pearling vessel but also a pirate and war vessel used in the eighteenth and nineteenth centuries, double-ended, with a fiddle-headed bow, a high sternpost and double forward-leaning masts; Musandam double-ended fishing vessel distinguished by its low pointed prow, high sternpost and projections

batus or battus – see *batellus*

bawra or bāwra – (fishermen's) anchor

belem – see *balam*

beylī – large dug-out canoe

bild – the plumb-line

bilūla – see *būlūle*

bir-rigʿa – square-sterned

bīṣ or bīs – a northern Gulf and Omani term for keel; the former part of a *battīl* keel

bo or po – a Chinese term for a seagoing vessel

bōt (pl bawātī) – an early nineteenth-century Hindi term for a sailing vessel

brīch or ibrīch – Indian cargo vessel with one or two masts belonging to Karachi and the Kutch Madvani coast

budgero or buggalow or bugle or bungalow – an Anglo-Indian term for the Arab *baghla*

būgāʿa or būqāʿa – the Kuwaiti and Bahraini small flat-bottomed vessel with a straight sternpost

buggalow – see *budgero*

bugle – see *budgero*

būlūle or bilūla – a crampoon

būm (pl abwām) – double-ended Kuwaiti cargo vessel distinguished by its straight, sharp-pointed stemhead painted black and white

būm al-māʾ – a water-carrying *būm*

būm al-qaṭṭāʿ – a transport *būm*

būm as-saffār – an ocean-cargo *būm*

būmiyya – the supporting knee to prop up the stem and sternposts

bungalow – see *budgero*

būqāʿa – see *būgāʿa*

burd – one side of the hull

burma (pl burmāt) – a medieval round ship of the Indian Ocean

būṣa (pl būṣāt) – an inch (unit of measure)

buti – a Swahili term for *jahāzī*

çâphan – Chaldean seagoing vessel

caravel – small trading Mediterranean vessel used in the late sixteenth century by the Portuguese and Spaniards for voyages of exploration

catur or chaturi or kaṭōrā – small Indian war vessel with oars (sixteenth and seventeenth centuries); light Malabarian rowing vessel

ç̣ᵉphînâh – a Hebrew term for seagoing vessel

chaftōh – the keelson

chāla (pl chāchīl or chāshīl) – double-ended fully decked craft used for transport, ferrying passengers and pearl-diving, with a peculiar stemhead and pointed stern similar to the *būm* and with projecting quarter strakes; see *tashshāla*

chalb or chalba – the cat beam (a carved wooden horn on the raised foredeck to secure mooring lines) chanta – the gunwale

charkh (also dūlāb or jarkh) – steering wheel which operates the compass

chaturi – see *catur*

chāwiya (pl chāwiyāt) – a 16-inch nail used to secure the floor timber to the keel

chunam – animal fat mixed with burned lime; see *shūna*

chyāla – an Emirati term for a double-ended fully decked craft, see *chāla*

cotia or kotia – the Indian type of cargo vessel, see Arab *kūtiyya*

dabūsa – the cabin for women passengers; a storage cabin

dagal (pl dagalāt or adgāl) – see *digil*

ḍalʿ (pl ḍulūʿ) – a classical Arabic term for rib

dāmir – a type of resin

dāneg (pl dawāneg) – an Iraqi river ferry boat

dangī (pl danākī) – Kuwaiti double-ended two-masted vessel with a slightly curved stem and a bird's head, the beak pointing aft at the stemhead

dangiyya (pl danāgī) – double-ended one-masted vessel with a low bow and high poop

dānūq (pl dawānīj) – small and narrow Kuwaiti boat for fishing and pleasure

daqal – see *daql*

ḍāqiya (pl ḍawāqī) – see *dhākiya*

daql or daqal (pl adqāl; coll daqala) – a classical Arabic term for mast

daraja or darija (pl darāyij) – see *dirīsha*

darīcha (pl darāyish) – see *dirīsha*

dariya – see *dirīsha*

darrāba (pl darārīb) – moveable weatherboard (a temporary planking fitted on top of the gunwale as a protection against the dhow's cargo falling over board)

dau (pl madau) – east African flat-bottomed boat

dau la mataruma – rib-constructed east African boat

dau la msomari – short-keeled east African boat with nailed planks dau la mtepe – sewn-hulled east African boat

daʿūma – cutwater; a wooden backhead (the bottom curve of the stempost joining the keel)

dāw – slave and trading vessel, also used as a war vessel or privateer; smaller than the *baghla* and *ghanja* with a long grab stem, a high stern and poop projecting over the rudder

dawba (pl duwab) – Ottoman war vessel used on the Nile

dawh – a medieval small ship of Persian origin

daww – a medieval ship of Persian origin

dawwār – the capstain

dawwārī – a type of sailors' song

dayl al-fār – plane

ḍēṅgā or ḍōṅgā – a generic term for a small sailing boat on the west coast of India; originally a native Indian canoe

dēra – see *dīra*

dhākiya (pl dhawākī) or ḍāqiya (pl ḍawāqī) – the Dhofari stitched boat employed during the sardine fishing season

dhakr (pl dhukūr) (also narr) – pintle fixed to the sternpost for hanging the rudder

dhangī – Indo-Pakistani trading cargo vessel

dhirāʿ (pl adhruʿ) – forearm's length (a measuring unit)

dhony – see *doney*

dhow – a generic term used by the west for any Indian Ocean type of craft

digil or dagal (pl dagalāt or adgāl) – the mast

id-digil il-ghulamī – the mizen-mast

id-digil il-ʿōd – the mainmast

dingey – large sailing vessel: two masts and two outboard sails (not to be confused with *dangī*)

dinghy – an Anglo-Indian term for a small wherry boat

diqil or diql (pl adqāl or daqalāt) – see *digil*

diql – see *diqil*

dīra or dēra (pl dīrāt) – the compass on a dhow

dirʿān – a Bahraini term for a gunwale of a boat

dirīsha or darīsha (pl darāyish) or daraja or darija (pl darāyij) – the port-hole (stern port for loading long poles into the hold of the vessel)

doney or dhony – south Indian dug-out craft

ḍōṅgā – see *ḍēṅgā*

droṇa – a Sanskrit term for boat

dūba (pl dawābī or adwāb or duwab or dawabāt) – large double-ended flat-bottomed harbour vessel for transport

dūlāb (also charkh or jarkh) – the steering wheel

dūmeh – a general term for a boat with oars

dūmi shirāʿ – a general term for a double-ended ocean-going sailing craft

durmēt – the 'sleeping' shelf (a stringer fixed inside the hull to add further support to the deck beams)

ʿēbāt – the support rail (wooden uprights alternating with iron bars)

fakhdh (pl afkhādh) – an aperture

fakhkha or fakhkh – a cramp

fālkī (also jāmlaw) – the handrail; bulk-head

fanaṣ – *Artocarpus hirsuta* or *Artocarpus integrifolia* 'jackwood': hard wood used for the dhow frames, selected for its natural bends

fanna – the fore or stern deck on boats raised above the main deck

fashīn – the tall stern-fins (a false sternpost) from which the rudder is hung

fatan – a centre-line plank

faydar – small Musandam rowing *battīl*

fils – the mast block

fīnī – *Palauium ellipticum* 'pali wood': wood ideal for stringers and other internal planks that strengthen the hull's frames

finṭās (also khazzān il-moy) – caulked water cistern tank

firmal (pl farāmil) – see *firman*

firman (pl farāmin) – the sail yard

firman ghulamī – the mizen yard

firman ʿōd – the main yard

firteh – Bahraini palm tree fibre beach boat punted by a pole

firteh chappār (pl chapāpīr) – see *firteh*

furma (pl furmāt) – template

furma d-digil – template (or key rib) positioned one third from the fore keel

furma kabirt – template (or key rib) positioned on the second third of the keel

furma l-wasṭ – third (middle) template (or key rib)

gadam (pl agdām) or qadam (pl aqdām) – a foot (unit of measure)

gādūpa – a Syriac term for oar

gāfiyya (pl gawāfī) – a block

gafla – the cross beam that rests on the aft stanchions

galam (pl aglām) – the compass (wooden fork for drawing parallel lines)

galami – see *ghulamī*

galbā – see *kalbā*

galeota – see *galliot*

galfat or ghalfat or kalfāt or kilfāt – caulking

gallāf (pl galālīf) or jallāf (pl jalālīf) – the dhow builder

galleon – seventeenth-century trading vessel

gallevat – see *gallivat*

galliot or galeota – small galley with oars, one mast and sail used in the seventeenth and eighteenth centuries

gallivat or gallevat or gallọuet – Perso-Arab or Indian single-masted warship or pirate ship built like the *ghurāb* with oars (eighteenth and nineteenth centuries)

gallouet – see *gallivat*

galmi – see *ghulamī*

galṣ (pl gulūṣ) or qalṣ (pl qulūṣ) – a lifeboat operated by oars or poles

galṣ lis-sibāq – a racing *galṣ*

gārib (pl gawārib) or kārib (pl kawārib) – a generic term for a small boat garookuh – Omani vessel with hybrid features of *zārūka* and *badan*, with a raked mast

gāyim – the bitt for the lower rigging (vertical stanchion fitted at the poop supporting the beam on which the mainmast rests when lowered)

gelba – sixteenth-century Portuguese vessel of the Red Sea and Indian Ocean

gelva – see *gelba*

gēṭān – a strake (an extra plank above the waterline wale)

ghādūf – a northern Gulf term for a spear-shaped oar

ghaff – *Acacia arabica*, wood used in dhow building in Oman

ghalfat – see *galfat*

ghanja (pl ghanjāt) or ghanye or ghinye (pl ghinyāt) – Suri ocean-going vessel distinguished by its curved stempost and a parrot's beak on the stemhead, and its square galleon-shaped stern with a high poop, similar to the *baghla*

ghanye (pl ghinyāt) – see *ghanja*

gharāb – a generic Fārsī term for launch

ghass or ghiss – the thole pin (peg inserted into the boat's gunwale to serve as a fulcrum for the oar when rowing)

ghawār – the auger

ghawṣ – diving

al-ghawṣ al-bārid – the cold (or short-) diving season

al-ghawṣ al-kabīr – the main pearl-diving season

al-ghawṣ aṣ-ṣaghīr – the short-diving season

ghawwāṣ (pl ghawāwīṣ) – a pearling dhow with sails and oars

ghinye (pl ghinyāt) – see *ghanja*

ghiss – see *ghass*

ghulamī or galmi or galami – the mizen mast

ghurāb (pl aghriba or ghirbān) (also grab) – galley with a low and sharp projecting prow and a square stern, two or three masts; also a Mediterranean galley

gilāfa or qilāfa – shipbuilding

gōz – the bow of a bow drill

grab – see *ghurāb*

gubēt or rās is-sidr – the stemhead of a *ghanja* and *baghla*

guddām or juddām – the front part of the dhow

gudri – padding

gudūm (pl gadāyim) – see *juddūm*

guful – the tongue (a ridge on the edge of one piece of wood used as a means of joining the groove of another piece of wood)

ḥalga (pl ḥalag) – an iron ring on deck for tying ropes

ḥalja (pl ḥalaj) – see *ḥalga*

ḥamāma – a medieval transport ship

hamar – hammer

ḥammāl (pl ḥammālīn) – a general term for transport ship

ḥammāl bāshī – the Kuwaiti harbour transport ship

ḥammāla – a medieval transport ship

ḥanda or ḥinda – improvised singing

handāza – brass quadrant (inscribed in degrees with a plumb line to calculate how far the stem and sternposts lean forward)

ḥāshya – a fixed spar (wooden support fixed to the gunwale to which the ropes are secure tied)

ḥayāb – see *ḥiyāb*

haykal (also jisad or jasad) – the hull

ḥfūt – Dhofari timber

ḥibāl al-qinnab – ropes of hemp

ḥinda – see *ḥanda*

hīrāb – a Dhofari term for keel

ḥīsa – the crossbar-stanchion

ḥiyāb or ḥayāb – the small bulwark (side of the middle part of the dhow from the keel to the deck)

ḥmār al-baḥr or ḥmār baḥḥār – the moveable spar (wooden support placed aft the foredeck used in the rigging of the dhow) ḥmār baḥḥār – see *ḥmār al-baḥr*

ḫmmāḷa – Moroccan harbour dredger

hody – Indian dug-out canoe similar to *tōnī*, see *doney*

hūrī (pl hawārī) – Malabarian dug-out canoe

hūrī ḥafar – a south-eastern Omani term for a dug-out *hūrī*

hūrī manshūr – a south-eastern Omani term for a dug-out *hūrī* to which are added planks for a gunwale and ribs

hūriyya – see *wāriyya*

huwayriyya – see *wāriyya*

ḥzām (pl ḥzāmāt) – an internal stringer

ibrīch – see *brīch*

ibrīch bākistānī – Pakistani *brīch*

imzawrī – someone who carries the timber from the yard to the dhow

irdabb (pl arādib) – an Egyptian dry measure

ʿiṭfa (pl ʿiṭaf) – see *ʿuṭfa*

iwlēid – a boy who gathers scraps of wood to use for a cooking fire

izmīl – chisel

jahazi – Zanzibari trading vessel, transport vessel and a ferry boat, with similar features to the *sanbūq*, with a circular ring-oculus painted on the moustache of the bows; a white circle oculus is painted on each side of the stern projections of a Red Sea craft

jahāzī or jehāzī or jihāzī – the Arabic term for Swahili *jahazi*; a medieval vessel

jāla – medieval Persian raft made of leathern bottles

jalba or jilaba (pl jilāb) – medieval light passenger boat from the Red Sea

jalbut – a Swahili term for *jālbūt*

jālbūt (pl jalābīt) – northern Gulf coastal boat characterized by its upright stem and transom stern; one mast

jālbūt lis-sibāq – racing *jālbūt*

jalbūt-shuāy – amalgamated features of the square stern of the *jālbūt* and the stem of the *shūʿī*

jālī (pl jawālī) – the hatch leading to the hold

jallāf (pl jalālīf) – see *gallāf*

jāmaʿa – the ramhead (a moveable tackle block with four grooved pulleys)

jāmlaw (also fālkī) – the handrail

jangalī – *Terminalia alata* or *Terminalia coriacea* 'jungle (laurel) wood'; grows to a height of about 90 feet, used for the keel, the lower and upper deck

jarīd saʿaf – the central spines of date-palm leaves

jarkh (also charkh or dūlāb) – steering wheel which operates the compass

jasad – see *jisad*

jase – a medieval stitched vessel from the Indian Ocean

jazra (pl jazrāt) – the stealer (tapered plank worked into the stern to fill a gap after the first seven planks have been erected)

jehāzī – see *jahāzī*

jihāzī – see *jahāzī*

jilaba (pl jilāb) – see *jalba*

jilinga (also sdīrī) – the v-shaped timber at the forecastle and aftercastle

jisad (also haykal) – the hull

jolly-boat – Anglo-Indian term for a Perso-Arab or Indian type of craft

jōz – see *gōz*

juddām – see *guddām*

juddūm or judūm (pl jadāyim) or gudūm (pl gadāyim) – the adze

judūm (pl jadāyim) – see *juddūm*

jūniyye – a sack (of dates)

kalb or kalba – see *chalb*

kalbā or galbā – Emirati vessel with a straight stem, a transom stern and a long keel

kalfāt – see *galfat*

kalikut ibrīch – a Calicut *brīch*, see *brīch*

kamar or kamir – the waterline wale

kambārī or kumbārī (pl kambāriyyāt) – a Dhofari stitched boat kamir – see *kamar*

kamira – the hatchway

kāna – the tiller (a piece of wood which fits into the rudder's head)

karab – bulbous ends of palm stalks

kārib (pl kawārib) (also selek) – large Musandam *battīl*

karwa – the semi-oval design at the bottom of the stern to fit a shaft and propeller; a knee

kashtīl is sidr – the foredeck or forecastle

kashtīl it-tifr – the aftercastle

katāt or kitāt – davits

kātlī – the wooden bench on the poopdeck

kaṭōrā – see *catur*

kawra (also milzāma) – the knee (wooden wedge)

kelek – Iraqi cargo and transport raft supported by skins and operated by oarsmen

keter or kitr – double-ended lifeboat

ketīre – rowing boat

khadd (pl khudūd) – the second garboard strake above the keel

khann (pl akhnān) – a degree (unit of measure)

khashaba (pl khashabāt or akhshāb) – a generic term for vessel

khaṭra – punting pole

khawr – fjord

khazzān il-moẏ (also finṭās) – the caulked water cistern tank

khīsa (pl khiyyīsa or khīyāsa) – the large aft stanchion supporting a horizontal beam on which the yard, when lowered, is rested

kilfāt – see *galfat*

kirsh – shark oil

kishtī – a fishing vessel

kīt – dug-out canoe

kitāt – see *katāt*

kitr – see *keter*

kōbār – the auger

kotia – see *cotia*

kumbārī (pl kambāriyyāt) – see *kambārī*

kunbār – see *qanbar*

kursī – the box or bench

kūtiyya (pl kuwātī or kūtiyyāt) – Kuwaiti and Bahraini ocean-going vessel similar to the *baghla* except for the parrot's head on the stemhead pointing backwards

kwēsiyya – the latter part of the *battīl* keel

lanch (pl lanchāt) or lanj (pl lanjāt) or ling (pl lingāt) – a generic term for fishing or cargo vessel

lanchāt hindiyya – Indo-Pakistani vessels

lanj (pl lanjāt) – see *lanch*

lawḥ or lōḥ (pl alwāḥ) – a generic term for a vessel; a plank

ling (pl lingāt) – see *lanch*

lingūtī – an iron rivet

lōḥ (pl alwāḥ) – see *lawḥ*

machwa – small Indian fishing and cargo boat on the north-west coast

māda (pl mādāt) (also nathiyya) – the gudgeon of a rudder which is attached to the pintle of the sternpost

madrī – a Omani and Emirati term for rollers to haul a boat into the sea

mafrāṣ – the chisel

magarr – the drainhole

maḥmil (pl maḥāmil) – see *meḥmel*

majdāḥ (pl majādiḥ) – see *migdāḥ*

makhāṭif – the main tackle

mākrī (pl mawākrī) – a stop-cleat (piece of wood which is secured to a horizontal beam on the foredeck)

mālich or mālich al-awwal (pl mawālich) – the first garboard strake above the keel mankaba (pl manākib) – wooden container

manṭīj – *Lagerstroemia lanceolata* 'benteak wood', used for planking

manẓara (pl manāẓir) – the rubbing strake (wale bolted to the side of the dhow); a bulwark (woodwork above the waterline wale preventing water from washing over the gunwales and to protect mariners from falling overboard)

marākib baḥriyya – deep-sea vessels; warships

marākib kabīra – large vessels

marākib khafīfa – lightly laden vessels

marākib khayṭiyya – stitched boats

marākib māshiya – fast vessels

marākib safariyya – deep-sea vessels

marākib ṣaghīra – small vessels

marākib shirāʿiyya or marākib bish-shirāʿ – sailing vessels

marākib thaqīla – heavily laden vessels

marākib at-tujjār – merchant ships

markab (pl marākib) – any sailing or motorized vessel of different hull design and size; also a modern foreign ship

marzabān – a kind of palm tree

marzām (pl marāzim) (also mirzāb) – a scupper

mashāy – fore and aft carling (piece of squared timber fitted between the deck beams)

mashḥūf – slender, flat-bottomed Iraqi longboat

mashua – all-purpose Zanzibari boat similar to a *jahazi* with an oculus on either side of the stempost

māshuwwa (pl mawāshī) – cargo and fishing vessel, square-sterned and broad-beamed with a single mast similar to the *jahāzī*; a small double-ended craft; a generic term for lifeboat

masula – stitched Madras boat

maṭraga (pl maṭārig) – hammer

maṭraga khashbiyya – wooden hammer

maṭraga umm nīr – ordinary hammer

maṭraga umm shaghwa – claw

mawsim (pl mawāsim) – monsoon; also, season

meḥmel or maḥmil (pl maḥāmil) – a general term for a seagoing vessel and coastal boat

meḥmel ʿūd – large Emirati vessel

mēl (pl amyāl) – the stem or stern

mēl is-sidr – the stempost

mēl it-tifr or mēl at-tufar – the sternpost

mīdāf (pl emyādīf) – a Dhofari term for oar

migdāf (pl magādīf) or miqdāf (pl makādīf) – northern Gulf term for oar

migdāḥ (pl magādiḥ) or majdāḥ (pl majādiḥ) – the bow drill

migdāḥ būrima – bow drill with narrow gaps

migdāḥ taysīr – bow drill with wider gaps

migdāḥ tifshīt – bow drill with two points at the tip of the drill

migsām umm idēn (pl magāsim umm idēn) – pit saw

milzama (pl malāzim) – vise

milzāma (also kawra) – the knee (wooden wedge)

mindī (pl manādī) – the prop

mingar (pl manāgir) – chisel

mingar kalfāt – the caulking iron

mingar wilāyti – chisel with changing blades

minshār umm idēn (pl manāshir umm idēn) – hand saw

miqdāf (pl makādīf) – see *migdāf*

mirzāb (pl marāzīb) (also marzām) – the scupper

mismār (pl masāmīr) – a handmade nail or iron spike

mismār bū fitir – a 7-inch nail

mismār bū shibir – a 9-inch nail

mismār jasad – a 12-inch nail for decking and planking

mismār maghlaṭānī – a 10-inch nail for planking in general

mismār ṣaff kibīr – a 5-inch nail

mismār saḥāra – a 2-inch nail

mismār satḥa – a 3-inch nail for decking only

mtepe – nineteenth-century, large sewn east African vessel with high stemhead

muʾakhkhar – the back end of the vessel

mudabbab – double-ended

mugaddam or mujaddam – the forward end of a vessel

muhayla – Iraqi river transport vessel

muhēle – see *muhayla*

mujaddam – see *mugaddam*

musaqqam – financier dealing with the pearl trade

mūshara (also wirsha) – shipbuilding yard

muwarsha – see *mūshara*

naʿal (pl nuʿūl) – the lowest stringer fitted close to the mast step

naʿāsh – the lowest stringer next to the keelson

nākhōda – the sea captain or owner of a dhow

nārjīl – coconut tree

narr (pl nurūr) (also dhakr) – pintle fixed to the sternpost for hanging the rudder

nashar – a Bahraini term for stern

nathiyya (pl nathiyyāt) (also māda) – the gudgeon of a rudder which is attached to the pintle of the sternpost

nauri – Indian vessel built on the Kathiawar coast, resembling the *būm* and the *dangī*; one feature like the *kūtiyya* is a curved parrot-head with a crest on the stemhead

nīm – the poopdeck or half deck

nūra – lime

ʿobīdār or ʿubaydār – the knight (heavy angled post anchored to an athwartship beam)

ʿōd or ʿūd (pl aʿwād) – a generic term for vessel; mast

ʿōma – see *ʿūma*

padão – Indian trading cargo vessel similar to the *cotia*

pahala – Indian type of vessel similar to the *cotia*

pāṭ – a Hindi term for board; plank

patamāri – swift-sailing Indian vessel

patela – clinker-built Indian vessel

pattamar – Indian coaster similar to the *cotia*

ploion – a classical Greek term for ship; a small fishing craft

po – see *bo*

qadam (pl aqdām) – see *gadam*

qādūm (also tāj) – see *yadūm*

qalf – a classical Arabic term for securing the ship's timbers with palm fibre

qalṣ (pl qulūṣ) – see *galṣ*

qanbar or qinbār or qunbār or kunbār – a classical Arabic term for coconut fibre thread; hemp

qanja – an Ottoman gondola-type

qaraṭ – *Acacia nilotica* or *Acacia indica* which grows at the foot of the mountains in the Musandam Peninsula, the Emirates and Al-Batinah region; a hard and strong wood employed for parts of a dhow

qārib (pl qawārib) – a classical Arabic generic term for a small boat; a large boat in the medieval period with multi-functional purposes, see *gārib*

qaṭāʿ (pl qaṭāʾiʿ) – a common term for the medieval Mediterranean and Red Sea galley

qaṭīra (pl qaṭāʾir) – coastal boat associated with the Red Sea

qaṭṭāʿ (pl qaṭāṭīʿ) – ocean-going vessel

qilāfa – see *gilāfa*

qinbār – see *qanbar*

qirba (pl qirab, qirbāt, or qirabāt) – inflated skin

qiṭʿ (pl aqṭāʿ, qiṭaʿ, or qaṭāʾiʿ) – see *qaṭāʿ*

qiṭʿa (pl aqṭāʿ, qiṭaʿ, or qaṭāʾiʿ) – see *qaṭāʿ*

qūfiyya (pl qawāfī) – see *gāfiyya*

qunbār – see *qanbar*

rāddeh – a Bahraini term for raft

ramás – a Somali term for raft

ramásh – see *ramás*

ramath (pl armāth, or rimāth or rawāmith) – the Socotran catamaran

ramísh – see *ramás*

ramsi – see *ramás*

randa – the plane

rass (also tanzīl al-alwāḥ) – the process of securing planks together

rāwī (pl rāwiyyīn) – the storyteller

rēl – the railing

ribsh – see *ribūsh*

ribūsh – the lower planking fitted to the outer railing of the poopdeck

rigʿa – the dhow's transom stern

rubbān – the navigator or skipper in south-east Oman and Dhofar

rummāna – the bollard (piece of timber fixed to the gunwale to which the mooring lines are made fast); a piece of timber fixed at the stemhead of a Kuwaiti *baghla*

ṣadir – see *sidr*

safīna (pl sufun or safāʾin or safīn) – a generic term for vessel; a classical Arabic term for ship

sagena – Byzantine galley

ṣāḥib al-markab – the shipowner

sāj – see *sāy*

sakūna – fishing boat with a very long and deep stemhead similar to the Adeni *sanbūq*

salāma – safety rope

salbīs – a stringer to shelf the deck beam; clamp

ṣall – shark liver oil

samʿa or ṣamʿa (pl samʿāt or ṣamʿāt) – Emirati fishing and pearling boat with similar features to the northern Gulf *sanbūq*, the stemhead painted white and black

samar – see *sumur*

sambucho (also zambuco or zambuk) – a Portuguese term for the sixteenth-century *sanbūq*, a small flat-bottomed coastal boat or large ocean-going vessel

sambūq – Mehri, Hadrami and Amharric cognates for *sanbūq*

sammāk (pl samāmīk) – fishing vessel

samn – castor oil

sampan – a Malay term for a small boat or skiff found on the Indian coast (as known to the Portuguese)

sanbūk (pl sanābīk) – see *sanbūq*

sanbūq (pl sanābīq) – a general term for any sailing boat or motorized vessel; identified in the northern Gulf by the low, curved, scimitar-shaped bow and a high square stern; also the double-ended vessel in Oman and the south Arabian coast, see *ṣunbūq*

sanbūq mukhayyaṭ – a stitched *sanbūq*

sanbūq ẓufārī – a stitched fishing boat of Dhofar

ṣandūg as-sankal – chain-box or cover

ṣanfīr (pl ṣanāfīr) – a sheave pin (grooved wheel around which revolves the mast head in a block)

sangal or ṣangal or sankal – chain pull

ṣāniʿ al-sufun (pl ṣunnāʿ al-sufun) – a classical Arabic term for shipbuilder

sankal – see *sangal*

sapīn(a)tu – Akkadian seagoing vessel

saredān or siridān – moveable wooden box open at the front for cooking

saṭaḥ – the deck of a vessel

saṭaḥ guddām or juddām – forecastle

sāṭūr or ṣāṭūr – the bow fender (projecting stemhead of a *būm*)

sāy or sāj – teak wood

sdīrī (also jilinga) – the v-shaped timber at the forecastle and aftercastle

selek (also kārib) – large Musandam *battīl*

sembuk – a Tigré cognate for *sanbūq*

shabāṣa – a pincer or iron clamp

shabbāk or shubbāk (pl shabābīk) – the stern port in the *baghla*

shācheh (pl shjāyech) – a nail of palm fibre

shaghghār (pl shaghāghīr) – the batten nailed temporarily to the sides of the keel to hold the planks in position

shaḥam (also wadach) – fat

shāḥūf (pl shawāḥīf) – double-ended fishing craft belonging to the east Emirati coast and Oman, similar to the *baqqāra* though smaller, with pointed stemhead and long upright sternpost

shāsha (pl shāshāt or shūsh) – Omani and Emirati beach palm tree-fibre canoe, operated with oars

shibir (pl ashbār) – a span of the hand (unit of measure)

shilmān (pl shalāmīn) – the rib (frame)

shīsh – a kind of date

shkhāsa – the stealer (tapered plank worked into the run of the vessel)

shubbāk – see *shabbāk*

shūʿī (pl shawāʿī or shwāʿ) – fishing vessel almost identical to the *sanbūq*, identified by its straight stem (the tip painted blue) ending in a double curve and transom stern with projecting quarter strakes looking like wooden fins

shūna – mixture of fat with lime, see *chunam*

shuwayʿī – double-ended Iraqi transport boat similar to a *chāla* and *muhayla*

sibāq al-marākib – boat race

sidir – see *sidr*

sidr or ṣadir or sidir – the bow (foremost end of a dhow)

sikk – the mast-step

sikkān – see *sukkān*

sinn (pl asnān) – the killick for anchoring on coral

ṣīrī – the hanging wooden ladder on an ocean-going dhow

siridān – see *saredān*

snawbar – *Pinus pinea*, 'pine wood', used for the yard

sufun al-jusur – medieval boat bridges

sufun al-rijjāla – medieval transport ships for foot-soldiers and weapons

sukkān or sikkān – rudder

sukkān bil-ḥibāl – rope steering mechanism

sukkōnī – see *sukkūnī*

sukkūnī – the helmsman

sumur or samar – *Acacia spirocarpa*, used in dhow building

ṣunbūq (pl ṣanābīq) – the small or large medieval boat found in the Mediterranean, Red Sea and the Indian Ocean, see *sanbūq*

ṣuwār al-muqaddama – foredeck crossbar

ṣuwār id-digil – mast crossbar

ṣuwār it-tifir – aftdeck crossbar

ṣwāra or swāra (pl ṣwārāt or swārāt; coll ṣuwār) – deck beam

ṣwāra kabirt – middle of the deck crossbar

ṭabla (pl ṭablāt) – aft platform (triangular shaped beam on either side of the stemhead)

tadrīkh (also tashdīb) – the process of smoothing the outer planks

tāj (also qādūm or yadūm) – the carving on the stemhead of a *ghanja* or *kūtiyya*

talbīs or tilbās – the plaited tress fitted to the railing on the gunwale

ṭaʿm (pl ṭuʿūm) – building block

tanzīl al-alwāḥ (also rass) – the process of securing the planks together

tarḥa – long plane

ṭārī (pl ṭawārī) – a crook of timber clamped to the garboard strakes and to the keel

ṭarīda (pl ṭarāʾid) – medieval Mediterranean transport ship, designed primarily to carry horses

ṭarrād – small and swift Iraqi river canoe

ṭarrād or ṭarrāda (pl ṭarrādāt) – fibreglass motorized boat

ṭarrāda – southern Iraqi reed boat; cruiser or warship

tashdīb (also tadrīkh) – the process of smoothing the outer planks

tashshāla or tashshāle (pl tashāshīl or tashāyil) – Kuwaiti and Bahraini term for a double-ended fully decked craft, see *chāla* and *tishāla*

tasqām – see *tisqām*

ṭawwāsh (pl ṭawāwīsh) – small rowing boat used by the pearl merchant or skipper

ṭayra – swift medieval boat

terraquin – see *trānkī*

ṭghār – an Iraqi unit of weight measure

thālith mālich – the third garboard strake

thoni – southern Indian boat

tilbās – see *talbīs*

tiʿrāḍa – the stout beam above the poopdeck onto which the ends of the main yard are lowered

tirrīch (pl tirrīchāt) – the sheer-strake (upper strake, topmost wale)

tishāla or tishshāle – an Emirati term for a double-ended fully decked craft, see *chāla* and *tashshāla*

tisqām or tasqām – loan (advance given to pearl-divers and sailors)

tōnī – a Tamil term for boat

trānkeh – small type of Iranian vessel, undecked double-ended used for pearl-fishing

trankey – see *trānkī*

trānkī or terraquin or trankey – large, fast and armed vessel but also a transport and trading vessel from the sixteenth to eighteenth centuries; very long and wide, with a low stempost and a very high stern, one mast

trincador – flat-bottomed coasting Portuguese vessel with a high stern

ṭunn (pl aṭnān) – a ton (unit of measure)

ṭunn musajjal – the registered ton

ʿubaydār – see *ʿobīdār*

ʿūd (pl aʿwād) – see *ʿōd*

ʿukayrī – Medieval Indian Ocean type of *ghurāb*

ʿūma or ʿōma – sardine

ustād or ustādh (pl istādiyya or istādhiyya) – master craftsman

ʿuṭfa (pl ʿuṭaf) or ʿiṭfa (pl ʿiṭaf) – floorboard rib (naturally grown floor rib placed alternately to the *shilmān*)

ʿuwaysī or ʿuwaysiyya – ocean-going vessel with two masts, a variety of *badan*

vallam – Tamil Nadu fishing boat

wadach (also shaḥam) – sheep fat mixed with lime, the paste of which is applied below the waterline of a dhow

wādira (pl wādirāt) – groove

wāhan – Indian vessel with a modern design of the *kūtiyya*

walajiyya – see *waljiyya*

waljiyya – a medieval boat

wāriyya or wariyya (pl wāriyyāt or wariyyāt) (also hūriyya or huwayriyya) – Kuwaiti palm-tree fibre beach boat, operated with oars

warjiyya (pl warjiyyāt) – see *wāriyya*

wirsha (pl wirash) (also mūshara) – shipbuilding yard

wisāda (pl wasāyid) – the cheek timber (one of the two pieces of timber on either side of the stemhead)

yadūm or qādūm (also tāj) – carving on the stemhead of a *ghanja* or *kūtiyya*

yāmiʿa – see *jāmaʿa*

yūnya – see *jūniyye*

zabdara – the gunwale

zaffān – a kind of date palm tree

zaʿīma (pl zaʿāyim) – a general term for sailing boat in Hadhramaut and Yemen; a large double-ended craft with a curved scimitar-styled stem like the *sanbūq*, a raked stern, one or two masts; an Omani rectangular reed coracle

ẓalla – see *ẓulla*

zambuco – see *sambucho*

zambuk – see *sambucho*

zand (pl zunūd) – the tie-beam (stout piece of crescent-shaped timber on either side of the foredeck where the anchor cable is laid) zanzīr – tassel of shells

ẓarrāb (pl ẓarrābīn) – the carpenter

zārūk – open-ended Yemeni boat with a sharp and pointed stem and stern, one or two masts; a slaver in the early part of the nineteenth century

zārūka or zārūk (pl zawārīk) – Musandam double-ended transport and fishing vessel with a high stern-piece like a dog's head

zaw – a medieval Chinese vessel

zawraka – see *zārūka*

zawraq (pl zawāriq or zawārīq) – a generic term for small boat

zaww – a small medieval Mesopotamian river boat

zīār – rope lashing

zōlī – see *zūlī*

zōr – a Bahraini term for a palm stem

zufāra – small Omani raft made of date palm spines which serves as a lifeboat

zūlī or zōlī – the semi-circular male latrine box, hanging from the bow or stern of the dhow

ẓulla or ẓalla (also ʿarsha) – awning (canvas or reed canopy)

BIBLIOGRAPHY

Abū Shāma, ʿAbd al-Raḥmān b Ismāʿīl. *Recueil des historiens des Croisades*, translated and edited by A. C. Bárbier de Meynard, Volumes I–IV (Paris: Imprimerie Nationale, 1872–98).

Al-ʿAbd al-Mughnī, ʿĀdil Muḥammad. *Al-Iqtiṣād al-kuwaytī l-qadīm* (Kuwait: al-Qabas, 1987).

ʿAbdallāh, Muḥammad ʿAlī. *Taqrīr bināʾ safīna battīl fī Qaṭar*, Volumes I–III (Doha: Markaz al-Turāth al-Shaʿbī li-Duwal al-Khalīj al-ʿArabiyya, 1987).

Abu Hakima, Ahmad Mustafa. *History of Eastern Arabia 1750–1800: The Rise and Development of Bahrain and Kuwait* (Beirut: Khayats, 1965).

Agius, Dionisius Albertus. *Arabic Literary Works as a Source of Documentation for Technical Terms of the Material Culture* (Islamkundliche Untersuchungen, No. 98) (Berlin: Klaus Schwarz, 1984).

—1997. 'Historical-linguistic reliability of Muqaddasī's information on types of ships' in *Across the Mediterranean Frontiers: Trade, Politics and Religion 650–1450*, edited by Dionisius A. Agius and Ian R. Netton (Turnhout: Brepols), 303–29.

—1998. 'Maqrīzī's evidence for the *ġurāb*: the galley of the Mamlūks' in *Law, Christianity and Modernism in Islamic Society*, edited by Urbain Vermeulen and Jan M. F. Van Reeth (Leuven: Peeters), 185–97.

—1999. 'Medieval Qalhat: travellers, dhows and stone anchors in South-East Oman' in *Archaeology of Seafaring: The Indian Ocean in the Ancient Period*, edited by Himanshu Prabha Ray (Delhi: Indian Council for Historical Research), 173–220.

Aḥmad, Ibrāhīm Fuʾād. *Qaṭar wa l-baḥr*, assisted by S. M. ʿAwartānī and B. T. Amīr ʿAlī (Doha, Qatar: Ministry of Information, 1987).

Amin, Abd al-Amir Muhammad. *British Interests in the Persian Gulf* (Leiden: E. J. Brill, 1967).

Anāstās Mārī l-Kirmilī. 'Al-kalim al-yūnāniyya fī l-lughat al-ʿarabiyya', *Al-Mashriq*, 3: 63–8 (1900).

Anscombe, Frederick F. *The Ottoman Gulf: The Creation of Kuwait, Saudi Arabia, and Qatar* (New York: Columbia University Press, 1997).

Aubin, Jean. 'Y-a-t-il eu interruption du commerce par mer entre le Golfe Persique et l'Inde du XIe au XIVe siècle' in *Océan Indien et Mediterranée* (Travaux du Sixième Colloque International d'Histoire Maritime et du

Deuxième Congrès de l'Association Historique Internationale de l'Océan Indien) (Paris: Sevpen, 1964), 165–71.
Badger, George Percy. *An English–Arabic Lexicon* (Beirut: Librairie du Liban, 1967); originally published by C. K. Paul & Co., 1889.
Bass, George F. (ed.) *A History of Seafaring based on Underwater Archaeology* (London: Thames & Hudson, 1972).
Belgrave, James H. D. *Welcome to Bahrain* (Manama: The Augustan Press, 1975).
Bent, James Theodore. *Southern Arabia*, assisted by Mabel Virginia Anna Bent (London: Smith Elder, 1900).
Bertram, George Colin Lawder. *The Fisheries of the Sultanate of Muscat and Oman* (Muscat, 1948).
Bidwell, Robin. *Dictionary of Modern Arab History* (London and New York: Kegan Paul International, 1998).
Blunt, Lady Anne. *A Pilgrimage to Nejd: The Cradle of the Arab Race* (London: Century, 1985), first published 1881.
The Book of Duarte Barbosa. Translated by Mansel Longworth Dames, Volumes I–II (London: The Hakluyt Society, 1918–21).
Brockett, Adrian. *The Spoken Arabic of Khābūra on the Bāṭina of Oman* (Journal of Semitic Studies, No 7) (Manchester: University of Manchester, 1985).
Broeze, Frank. (ed.) *Gateways of Asia: Port Cities of Asia in the 13th–20th Centuries* (London: Kegan Paul International, 1997).
Brunot, Louis. *Notes lexicologiques sur le vocabulaire maritime de Rabat et Salé* (Paris: E. Leroux, 1920a).
—1920b. *La mer dans les traditions et les industries indigènes à Rabat et Salé* (Paris: E. Leroux).
Bū Shahrī, ʿAlī Akbar. *Al-taʾrīkh al-qadīm lil-Baḥrayn wa l-Khalīj al-ʿArabī* (Bahrain: Al-Waṭaniyya, 1407/1987).
Buckingham, James Silk. *Travels in Assyria, Media and Persia etc.* (London: H. Colburn, 1829).
Burckhardt, Johann Ludwig. *Travels in Nubia* (London: J. Murray, 1822).
—1829. *Travels in Arabia*, Volumes I–II (London: H. Colburn).
Burton, Richard F. *Personal Narrative of a Pilgrimage to Al-Madinah and Mecca*, edited by Isabel Burton, Volumes I–II (New York: Dover, 1964); first published 1893.
Buzurg b Shahriyār al-Rāmhurmuzī, see under al-Rāmhurmuzī.
Casson, Lionel. 'The river boats of Mesopotamia', *The Mariner's Mirror*, 53, iii: 286–8 (1967).
Cathay and the Way Thither. Translated and edited by Henry Yule, Volumes I–II (London: The Hakluyt Society, 1866).

Chau Ju-Kua: His Work on the Chinese and Arab Trade in the Twelfth and Thirteenth Centuries. Entitled *Chu-Fan-chi*, translated from the Chinese and annotated by Friedrich Hirth and W. W. Rockhill (St. Petersburg: Imperial Academy of Sciences, 1911).

Chaudhuri, K. N. *Trade and Civilization in the Indian Ocean* (Cambridge: Cambridge University Press, 1985).

Chesney, Francis Rawdon. *The Expedition for the Survey of the Rivers Euphrates and Tigris*, Volumes I–II (London: Longman, Brown, Green and Longman, 1850).

Chronicle of Events between the Years 1623–1733 relating to the Settlement of the Order of Carmelites in Mesopotamia. Edited by H. Gollancz, Volumes I–II (London: np, 1927).

Colomb, Philip Howard. *Slave Catching in the Indian Ocean. A Record of Naval Experiences* (London: Dawsons of Pall Mall, 1968); a reprint of 1873.

The Commentaries of the Great Alfonso Dalboquerque. Translated from Portuguese by Walter De Gray Birch, Volumes I–IV (London: The Hakluyt Society, 1875–84); Portuguese edition 1774.

Coupland, Reginald. *East Africa and its Invaders, from the Earliest Times to the Death of Seyyid Said in 1856* (Oxford: Clarendon Press, 1938).

—1939. *The Exploitation of East Africa, 1856–1890; The Slave Trade and the Scramble* (London: Faber & Faber).

Crawford, Harriet. *Dilmun and its Gulf Neighbours* (Cambridge: Cambridge University Press, 1998).

Crumlin-Pedersen, Ole. 'The Vikings and the Hanseatic merchants: 900–1450' in *A History of Seafaring based on Underwater Archaeology*, edited by George F. Bass (London: Thames & Hudson, 1972), 181–204.

Da Silva, Fernando J. *Dicionário da Língua Portuguesa* (Porto: Domingos Barreira, nd).

Dale, Stephen. 'The Hadhrami diaspora in south-western India: the role of the Sayyids of the Malabar Coast' in *Hadhrami Traders, Scholars and Statesmen in the Indian Ocean, 1750s–1960s*, edited by Ulrike Freitag and William G. Clarence-Smith (Leiden: E. J. Brill, 1997), 175–84.

Danvers, Frederick Charles. *The Portuguese in India*, Volumes I–II (London: Frank Cass, 1966); first published 1894.

De Goeje, Michael Jan. *Indices, glossarium ed addenda et emendanda ad partes I–III* (Bibliotheca Geographorum Arabicorum, IV) (Leiden: E. J. Brill, 1967); first published 1879.

De Graeve, Marie-Christine. *The Ships of the Ancient Near East* (*c. 2000–500 BC*) (Orientalia Lovaniensia Analecta, 7) (Leuven: Departement Oriëntalistiek, 1981).

De Landberg, Comte. *Glossaire Daṯînois*, Volumes I–III (Leiden: E. J. Brill, 1920–42).
Dickson, Harold R. P. *The Arab of the Desert* (London: George Allen & Unwin, 1949).
Diodorus, Siculus. *Bibliotheca historica*, translated by C. H. Oldfather, Volumes I–X (London and New York: William Heinemann and G. P. Putnam, 1933).
Donaldson, William James. 'Fishing and fish marketing in northern Oman: a case study of artisanal fisheries development' (Ph.D. Thesis, University of Durham, 1979).
—1980. 'Enterprise and innovation in an indigenous fishery: the case of the Sultanate of Oman', *Development and Change*, 11: 479–95.
—2000. 'Erythraean Ichthyophagi: Arabian fish-eaters observed', *New Arabian Studies*, 5: 7–32.
Dozy, Reinhart P. A. *Supplément aux dictionnaires arabes*, Volumes I–II (Leiden: E. J. Brill, 1967); a reprint of the 1887 edition.
Al-Dujaylī, Kāẓim. 'Al-sufun fī l-ʿIrāq', *Lughat al-ʿArab*, 2, iii: 93–103 (1912a).
—1912b. 'Ashbāh al-sufun fī l-ʿIrāq', *Lughat al-ʿArab*, 2, iv: 152–5.
—1912c. 'Asmāʾ mā fī l-safīna', *Lughat al-ʿArab*, 2, v: 198–205.
—1912d. 'Adawāt al-safīna', *Lughat al-ʿArab*, 2, vi: 393–403.
—1913. 'Rijāl al-safīna l-ʿIrāqiyya', *Lughat al-ʿArab*, 3, ii: 82–6.
Edye, John. 'Description of the various classes of vessels constructed and employed by the natives of the coasts of Coromandel, Malabar, and the Island of Ceylon for their coasting navigation', *Journal of the Royal Asiatic Society*, I: 1–14 (1835).
Facey, William. *Oman: A Seafaring Nation* (Muscat: Ministry of Information, 1979).
—1987. 'The boat carvings at Jabal al-Jussasiyah, Northwest Qatar', *Seminar for Arabian Studies*, 17: 199–222.
Farrar, Austin. 'Ancient Mediterranean ship design', *The Mariner's Mirror*, 83, ii: 211–5 (1997).
Ferrand, Gabriel. 'L' élément persan dans les textes nautiques arabes des XVe et XVIe siècles', *Journal Asiatique*, 204: 193–257 (1924).
Fraenkel, Siegmund. *Die Aramäischen Fremdwörter im Arabischen* (Hildesheim: Georg Olms, 1962); first published Leiden 1886.
Frayḥa, Anīs. *Muʿjam al-alfāẓ al-ʿarabiyya* (Beirut: Maktabat Lubnān, 1973).
Freeman-Grenville, Greville Stewart Parker. *The East African Coast: Select Documents from the First to the Earlier Nineteenth Century* (Oxford: Clarendon Press, 1962).

Glidden, Harold W. 'A comparative study of the Arabic nautical vocabulary from al-Aqabah, Transjordan', *Journal of the American Oriental Society*, 62: 68–72 (1942).

Greenhill, Basil. *The Archaeology of Boats and Ships* (London: Conway Maritime Press, 1995); first published by A & C Black, 1976.

Grosset-Grange, Henri. *Glossaire nautique arabe ancien et moderne de l'océan indien* (Paris: Comité des Travaux Historiques et Scientifiques, 1993).

Haines, Stafford Bettesworth. 'Memoir of the South and East Coasts of Arabia', *Geographical Journal*, 15: 136–41 (1847).

Handal, Falih. 'A glossary of the dialect of the United Arab Emirates, translated and arranged according to the English alphabet' (Ph.D. Thesis, University of Exeter, 1987).

Hārūn, ʿAbd al-Salām *et al. Muʿjam al-wasīṭ*, Volumes I–II (Cairo: Maṭbaʿat Miṣr, 1960–61).

Ḥasan Tāj al-Dīn. *The Islamic History of the Maldive Islands*, edited by Hikoichi Yajima (Studia Culturae Islamicae, No. 22), Volumes I–II (Tokyo: Institute for the Study of Languages and Cultures of Asia and Africa, 1982-84).

Hasslöf, Olof. 'Portuguese influences on ship-building in the Persian Gulf', *The Mariner's Mirror*, 48, i: 58–63 (1962).

Hawkins, Clifford. *The Dhow* (Lymington: Nautical Publishing Company, 1977).

Hawley, Donald. *Oman and its Renaissance* (London: Stacey International, 1995); revised jubilee edition, first published 1977.

Heard-Bey, Frauke. *From Trucial States to UAE* (London: Longman, 1981).

Herodotus. *The History of Herodotus*, translated by A. D. Godley, Volumes I–IV (London and New York: William Heinemann and G. P. Putnam, 1921).

—1996. *The Histories*, translated by A. De Sélincourt, revised by J. Marincola (London: Penguin); first published 1954.

Heyerdahl, Thor. *The Kon-Tiki Expedition by Raft across the South Seas*, translated from Norwegian by F. H. Lyon (London: George Allen & Unwin, 1950).

—1971. *The Ra Expeditions* (London: George Allen & Unwin).

—1982. *The Tigris Expedition* (London: George Allen & Unwin).

—1986. *The Maldive Mystery* (London: George Allen & Unwin).

Al-Ḥijjī, Yaʿqūb Yūsuf. *Ṣināʿat al-sufun al-shirāʿiyya fī l-Kuwayt* (Doha, Qatar: Markaz al-Turāth al-Shaʿbī, 1988).

—1997. *Al-Muhallab al-jadīd* (Kuwait: Al-Dīwān al-Amīrī).

Hill, A. H. 'Some early accounts of the oriental boat', *The Mariner's Mirror*, 44, iii: 201–17 (1958).

Holes, Clive. *Language Variation and Change in a Modernising Arab State* (Library of Arabic Linguistics, No. 7) (London: Kegan Paul International, 1987).

The Holy Qurʾan: Text. Translation and commentary by Abdullah Yusuf Ali, Volumes I–II (New York: Hafner, 1946); first edited 1934.

Hornell, James. 'The origins and ethnological significance of Indian boat designs', *Memoirs of the Asiatic Society of Bengal*, 7, iii: 139–256 (1920).

—1941. 'The sea-going Mtepe of the Lamu Archipelago', *The Mariner's Mirror*, 27, i: 54–68.

—1942. 'A tentative classification of Arab sea-craft', *The Mariner's Mirror*, 28, i: 11–40.

—1946. 'The sailing craft of western India', *The Mariner's Mirror*, 32, iv: 195–217.

Hourani, George Fadlo. *Arab Seafaring in the Indian Ocean in Ancient and Early Medieval Times* (Beirut: Khayats, 1963); first published Princeton 1951.

Howard-Carter, Theresa. 'The Arab-Iranian Gulf', *Archaeology*, 26: 16–23 (1973).

Howarth, David. 1977. *Dhows* (London: Quartet).

Hunter, Frederick Mercer. *An Account of the British Settlement at Aden, in Arabia* (London: Trübner & Co, 1877).

Hyde, Thomas. *Syntagma dissertationum quas olim auctor doctissimus*, Volumes I–II (Oxford: Clarendon Press, 1767).

Ibn al-Daybaʿ, Abū ʿAbdallāh. *Al-faḍl al-mazīd ʿalā bughyat al-mustafīd fī akhbār madīnat Zabīd*, edited by Muḥammad ʿĪsā Ṣāliḥiyya (Kuwait, 1983).

Ibn al-Mujāwir, Jamāl al-Dīn Muḥammad al-Shaybānī. *Descriptio arabiae meridionalis* (Taʾrīkh al-mustabṣir), edited by Oscar Löfgren (Leiden: E. J. Brill, 1954).

Ibn Baṭṭūṭa, Abū ʿAbdallāh Muḥammad. *The Travels of Ibn Baṭṭūṭa A.D. 1325–1354*, translated with revision and notes from the Arabic text edition of C. Defrémery and B. R. Sanguinetti by H. A. R. Gibb, in four volumes; Volume I, 1958; Volumes II and III reprint 1995; Volume IV 1994, translation completed with annotations by C. F. Beckingham (London: The Hakluyt Society).

—1968. *Voyages d'Ibn Battûta*, Arabic text with translation by C. Defrémery and B. R. Sanguinetti, Volumes I–IV (Paris: Anthropos); first published in 1853–58.

Ibn Ḥawqal, Abū l-Qāsim. *Kitāb ṣūrat al-arḍ*, edited by Michael Jan de Goeje (Bibliotheca Geographorum Arabicorum, II) (Leiden: E. J. Brill, 1873).

Ibn Jubayr, Abū l-Ḥasan Muḥammad. *Riḥlat Ibn Jubayr*, edited by W. Wright and revised by Michael Jan de Goeje (E. J. W. Gibb Memorial Series, V) (Leiden: E. J. Brill, 1907); first edition 1852.

—1952. *Riḥla. The Travels of Ibn Jubayr*, translated by R. J. C. Broadhurst (London: Jonathan Cape).

Ibn Mājid, Shihāb al-Dīn Aḥmad. *Kitāb al-fawā'id fī uṣūl ʿilm al-baḥr wa l-qawāʿid*, edited by Ibrāhīm Khūrī (Damascus: np, 1971).

Ibn Mammātī, Asʿad. *Kitāb qawānīn al-dawāwīn* (Bulaq: Maṭbaʿat al-Waṭan, 1299AH).

—1943. *Kitāb qawānīn al-dawāwīn*, edited by ʿAzīz Suryāl ʿAtiyya (Cairo).

Ibn Manẓūr, Abū Faḍl Jamāl al-Dīn Muḥammad b Mukarram. *Lisān al-ʿArab*, edited by ʿAbdallāh ʿAlī l-Kabīr, Muḥammad Aḥmad Ḥasaballāh and Hāshim Muḥammad al-Shādhlī, Volumes I–VI (Cairo: Dār al-Maʿārif, nd).

—1955–56. *Lisān al-ʿArab*, Volumes I–XV (Beirut: Dār Bayrūt).

Ibn Miskawayh, Abū ʿAlī Aḥmad b Muḥammad. *Kitāb tajārub al-umam*, edited by H. F. Amedroz, Volumes I–II (Cairo: Sharikat al-Tamaddun al-Ṣināʿiyya, 1914–15).

Ibn Razīk, Salīl. *History of the Imâms and Sayyids of ʿOman*, translated by George Percy Badger (London: The Hakluyt Society, 1871).

Ibn Sīda, Abū l-Ḥasan ʿAlī b Ismāʿīl. *Kitāb al-mukhaṣṣaṣ*, Volumes I–XVII (Bulaq, 1893–1903).

Inalcik, Halil. *The Ottoman Empire. The Classical Age 1300–1600* (London: Weidenfeld and Nicholson, 1973).

Al-Iṣṭakhrī, Abū Isḥāq Ibrāhim b Muḥammad. *Kitāb masālik al-mamālik*, edited by Michael Jan de Goeje (Bibliotheca Geographorum Arabicorum, I). (Leiden: E. J. Brill, 1870).

Ives, Edward. *Journey from Persia to England* (London: Edward and Charles Dilly, 1758).

Jahn, Alfred. *Die Mehri-Sprache in Südarabien* (Vienna: A. Hölder, 1902).

Jal, Auguste. *Archéologie navale*, Volumes I–II (Paris: A. Bertrand, 1840).

—1848. *Glossaire nautique: répertoire polyglotte de termes de marine anciens et modernes* (Paris: Firmin Didot).

Al-Jawālīqī, Abū Manṣūr Mawhūb b Aḥmad b Muḥammad. *Al-muʿarrab min kalām al-aʿjamī ʿalā ḥurūf al-muʿjam*, edited by A. M. Shākir (Tehran: Dār al-Kutub, 1969).

Al-Jawharī, Abū Naṣr Ismāʿīl b Ḥammād. *Tāj al-lugha wa ṣiḥāḥ al-ʿarabiyya*, edited by Aḥmad ʿAbd al-Ghafūr ʿAttār, Volumes I–VI (Beirut: Dār al-ʿIlm lil-Malāiyyīn, 1984); first published 1956.

Jayakar, A. S. G. 'The O'mánee dialect of Arabic: Parts I–II', *Journal of the Royal Asiatic Society*, 21: 649–87; 811–80 (1889).

Jenour, Matthew. *The Route to India through France, Germany, Hungary, Turkey, Natolia, Syria and the Desert of Arabia* (London, 1791).

Jewell, John H. A. *Dhows at Mombasa* (Nairobi: East African Publishing House, 1969).

Johnstone, T. M. and J. Muir. 'Portuguese influences on shipbuilding in the Persian Gulf', *The Mariner's Mirror*, 48, i: 58–63 (1962).
—1964. 'Some nautical terms in the Kuwaiti dialect of Arabic', *Bulletin of the School of Oriental and African Studies*, 27: 299–332.
Jones, Vincent. *Sail the Indian Sea* (London and New York: Gordon and Cremonesi, 1978).
Kahane, Henry, Renée Kahane and Andreas Tietze. *The Lingua Franca in the Levant* (Hildesheim: Georg Olms, 1958).
Kamioka, Koji and Hikoichi Yajima. *The Inter-Regional Trade in the Western Part of the Indian Ocean* (Studia Culturae Islamicae, No. 9) (Tokyo: Institute for the Study of Languages and Cultures of Asia and Africa, 1979).
Kapel, Hans. 'Rock carvings at Jabal Jusasiyah, Qatar', *Arrayan*, 8: 1–126 and Appendix 1–53 (1983).
Katzev, Michael L. 'The Kyrenia ship' in *A History of Seafaring based on Underwater Archaeology*, edited by George F. Bass (London: Thames & Hudson, 1972), 50–64.
Kay, Shirley. *Seafarers of the Gulf* (London: Motivate, 1994); reprint of 1992 edition.
Al-Kāẓimī, Ẓamyāʾ al-Kāẓim. *Al-Ṣināʿāt al-shaʿbiyya fīl-Khalīj al-ʿArabī* (Basra: Markaz Dirāsāt al-Khalīj al-ʿArabī, 1981).
Kemp, Peter. *The Oxford Companion to Ships and the Sea* (Oxford: Oxford University Press, 1992); first published 1976.
Kentley, Eric. 'Some aspects of the masula surf boat' in *Sewn Plank Boats* (BAR International Series, 276) (Greenwich: National Maritime Museum, 1985), 303–17.
Al-Khafājī, Shihāb al-Dīn Aḥmad. *Shifāʾ al-ghalīl fī mā fī kalām al-ʿArab min al-dakhīl* (Cairo: al-Maṭbaʿat al-Wahabiyya, 1282/1865).
Al-Khalifa, Shaikha Haya ʿAli and Michael Rice (eds.). *Bahrain through the Ages: The Archaeology* (London: Kegan Paul International, 1986).
—1993. *Bahrain through the Ages: The History* (London: Kegan Paul International).
Kindermann, Hans. *'Schiff' im Arabischen Untersuchung über Vorkommen und Bedeutung der Termini* (Bonn: Zwickau, 1934).
Lane, Edward William. *Arabic–English Lexicon* (Cambridge: Islamic Texts Society Trust, 1984); a reprint of London 1863–93 edition.
LeBaron Bowen, Richard. 'Arab dhows of eastern Arabia', *The American Neptune*, 9, i: 87–132 (1949).
—1951. 'The pearl fisheries of the Persian Gulf', *The Middle East Journal*, 5, ii: 161–180.
—1952. 'Primitive watercraft of Arabia', *The American Neptune*, 12, iii: 186–221.

—1957. 'Arab anchors', *The Mariner's Mirror*, 43, iv: 288–93.

—1963. 'Early Arab ships and rudders', *The Mariner's Mirror*, 49, iv: 302–4.

—1966. 'Early Arab rudders', *The Mariner's Mirror*, 52: 172.

Le Strange, Guy. *The Lands of the Eastern Caliphate* (London: Frank Cass, 1966); first edition 1905.

Leitão, H. and J. Vicente Lopes. *Dicionário da linguagem de marinha antiga e actual* (Lisbon: Centro de Estudios Históricos Ultramarinos, 1963).

Leslau, Wolf. *Lexique soqotri (sudarabique moderne) avec comparisons et explications étymologiques* (Paris: Librairie C. Klincksieck, 1938).

Lewis, Archibald. 1973. 'Maritime skills in the Indian Ocean 1368–1500', *Journal of the Economics and Social History of the Orient*, 16, ii–iii: 238–64.

Lewis, Charlton T. and Charles Short. *A Latin Dictionary* (Oxford: Clarendon Press, 1975); first edition 1879.

Liddell, Henry George and Robert Scott. *A Greek–English Lexicon*, revised by Henry Stuart Jones with Roderick McKenzie (Oxford: Clarendon Press, 1953); revised edition 1940; first edition 1843.

Lorimer, John Gordon (ed). *Gazetteer of the Persian Gulf, Oman and Central Arabia*, Volume I, Parts ia, ib, iia, iib, iii, Volume IIa, IIb, IIc. (Westmead, Farnborough: Gregg International, 1986); first published Calcutta 1908–1915.

Low, Charles Rathbone. *History of the Indian Navy (1613–1863)*, Volumes I–II (London: R. Bentley, 1877).

Māhir, Suʿād. *Al-baḥriyya fī Miṣr al-islāmiyya wa āthāruhā l-bāqiya* (Cairo: Wizārat al-Thaqāfa - Dār al-Kātib al-ʿArabī, 1967).

Al-Maqrīzī, Taqī l-Dīn. *Al-Mawāʿiẓ wa l-iʿtibār fī dhikr al-khiṭaṭ wa l-āthār*, edited by M. Q. al-ʿAdawī, Volumes I–II (Bulaq, 1270/1853).

—1911–24. *Al-mawāʿiẓ wa l-iʿtibār fī dhikr al-khiṭaṭ wa l-āthār*, edited by M. Gaston Wiet, Volumes I–IV (Cairo: Institut Français d'Archéologie Orientale).

—1957–64. *Kitāb al-sulūk li maʿrifat duwal al-mulūk*, edited by Muḥammad Muṣṭafā Ziyāda, Volumes I–II (Cairo).

Marco Polo, *see The Travels of Marco Polo*.

Marx, Eric. 'The derivation of the words 'dhow' and 'junk'', *The Mariner's Mirror*, 32, iii: 185 (1946).

Al-Maʿshinī, Saʿīd bin Masʿūd bin Muḥammad. *Al-ṣināʿāt al-taqlīdiyya fī Ẓufār* (Salalah: Al-Kunūz, 1992).

Al-Masʿūdī, Abū l-Ḥasan b al-Ḥusayn. *Murūj al-dhahab wa maʿādin al-jawhar*, edited by Yūsuf Asʿad Dāghir, Volumes I–IV (Beirut: Dār al-Andalus, 1983).

Miles, Samuel Barrett. *The Countries and Tribes of the Persian Gulf* (Reading: Garnet Publishing, 1994); first published 1919 and reprinted in two volumes 1920.

Montgomery, James E. *The Vagaries of the Qaṣīdah. The Tradition and Practice of Early Poetry* (E. J. W. Gibb Literary Studies, No. 1) (Warminster: Aris Phillips, 1997).

Mookerji, Radhakumud. *Indian Shipping* (London and New York: Longman, 1912).

Moore, Alan. 'The craft of the Red Sea and the Gulf of Aden', *The Mariner's Mirror*, 6: 73, 98, 136 (1920).

—1925. *Last Days of Mast and Sail* (Oxford: Clarendon Press).

Moreland, William Harrison. 'The ships of the Arabian Sea about A.D. 1500', *Journal of the Royal Asiatic Society*, 63–74; 173–92 (1939).

Muir, John. 'Early Arab seafaring and rudders', *The Mariner's Mirror*, 51: 357–9 (1965).

Al-Muqaddasī, Muḥammad b Aḥmad. *Kitāb aḥsan al-taqāsīm fī maʿrifat al-aqālīm*, edited by Michael Jan de Goeje (Bibliotheca Geographorum Arabicorum, III). (Leiden: E. J. Brill, 1906); first published 1877.

—1994. *The Best Divisions for Knowledge of the Regions*, translated by Basil Anthony Collins and Muhammad Hamid al-Tai (Reading: Garnet Publishing).

Musāmiḥ, ʿAbd al-Raḥmān. 'Ḥaḍāra wa luʾluʾ wa tijāra', *Al-Ayyām* (23 November): 13–14 (1989).

Nadvi, Syed Sulaiman. *The Arab Navigation*, translated by Syed Sabahuddin Abdur Rahman (Lahore: Sh. Muhammad Ashraf, 1966).

Al-Nahrawālī, Quṭb al-Dīn Muḥammad b Aḥmad. *Al-Barq al-yamānī fī l-fatḥ al-ʿuthmānī* (Beirut: Manshūrāt al-Madīna, nd).

Nakano, Akiʾo. *Comparative Vocabulary of Southern Arabic–Mahri, Gibbali and Soqotri* (Studia Culturae Islamicae, No. 43) (Tokyo: Institute for the Study of Languages and Cultures of Asia and Africa, 1986).

Al-Nakhīlī, Darwīsh. *Al-sufun al-islāmiyya ʿalā ḥurūf al-muʿjam* (Cairo: Al-Ahrām al-Tijāriyya, 1974).

Nicolle, David. 'Shipping in Islamic art: seventh through sixteenth century AD', *The American Neptune*, 49, iii: 168–97 (1989).

Niebuhr, Carsten. *Beschreibung van Arabien* (Copenhagen: N. Möller, 1772).

—1774. *Reisebeschreibung nach Arabien und andern umliegenden Ländern*, Volumes I–II (Copenhagen: N. Möller).

Al-Nuwayrī, Aḥmad b ʿAbd al-Wahhāb. *Nihāyat al-arab fī funūn al-adab*, Volumes I–XVIII (Cairo: Dār al-Kutub, 1923–55).

Al-Nuwayrī l-Iskandarānī, Muḥammad b al-Qāsim. *Kitāb al-ilmām bil-iʿlām fī mā jarat bihi l-aḥkām wa l-umūr al-muqḍiyya fī waqʿāt al-Iskandariyya*, Volumes I–VI (Hyderabad: Osmania University, 1969).

Osgood, Joseph Barlow Felt. *Notes of Travel; or, Recollections of Majunga, Zanzibar, Muscat, Aden, Mocha, and other Eastern Ports* (Salem, Mass: G. Creamer, 1854).

O'Shea, Raymond. *Sand Kings of Oman* (London: Methuen, 1947).

Oxford English Dictionary, Volumes I–II (Oxford: Oxford University Press, 1982); compact edition; first published 1971.

Palgrave, William Gifford. *A Year's Journey through Central and Eastern Arabia (1862–3)*, Volumes I–II (London: Macmillan, 1865).

Pâris, François Edmond. *Essai sur la construction navale des peuples extra-européens* (Paris: Arthur Bertrand, 1841).

—1975. *Souvenirs de plans ou dessins de navires et de bateaux anciens ou modernes existants ou disparus*, Parts I–III (Grenoble: 4 Seigneurs); first published 1882.

Parsons, Abraham. *Travels in Asia and Africa etc.* (London: Longman, Hurst, Rees, and Orme, 1808).

Pellegrini, Giovan Battista. 'Terminologia marinara di origine araba in italiano e nelle lingue europee' in *La navigazione mediterranea nell' alto medioevo* (Settimana di Studio del Centro Italiano di Studi sull'Alto Medioevo), Volumes I–II (Spoleto, 1978), II: 797–841.

Pengelley, W. M. 'Remarks on a portion of the eastern coast of Arabia between Muscat and Sohar', *Transactions of the Bombay Geographical Society*, 16: 30–9 (1860).

Periplus Maris Erythraei. Translated by Wilfred H. Schoff (New York: Longman, Green and Co, 1912).

—1989. Translated by Lionel Casson (Princeton, New Jersey: Princeton University Press).

Plinius Secundus. *Historia Naturalis*, translated in 10 volumes, H. Rackham [1, 5, 9], W. H. S. Jones [6–8], D. E. Eichholz [10] (London: Heinemann, 1938–63).

Potts, Daniel. T. 'Watercraft of the Lower Sea' in *Beiträge zur Kulturgeschichte Vorderasiens: Festschrift für Rainer Michael Boehmer*, edited by U. Finkbeiner, R. Dittmann and H. Hauptmann (Mainz, 1995), 559–71.

Prados, Edward. 'Indian Ocean littoral maritime evolution: the case of the Yemeni *huri* and *sambuq*', *The Mariner's Mirror*, 83, ii: 185–98 (1997).

Prins, Adriaan Hendrick Johan. *Sailing from Lamu: A Study of Maritime Culture in Islamic East Africa* (Assen: Von Gorcum, 1965).

—1965–6. 'The Persian Gulf dhows: two variants in maritime enterprise', *Persica*, 2: 1–18.

—1970. 'Maritime art in an Islamic context: oculus and theron in Lamu ships', *The Mariner's Mirror*, 56, iii: 327–39.

—1972–4. 'The Persian Gulf dhows: new notes on the classification of mid-eastern sea-craft', *Persica*, 6: 157–65.

Al-Qasimi, Sultan bin Muhammad. *The Myth of Arab Piracy in the Gulf* (London: Croom Helm, 1986).

Al-Qināʿī , Najāt ʿAbd al-Qādir al-Jāsim and Badr al-Dīn ʿAbbās al-Khuṣūṣī. *Tārīkh ṣināʿat al-sufun fī l-Kuwayt wa anshiṭatuhā l-mukhtalifa* (Kuwait: Muʾassasat al-Kuwayt lil-Taqaddum al-ʿIlmī, 1982).

Qureshi, Bashir A. *Standard Dictionary: Urdu into English* (Lahore: Kitabistan, nd).

Al-Qurṭubī, ʿArīb b Saʿd. *Ṣilat taʾrīkh al-Ṭabarī. Tabari continuatus*, edited by Michael Jan de Goeje (Leiden: E. J. Brill, 1897).

Al-Quṭāmī, ʿIsā. *Dalīl al-mukhtār fī ʿilm al-biḥār* (Kuwait: Maktabat al-Ḥukūma, 1964); third edition; Cairo 1950 first edition.

Al-Rāmhurmuzī, Buzurg b Shahriyār. *Kitāb ʿajāʾib al-Hind (Le Livre des merveilles de l'Inde)*, edited by P. A. Van der Lith and translated by L. M. Devic (Leiden: E. J. Brill, 1883–86).

—1981. *Kitāb ʿajāʾib al-Hind (The Book of Wonders of India)*, edited and translated by Greville S. P. Freeman–Grenville (London and the Hague: East–West Publications).

Reinaud, Joseph Toussaint. *Relation des voyages faits par les arabes et les persans dans l'Inde et la Chine*, Arabic text with translation, 2 volumes in 1 (Paris: L'Imprimerie Royale, 1845); first published by Louis Mathieu Langlès, 1811.

Al-Rifāʿī, Ḥussa l-Sayyid Zayd. *Aghānī l-baḥr: dirāsa fūlklūriyya* (Kuwait: Dhāt al-Salāsil, 1985).

Al-Riḥānī, Amīn. *Mulūk al-ʿArab*, Volumes I–II (Beirut: Dār al-Riḥānī, 1960); fourth edition.

Ritter, Helmut. 'Mesopotamische Studien 1. Arabische Flussfahrzeuge auf Euphrat und Tigris', *Der Islam*, 9: 121–43 (1919).

Al-Rūmī, Aḥmad al-Bishr. *Muʿjam al-muṣṭalaḥāt al-baḥriyya fī l-Kuwayt* (Kuwait: Markaz al-Buḥūth wa l-Dirāsāt al-Kuwaytiyya, 1996).

Al-Saʿīdān, Ḥamad Muḥammad. *Al-mawsūʿa l-kuwaytiyya l-mukhtaṣira*, Volume I– (Kuwait: al-Maṭbaʿa l-ʿAṣriyya, 1970).

Saldanha, Jerome Antony. *Selections from State Papers, Bombay regarding the East India Company's Connection with the Persian Gulf* (Calcutta: Superintendent of Government Printing, 1908).

Salonen, Armas. 'Zum Verständnis des sumerischen Schiffbautextes AO 5673 mit Berücksichtigung des Textes VAT 7035', *Studia Orientalia*, 8, iii: 3–23 (1938).

—1939. 'Die Wasserfahrzeuge in Babylonien nach sumerisch-akkadischen Quellen (mit besonderer Berücksichtigung der 4 Tafel der Serie ḪAR-ra-ḫubullu). Eine lexikalische und kultürgeschichtliche Untersuchung', *Studia Orientalia*, 8, iv: 1–199.

—1942. 'Nautica Babyloniaca', *Studia Orientalia*, II, i: 1–118.

Sassoon, Caroline. 'The dhows of Dar es Salaam', *Tanzania Notes and Records*, 71: 185–7 (1970).

Serjeant, Robert Bertram. *The Portuguese off the South Arabian Coast* (Oxford: Clarendon Press, 1974); a reprint of the 1963 edition with minor corrections.

Severin, Tim. *The Sindbad Voyage* (London: Hutchinson, 1982).

Severin, Tim and Korkis Awad. 'The Sindbad Voyage: an experiment in nautical archaeology', *Al-Watheekah*, 6: 198–205 (1985).

Al-Shamlān, ʿAbdallāh Khalīfa. *Bināʾ al-sufun al-khashabiyya fī dawlat al-Baḥrayn* (Bahrain: Markaz al-Baḥrayn lil-Dirāsāt wa l-Buḥūth, 1990).

Al-Shamlān, Sayf Marzūq. *Taʾrīkh al-ghawṣ ʿalā l-luʾluʾ fī l-Kuwayt wa l-Khalīj al-ʿArabī*, Volumes I–II (Kuwait: Ḥukūmat Kuwayt, 1975–8).

Shihāb, Ḥasan Ṣāliḥ. *Ṭuruq al-milāḥa l-taqlīdiyya fī l-Khalīj al-ʿArabī* (Kuwait: Qism al-Jughrāfiyā, Jāmiʿat al-Kuwayt, 1983).

—1987. *Al-marākib al-ʿarabiyya: taʾrīkhuhā wa anwāʿuhā* (Kuwait: Muʾassasat al-Kuwayt lil-Taqaddum al-ʿIlmī).

Shīr, Addī. *Muʿjam al-alfāẓ al-fārisiyya l-muʿarraba* (Beirut: Maktabat Lubnān, 1980); a reprint of 1908 edition.

Silsilat al-tawārīkh, see Reinaud, J. T.

Slot, B. J. *The Arabs of the Gulf: 1602–1784* (Abu Dhabi and The Hague: Cultural Foundation and Centre for Documentation and Research, 1991).

Smith, Rex. 'Ibn Mujāwir's 7th/13th-century guide to Arabia: the eastern connection' in *Occasional Papers of the School of Abbasid Studies*, No. 3. (St. Andrews: University of St. Andrews, 1990), 71–88.

—1997. *Studies in the Medieval History of the Yemen and South Arabia* (Variorum Collected Studies Series) (Aldershot: Ashgate Publishing Ltd.).

Stark, Freya. *The Southern Gates of Arabia: A Journey in the Hadhramaut* (London: John Murray, 1957); first edition 1936.

Steensgaard, Niels. *The Asian Trade Revolutions of the Seventeenth Century. The East India Companies and the Decline of the Caravan Trade* (Copenhagen, 1975); second edition.

Steingass, Francis Joseph. *A Comprehensive Persian–English Dictionary* (New Delhi: Cosmo, 1977).

Stiffe, Arthur William. 'Former trading centres of the Persian Gulf', *The Geographical Journal*, 13: 294–7 (1899).

Stocqueler [Siddons], Joachim Heyward. *Fifteen Months' Pilgrimage through Untrodden Tracts of Khuzistan and Persia etc.*, Volumes I–II (London: Saunders and Otley, 1832).

Strabo. *The Geography of Strabo*, translated by Horace Leonard Jones, based in part upon the unfinished version of J. R. S. Sterrett, Volumes I–VIII (London and New York: William Heinemann and G. P. Putnam, 1917).

Strong, James. *Exhaustive Concordance together with Dictionaries of the Hebrew and Greek Words* (Second Rapids, Michigan: Baker Book House, 1982); a reprint.

Al-Ṭabarī, Abū Jaʿfar Muḥammad b Jarīr. *Taʾrīkh al-rusul wa l-mulūk*, edited by Michael Jan de Goeje *et al.*, Volumes I–XV (Beirut: Khayats, 1965); first published Leiden 1879–1901.

Tabrīzī, Muḥammad Ḥusayn. *Burhān-e Qāṭeʿ*, edited by M. Moʿīn, Volumes I–V (Tehran: Amīr Kabīr, 1982).

Temple, Richard. *Sixteen Views of Places in the Persian Gulf, Taken in the Years 1809–10* (Bombay: np, 1811).

Theophrastus. *Enquiry into Plants*, translated by Arthur Hort, Volumes I–II (London and New York: William Heinemann and G. P. Putnam, 1916).

Thesiger, Wilfred. *The Marsh Arabs* (London: Penguin, 1967); first published 1964.

Thomas, Bertram. *Alarms and Excursions in Arabia* (London: George Allen and Unwin, 1931).

Thomas, R. Hughes (ed). *Arabian Gulf Intelligence: Selections from the Records of the Bombay Government*, Volume XXIV (Cambridge: Oleander, 1985); first published 1856.

The Thousand and One Nights. Translated by Edward William Lane, edited by Edward Stanley Poole, Volumes I–III (London: East-West Publications, 1979); first published 1838.

Three Voyages of Vasco Da Gama and his Viceroyalty. From the Lendas da India of Gaspar Correa. Translated by Henry E. J. Stanley (London: The Hakluyt Society, 1869).

Tibbetts, Gerald R. 1981. *Arab Navigation in the Indian Ocean before the Coming of the Portuguese being a Translation of Kitāb al-fawāʾid fī uṣūl al-baḥr wa l-qawāʿid of Aḥmad b Mājid al-Najdī* (London: The Royal Asiatic Society of Great Britain and Ireland, 1981); first published 1971.

Toreen, Olof. *A Voyage to Suratte, China, 1750–1752* (London: np, 1771).

The Travels of Ludovico di Varthema in Egypt, Syria, Arabia Deserta and Arabia Felix, in Persia, India and Ethiopia, A.D. 1503 to 1508. Translated

by John Winter Jones and edited by George Percy Badger (London: The Hakluyt Society, 1863).
The Travels of Marco Polo. Translated by Ronald Latham (New York: Abaris, 1982); first published 1958.
The Travels of Pietro della Valle in India. Translated by G. Havers, edited by Edward Grey (London: The Hakluyt Society, 1892).
ʿUthmān, Shawqī ʿAbd al-Qawī. *Tijārat al-muḥīṭ al-hindī fī ʿaṣr al-siyāda l-islāmiyya (41–904/661–1498)* (Kuwait: ʿĀlam al-Maʿrifa, 1990).
Van Doorninck, Frederick. 'Byzantium, mistress of the sea: 330–641' in *A History of Seafaring based on Underwater Archaeology*, edited by George F. Bass (London: Thames & Hudson, 1972), 133–58.
Villiers, Alan John. *Sons of Sinbad* (New York: C. Scribner's Sons, 1940).
—1948a. 'Dhow-builders of Kuwait', *The Geographical Magazine*, 20, ix: 345–50.
—1948b. 'Some aspects of the Arab dhow trade', *The Middle East Journal*, 2, iv: 399–416.
—1952. *The Indian Ocean* (London: Museum Press).
—1962. 'Voyage in a Kuwait boom', *The Mariner's Mirror*, 48, ii: 112–28; 48, iv: 264–75.
Vollers, Karl. 'Beiträge zur Kenntniss der lebenden arabischen Sprache in Ägypten, ii. über Lehnwörter. Fremdes und Eigenes', *Zeitschrift der Deutschen Morgenländischen Gesellschaft*, 50: 607–57 (1896).
Von Soden, Wolfram. *Akkadisches Handwörterbuch*, Volumes I–XI (Wiesbaden: Otto Harrassowitz, 1959–81); a revised work of Bruno Meissner.
Vosmer, Tom. 'Maritime archaeology, ethnography and history in the Indian Ocean: an emerging partnership' in *Archaeology of Seafaring: The Indian Ocean in the Ancient Period*, edited by Himanshu Prabha Ray (Delhi: Indian Council for Historical Research, 1999), 291–312.
Vosmer, Tom, D. A. Agius, P. Baker and J. Carpenter. *Field Report, Oman 1998* (Western Australian Maritime Museum Report, No. 144) (Perth, 2000).
Voyage du marchand arabe Sulayman en Inde et en Chine rédigé; en 851, suivi de remarques par Abû Zayd Ḥasan (vers 916). Translated by Gabriel Ferrand (Paris: Bossard, 1922).
The Voyage of Floris. (London: The Hakluyt Society, 1934).
Vullers, Ioannes Augustus. *Lexicon Persico-Latinum Etymologicum*, Volumes I–II (Graz: Akademische Druck, 1962); first published Bonn 1855–64.
Ward, Philip (ed). *Travels in Oman on the Track of the Early Explorers* (Cambridge: Oleander, 1987).
Wehr, Hans. *A Dictionary of Modern Written Arabic*, edited by J. Milton Cowan (Wiesbaden: Otto Harrassowitz, 1966); first published 1961.

Wellsted, James Raymond. *Travels in Arabia*, Volumes I–II (London: J. Murray, 1838).
—1840. *Travels to the City of the Caliphs along the Shores of the Persian Gulf and the Mediterranean* (London: H. Colburn).
Western Arabia and the Red Sea. Admiralty Naval Intelligence Division (Geographical Handbook Series) (Oxford: H. M. Stationery Office, 1946).
Wiebeck, E. *Indische Boote und Schiffe* (Rostock: np, 1987).
Wilson, Arnold. T. *The Persian Gulf* (London: George Allen and Unwin, 1954); first published 1928.
Winder, R. Bayly. *Saudi Arabia in the Nineteenth Century* (London: Macmillan, 1965).
Woodhead, Daniel R. and Wayne Beene. *A Dictionary of Iraqi Arabic–English* (Washington, D.C.: Georgetown University Press, 1967).
Wrede, Adolf von. *Reise in Hadhramaut*, edited by Heinrich Freiherr von Maltzan (Braunschweig, 1870).
Wüstenfeld, Fend. 'Namen der Schiffe im Arabischen' in *Nachrichten von der königlichen Gesellschaft der Wissenschaften und der G. A. Universität zu Göttingen* (Göttingen, 1880), 133–43.
Yajima, Hikoichi. *The Arab Dhow Trade in the Indian Ocean* (Studia Culturae Islamicae, No. 3) (Tokyo: Institute for the Study of Languages and Cultures of Asia and Africa, 1976).
Al-Yaʿqūbī, Aḥmad b Abī Yaʿqūb b Wāḍiḥ. *Kitāb al-buldān*, edited by Michael Jan de Goeje (Bibliotheca Geographicorum Arabicorum, VII) (Leiden: E. J. Brill, 1892).
Yāqūt b ʿAbdallāh al-Rūmī. *Kitāb muʿjam al-buldān*, edited by T. Wüstenfeld, Volumes I–VI (Leipzig: F. A. Brockhaus, 1866–73).
Young, Gavin. *Return to the Marshes* (London: Penguin, 1989); first published 1983.
Yule, Henry and Arthur C. Burnell. *Hobson-Jobson. A Glossary of Colloquial Anglo–Indian Words*; edited by William Crooke with a historical perspective by Nirad C. Chaudhuri (Sittingbourne, Kent: Linguasia, 1994); first published 1886; second edition 1903.
Al-Zabīdī, Abū l-Fayḍ al-Sayyid Muḥammad Murtaḍā b Muḥammad. *Tāj al-ʿarūs min jawāhir al-qāmūs*, Volume I– (Kuwait: Ministry of Information, 1965–); Volume III, edited by ʿAbd al-Karīm al-ʿIzbāwī, revised by Ibrāhīm al-Sāmarāʾī Aḥmad Farrāj (1967); Volume IV, edited by ʿAbd al-ʿAlīm al-Ṭaḥāwī, revised by Muḥammad Bahjat al-Atharī and ʿAbd al-Sattār Aḥmad Farrāj (1968); Volume V, edited by Muṣṭafā Ḥijāzī, revised by ʿAbd al-Sattār Aḥmad Farrāj (1969); Volume VI edited by Ḥusayn Naṣṣār, revised by Jamīl Saʿīd ʿAbd al-Sattār Aḥmad Farrāj

(1969); Volume XIV, edited by ʿAbd al-ʿAlīm al-Ṭaḥāwī, ʿAbd al-Karīm al-ʿAzabāwī, ʿAbd al-Sattār Aḥmad Farrāj (1974); Volume XVI, edited by Muḥammad Muḥammad al-Ṭanāḥī, revised by Muṣṭafā Ḥijāzī and ʿAbd al-Sattār Aḥmad Farrāj (1976); Volume XVII, edited by Muṣṭafā Ḥijāzī (1977); Volume XXIII, edited by ʿAbd al-Fattāḥ al-Ḥalw, revised by Muṣṭafā Ḥijāzī (1986); Volume XXIV, edited by Muṣṭafā Ḥijāzī (1987); Volume XXV, edited by Muṣṭafā Ḥijāzī (1989); Volume XXVII, edited by Muṣṭafā Ḥijāzī (1993); Volume XXIX, edited by ʿAbd al-Fattāḥ al-Ḥalw, revised by Aḥmad Mukhtār ʿUmar and Khālid ʿAbd al-Karīm Jumʿa (1997).

Zahlan, Rosemarie Said. *The Making of the Modern Gulf States* (Reading: Ithaca Press, 1998); first edition 1989.

Zayyāt, Ḥabīb. 'Muʿjam al-marākib wa l-sufun fī l-Islām', *Al-Mashriq*, 43, iii–iv: 321–64 (1949).

Zenker, Julius Theodor, *Türkisch–Arabisch–Persisches Handwörterbuch* (Hildesheim: Georg Olms, 1979); a reprint of Leipzig, 1866–76 in two volumes.

INDEX†

A

B

†Note: names of authors, rulers and sultans follow the Library of Congress system; other names of interviewees follow the country's official transliteration system.

C